PENTECOSTAL
TRAILBLAZER AND
REVERED PASTOR
OF THE AZUSA
STREET REVIVAL

WILLIAM J.
SEYMOUR

LARRY MARTIN

WHITAKER
HOUSE

WILLIAM J. SEYMOUR
Pentecostal Trailblazer and Revered Pastor of the Azusa Street Revival

Larry E. Martin
River of Revival Ministries, Inc.
Christian Life Books
P.O. Box 5
Duncan, OK 73534
drlarrymartin.com
azusastreet.org
pentecostalgold.com

ISBN: 979-8-88769-139-8
eBook ISBN: 979-8-88769-138-1
Printed in the United States of America
© 2024 by Larry E. Martin

Whitaker House
1030 Hunt Valley Circle
New Kensington, PA 15068
www.whitakerhouse.com

Library of Congress Control Number: 2023951680

1 2 3 4 5 6 7 8 9 10 11 ⨇ 30 29 28 27 26 25 24

CONTENTS

Preface.. 5

1. The Message: A New Pentecost 11

2. The Background: Life in Southern Louisiana 17

3. The Roots: The Seymour Family 27

4. The Sojourn Begins: Seymour Heads North 35

5. The Sanctified Life: The Saints and the Revivalists..................... 43

6. The Divine Appointment: Parham and Seymour 53

7. The Call: Seymour Goes West... 59

8. The City: Los Angeles, California... 63

9. The Preparation: Hunger for God 69

10. The Unexpected Reception: Rejected in Los Angeles 77

11. The Unsung Leader: Edward S. Lee 81

12. The Prayers Answered: Holy Ghost Outpouring........................ 85

13. The Place: "Old Azusa" 93

14. The Beginning: The First Weeks of Revival 99

15. The Revival: Heaven on Earth... 103

16. The Word: Seymour's Preaching.................................... 117

17. The Pilgrims: Williams, Mason, and Cashwell.......................... 123

18. The Commission: Into All the World 143

19. The First Challenge: Opposition................................... 153

20. The Second Challenge: Division 161

21. The Apostolic Ministry: Seymour's Travels................................ 177

22. The Homegoing: William Seymour Receives His Reward 187

23. The End: When the Battle's Over................................. 199

24. The Legacy: The Fire That Still Burns 209

About the Author.. 215

Endnotes... 217

PREFACE

In September 1999, I visited the National Archives in Washington, D.C., in search of information on Simon Seymour, the father of William Seymour. I had been studying William Seymour for several years but had stumbled upon some new information. This was before a lot of genealogical information was available online, and searches were difficult.

I had previously visited Seymour's hometown of Centerville, Louisiana, and met the wife of Van Seymour, William's nephew. She shared with me the circumstances of his mother's death. After the meeting, I obtained a death certificate for William's mother; I suspect I am the first researcher who found it.

One answer on the death certificate surprised me. It asked if she was a veteran of past wars, and the word "civil" was scribbled in the space. I knew that was impossible; no women served in the military in the Civil War. I wondered if Simon could've been a veteran. I didn't think so. There were Black soldiers in the war, but they were Union soldiers. Simon lived in the Deep South—about as far south as you could go.

Following the new clues, I searched the web. Someone had catalogued a list of soldiers who served in the United States Colored Troops during the Civil War. There it was: Simon Seymour, from Louisiana. I still couldn't be sure it was "the" Simon Seymour.

Within days I was in Washington, D.C. The archivist brought me a folder with Simon Seymour's name on it. The red tape that sealed the file had literally been cut, hence the expression "cutting through the red tape." In the folder was information that had not been seen in decades. Quite likely it had been decades since anyone viewed the contents of the folder. I discovered never-known facts about Seymour's father, mother, and siblings. For a historian it was better than a gold mine.

Needless to say, I was on cloud nine. As you leave the Archives, there are two sixty-five-ton statues guarding the front doors. The statues by Robert Aiken represent the future and the past. As you exit on your right, *Future* is a "youthful woman gazing in contemplation of things to come. She holds an open book symbolizing what has yet to be written." On the left, *Past* is an "old man gazing down the corridors of time. He holds a closed book representing history." Inscribed on the pedestal beneath *Past* is this paraphrase of Confucius: "Study the Past."[1]

That phrase pretty well sums up my life. I love history. I love to study the past. When I was in grade school, we had an opportunity to earn a certificate for every twenty-five books we read. One year I read one hundred—most of them biographies. I still get excited knowing that a great man or woman can come alive in the page of a good book.

I also love revival—red hot, blood-bought, Holy Ghost and fire, Pentecostal revival. I was born in a revival. Well, I was actually born in a hospital, but my home church was in revival services when I was born. I had a deformity in my feet, and I received healing when the church prayed for me. Why wouldn't I love revival?

When a love for revival and a love for biography meet in one heart, you get a book like this one. It is the story of one of the greatest revivalists in church history, William J. Seymour.

Seymour is my hero. I believe he is one of the purest, saintliest, and humblest men who ever lived. He grew up in poverty and oppression. He knew the bitter sting of racism and pure hatred. He suffered from a life-threatening illness that left him blind in one eye. The odds were against him, yet he prevailed. He is an almost perfect example of what it means to be a faithful Christian. Seymour could have said, "Follow me as I follow

Christ," as Paul did, but he probably wouldn't have. (See 1 Corinthians 11:1 MEV.) I want to follow him anyway.

When I first released *The Life and Ministry of William J. Seymour* in late 1999, it was the first full biography of Seymour ever published. That is not to say others had not written about him. Douglas Nelson wrote a dissertation on his life that was very helpful in my research. Cecil M. Robeck has been studying Azusa Street and Seymour longer than me. His published works have also guided me. I give these men credit for leading the way.

It has been more than twenty years since I published that book. This rewritten book was quite a project but also an opportunity to make revisions and additions and to address errors and omissions to further clarify Seymour's life and legacy.

I didn't want to just present an old book with a new publisher. I wanted someone who had already read the original to want to read this edition. I wanted it to be a new book. I believe it is. There are new chapters, new background material, and new photos. The word count is 25 percent higher than the original book. This is a better book. I pray you will enjoy it.

When Whitaker House published my book *Charles Fox Parham: The Unlikely Father of Modern Pentecostalism*, we began to discuss the re-release of my Seymour book. My friend Tim Enloe encouraged me to pursue it and encouraged a friend at Whitaker House. I realize it is a big deal for a major publisher to release a book that has already been in print, even if it was self-published. I was unsure if this book would be published, but Whitaker House removed my doubts. I feel honored by their consideration of the book.

Having collected materials for thirty years or more, I find it hard to know whom to thank for their help. I have prowled in dusty courthouse basements, public libraries, seminaries, and universities from coast to coast. I not only researched at the National Archives in three different locations; I also visited eight different state archives and at least four denominational archives. I have made dozens of phone calls, written hundreds of letters and emails, and spent hours trying to read faded microfilmed newspapers and periodicals. More recently my search has kept me in front of a computer for days at a time. Would I be exaggerating if I said a thousand people have helped in some way? Perhaps not.

One person, however, stands out above all the others. Glenn Gohr at the Flower Pentecostal Heritage Center in Springfield, Missouri, has been an immeasurable asset in all my research. Glenn knows more about Pentecostal history than anyone I know, and he shares it with an unparalleled lack of selfishness. Glenn is a dear and trusted friend. I remember more than twenty-five years ago when Glenn let me hold and read the original editions of the *Apostolic Faith* newspaper for the first time. I was amazed. I still am.

I also want to thank my family. Sharing a home with a fanatical researcher and writer can be a sacrifice. That doesn't even begin to count the financial burden my expensive hobby has cost us. I have had no universities to sponsor me; I have had no grants. This has been my passion, and one that my precious family has borne well.

I closed the preface to the original book by saying, "Let us all pray that the love, humility, tears, hunger, and Pentecostal power that were the spirit of Azusa will visit us again. Our world, our nation, our churches need Holy Ghost revival."

I could not say it better today than I said it then. Grant it, Lord. Amen.

William Joseph Seymour

The first known image of the
Apostolic Faith Mission - 312 Azusa.
Notice the "For Sale" sign.
Used by permission
United Pentecosal Church Archives

Willam Seymour in front of the
Azusa Street Mission.

"Whosoever Will May Come."
The sign on the Mission.

Both photos used by permission Flower Pentecostal Heritage Center

One of the last photos of the Mission.
Larry Martin Collection
Courtesy of the Apostolic Faith Church - Portland, Oregon

1

THE MESSAGE:
A NEW PENTECOST

The words "Azusa Street" have become synonymous with the origin of the Twentieth-Century Pentecostal Revival. From the Apostolic Faith Gospel Mission at 312 Azusa Street, Los Angeles, California, the fire of Pentecost swept the world; yet the flame did not begin at Azusa Street. Like an Olympic runner with a torch, William Joseph Seymour brought the flame to Los Angeles from Houston, Texas. The same fire had been carried to Houston by Charles Fox Parham, the founder of the Apostolic Faith.

Parham was born June 4, 1873, in Muscatine County, Iowa.[2] When he was five, his family loaded a covered wagon and moved to Kansas, where Parham spent most of his life. As a child, Parham experienced many debilitating illnesses including tapeworms, spasms, inflammatory rheumatism, bad eyesight, sick headaches, abscesses of the liver, heart failure, and a "wrecked mind."[3] As a sickly child, Parham was abnormally close to his mother, who passed in 1885. On her deathbed she asked her son to promise to meet her in heaven.[4] These unfortunate confrontations with pain, and even death, would greatly impact his adult life.

Parham felt a call to the ministry at nine, four years before his conversion at thirteen. He began conducting revival meetings in local Methodist churches when he was fifteen.[5] In 1890 he started his formal ministerial training at Southwest Kansas College, a Methodist institution in Winfield, Kansas.[6]

A year later, Parham turned his back on God and on the ministry. Deciding that he would prefer the income and social standing of a physician, he began to lean toward medical studies.[7]

Soon his rheumatism returned, and it did not seem that Parham would recover. For months he suffered the "torments of hell." He had become addicted to the morphine prescribed for pain and wished for death.[8]

After he trusted God for his healing, the pain and fever that had tortured his body for months immediately disappeared. However, the healing was not yet complete. Months of inactivity had left Parham a virtual cripple. His ankles were too weak to support the weight of his body, so he staggered about, walking on the sides of his feet. In December 1891, Parham renewed his commitments to God and the ministry, and he was instantaneously and totally healed.[9]

Parham served a brief term as a Methodist pastor in Eudora, Kansas, but left the organization after a falling-out with his ecclesiastical superiors. He then became loosely affiliated with the Holiness movement that had split from the Methodists late in the nineteenth century. He never returned to structured denominationalism.[10]

On December 31, 1896, Parham married Sarah Eleanor Thistlethwaite, a devout Quaker.[11] The young couple worked together in the ministry, conducting revival campaigns in several Kansas cities. Influenced by a number of successful faith healers, Parham's Holiness message evolved to include an ever-increasing emphasis on divine healing. After Parham received another miraculous healing, he became convinced that the use of medicines was forbidden in the Bible.[12]

For a brief tenure Parham pastored a small Presbyterian church in Media, Kansas. Even while serving the church, he continued his revival ministry.[13]

In the summer of 1898, the aspiring evangelist moved his family to Topeka and opened Bethel Healing Home. For almost two years, the home served both the physical and spiritual needs of the city. Included in the services that Parham's ministry offered were an infirmary, a Bible institute, an adoption agency, and even an unemployment office. Parham also co-published a religious periodical, *The Apostolic Faith*. In only a few years, this would become the first Pentecostal journal.[14]

In the summer of 1900, Parham took a sabbatical from the healing home to embark on a spiritual odyssey throughout the northeastern United States. For three months he visited some of the most prominent ministries in the nation, including those of John Alexander Dowie, J. Walter Malone, and A. B. Simpson. None had a greater impact on his theology than the ministry of Frank W. Sandford of Durham, Maine.[15]

Along his spiritual journey, Parham also developed some extreme, unorthodox doctrines. For example, he taught the total annihilation of the wicked. His teachings on white superiority also included Anglo-Israelism, a cultic doctrine which argues that Anglo-Saxons are the ten lost tribes of Israel. He also believed that interracial marriages caused the flood of Noah's day.[16]

When the preacher returned to Topeka early in the fall of 1900, he found that the colleagues he had left in charge of the healing home had staged a religious coup d'état and gained control of the facility.[17] Not deterred by their disloyalty, in October, Parham relocated to an elaborate fifteen-room house in Topeka. The financial misfortunes of the home's original builder led local residents to give the castle-like structure the dubious nickname "Stone's Folly." With thirty-four students, Parham began Bethel Bible College, a Bible school that would emphasize healing, sanctification, and a Holy Spirit baptism.[18]

Parham said, "Our purpose in this Bible school was not to learn things in our head only but have each thing in the Scriptures wrought out in our hearts."[19] All students (mostly mature, seasoned gospel workers) were expected to sell everything they owned and give the proceeds away so each could trust God for daily provisions. From this humble college, a theology was developed that would change the face of the Christian church forever.

After a study of the book of Acts, the students entered a time of prayer and waiting on God. On January 1, 1901, Agnes Nevada Ozman, a thirty-year-old student, received the baptism in the Holy Ghost with the evidence of speaking in a language she did not know (known as glossolalia).[20] In the days following, Parham and a few other students received the experience and spoke with tongues.[21]

This episode at Stone's Mansion initiated the modern Pentecostal revival. This is not to suggest that this was the first modern incident of speaking in tongues. In fact, from the time of the apostles until today there have been occasions when believers, caught up in the Spirit, spoke in tongues. The Huguenots in France and Irvingites in England both shared the experience. The great revivals of Wesley, Finney, and Moody were sometimes accompanied by manifestations of spiritual gifts.[22]

By the latter nineteenth century, there had been numerous occurrences of speaking in tongues. Confirmed reports came from Minnesota, North Carolina, Texas, and Tennessee in the decade before Parham's group received their baptism in the Holy Ghost.

Yet the experience at Bethel College was unique. Parham and his students reached the theological conclusion that speaking in other tongues was the scriptural evidence of the Holy Spirit baptism. Earlier, tongues had been viewed as a demonstration of the Spirit, similar to weeping, shouting, or shaking. Parham's group received the baptism with evidential tongues while earnestly seeking the experience. Unlike his predecessors, Parham taught that those who did not speak in tongues had never received the fullness of the Holy Spirit.

The facts leave no doubt that Parham was the father or founder of modern Pentecostalism, and that the movement was born in Topeka, Kansas. Many prefer William Seymour and the Azusa Street Revival, but it is only that—a preference, and one that ignores the authentic historical record. For instance, noted Pentecostal historian Cecil M. Robeck says he has "chosen to highlight the Azusa Street Mission as the birthplace of global Pentecostalism" because few or no missionaries were sent out by Parham in the years before 1906. Despite the bias of Robeck and many others, it would be more accurate to say the Pentecostal movement began under Parham and became a global movement under Seymour, acknowledging the important role both men played in the formation of the movement.[23]

There are multiple historical elements that point to the early leadership of Parham. One of the many examples would be a list of church groups in America assembled by the United States Department of Commerce and

Labor in 1906. The Apostolic Faith is listed along with hundreds of other religious bodies. The headquarters are reported to be in Los Angeles, tying the movement to Apostolic Faith Mission on Azusa Street, which was widely publicized at the time. The official government report also states clearly that Charles F. Parham was the founder of the movement.[24]

After the initial revival in Topeka the young preacher accompanied a team of evangelists who went forth from Topeka to share what Parham called the "Apostolic Faith" message. Unfortunately, their earliest attempts at spreading the news were less than successful. After the tragic death of Parham's youngest child, Bethel College closed, and Parham entered a period of introspection.

The years immediately after Topeka were very difficult for Parham. He faced much opposition and hardship. At times there was barely food for the family. Yet, during this dark time, he wrote and published what became the first book of Pentecostal theology, *Kol Kare Bomidbar: A Voice Crying in the Wilderness*.[25]

Parham's fortunes changed dramatically when he hosted revival meetings in Eldorado Springs, Missouri. Mary Arthur, an elderly lady with many physical ailments, had visited the mineral springs in hopes of finding relief from her maladies. When Parham prayed for her, she was instantly and completely healed.

Arthur invited Parham to her home in Galena, Kansas, where the evangelist saw his first truly successful Pentecostal meetings. Additional campaigns were conducted in Baxter Springs, Kansas; Joplin, Missouri; and surrounding areas throughout 1903 and 1904. Hundreds of people were saved, healed, and baptized in the Holy Spirit as Parham preached to thousands in the booming mine towns.[26]

Following the fruitful meetings in Kansas and Missouri, Parham set his eyes on the Lone Star State. In the spring and summer of 1905, the evangelist conducted a highly successful crusade in Orchard, Texas, and then he moved his team to the Houston-Galveston area. After returning to Kansas for a few months, he moved his entire enterprise to Houston and opened another Bible college. "The Bible Training School," as it was called, provided several weeks of intensive Pentecostal indoctrination.[27]

When he moved his headquarters to Houston, Parham had no way of knowing that in less than three years, the Apostolic Faith message would spread worldwide, yet he would become much less relevant to the movement he had founded.

2

THE BACKGROUND: LIFE IN SOUTHERN LOUISIANA

The great American poet Ralph Waldo Emerson once said, "An institution is the lengthened shadow of one man."[28] The same thing can be said about a revival or a spiritual movement, and the Pentecostal/Charismatic renewal of the twentieth century is an extension of the shadow of a humble Black pastor named William Joseph Seymour.

Seymour was born in Centerville, Louisiana, on May 2, 1870, only five years after General Lee's surrender at Appomattox ended the Civil War.[29] Centerville was, and still is, a sleepy little town in southern Louisiana, situated about midway between Lafayette and Houma. Located in St. Mary Parish, Centerville is about five miles from Franklin, the center of parish government.[30]

St. Mary Parish had a total population of 13,860. After the Civil War there were 4,202 white people and 9,658 Blacks living in the parish. Of the five parishes that made up the Attakapas section, only St. Mary had a Black majority.[31]

The tiny town is located on the Bayou Teche, called "the most elegant of all the bayous." For those unfamiliar with the geographical phenomenon, a bayou has been defined as "a place that seems often unable to make up its mind whether it will be earth or water, and so it compromises." The

Bayou Teche, sometimes 200 feet wide, meanders for nearly 100 miles through Louisiana. It is graced by the largest and most beautiful moss-draped live oak trees in the state. Some are twenty feet wide at the trunk.[32]

At the time of Seymour's birth, the principal industries of the area were cotton, corn, rice, sugar cane, and cattle. Before the Civil War, St. Mary Parish boasted the "most flourishing" plantations in the state.

In 1869, Colonel Samuel H. Lockett, a professor of engineering at Louisiana State Seminary, began traveling throughout Louisiana preparing an official survey. July found him in St. Mary Parish, where he reported, "As an agricultural district, it is difficult to conceive of its superior. And yet, a want of labor caused much of even this fine country to be lying untilled and idle." Further, he said, "Much of this excellent country is lying waste, the fields grown up in cocklebur and other weeds, roads reduced to narrow trails, plantation houses and fences in a dilapidated condition. A general air of desertion and desolation pervades the scene." Lockett described Centerville as a "neat little village."[33]

Trying to attract settlers, one resident described the parish in most flattering terms: "The climate is salubrious, the lands fertile. All the year round he can have fresh vegetables, his cattle can feed out in the fields from January to December and he has ample leisure to fish and hunt, game abounding on all sides."[34]

It was in this place and on this land that William J. Seymour was born.

Yet, to fully understand the circumstances that shaped young Seymour's life, it is important to look beyond the geography and topography and to see the cauldron of boiling racial hatred that characterized Antebellum and Reconstruction Louisiana. Few, if any, southern states were more repressive in the treatment of Black people.

The undisguised hatred of Black people was evident in every area of society. In words that should have been considered too ugly to be published, *The Planter's Banner* in St. Mary parish printed:

But to place a race of human beings with wooly heads, thick lips; thick skulls and flat noses upon a level with white men, and pretend that God made them with as good intellects as the whites, and capable of maintaining as dignified positions in society is non-sense, and a low order of nonsense at that.[35]

Before the Civil War, two out of five white families in Louisiana owned slaves. Ownership of slaves, however, was not limited to private citizens. The State of Louisiana also owned slaves, utilizing them in road building and similar enterprises. Forty-seven percent of the state's total population were slaves. In St. Mary Parish, more than four hundred people owned nearly 13,000 slaves. Some slave owners had only one or two slaves while others had as many as four hundred.[36]

The Planter's Banner, Franklin's weekly newspaper, carried regular notices of slave auctions at the town center. Slaves of all ages, including those as young as infants, were placed on the auction block. It was not uncommon for slaves to be listed with other property. One listing said, "31 likely Slaves of both sexes, 9 horses, 6 mules, 12 work oxen, 300 hogs, stock and sheep."[37]

Slaves in St. Mary Parish were as expensive as they were plentiful. The Franklin newspaper announced that one "Negro in no way remarkable" brought a price of $2,300.[38]

Laws regulating slaves were inhuman at best and barbaric at worst. A Black person could be killed for hitting a white person hard enough to cause a bruise. Striking a white person a third time, regardless of the severity of the attack or the circumstances that precipitated it, was also cause for death.

A fleeing slave could be shot if they did not stop when a white person ordered them to do so. The Louisiana Supreme Court cautioned against trying to inflict a mortal wound but made it clear that if the slave died there would be no charges, since "the homicide is a consequence of the permission to fire upon him." [39]

Slaveholders had little regard for Black family life. Husbands and wives were often sold separately. In Louisiana, the only exception was that children under ten years of age were required to be sold or imported with their mother.

Unfortunately, all the cruelty of slavery was often adorned in the trappings of Christianity. An article in *The Planter's Banner* quoted numerous

Bible verses to justify the forced servitude, saying, "I shall proceed to show that slavery is…no sin." The author further boasted, "You tell us that slavery is a great evil. Why, so, sir? Was it an evil to the slave to be brought from the barbarous cruelty of infanticide and cannibalism in his native wilds, to the mild treatment and personal security of a Christian land! — from heathen worship to Christianity!"[40]

One writer in St. Mary Parish described the treatment of slaves in the area: "I have known Negroes to remain weeks, with their bodies exposed to the severest of our cold weather, and in the warmest and sultriest, in the same clothing, until it became thick with filth exuded from their skins, and gathered from that with which they were surrounded."[41]

If, for some act of charity, a Louisiana slave was freed by their master, they had to leave the state within thirty days. In 1852, the law was amended to require that the former slaves leave the United States. The law was changed again in 1857, totally banning private emancipation. The southern attitude toward Black people can be summed up in the words of the Chancellor of the South Carolina Court of Appeals: "A free African population is a curse to any country."[42]

It is obvious that losing a bloody war, seeing their economy devastated, witnessing the emancipation of slaves, and being forced into a despised reconstruction did not improve the southern white man's attitude toward his Black neighbors. Rich white people despised the formerly enslaved, and poor white people hated them for taking the few menial jobs available to their class. The Civil War and its aftermath were especially devastating to rice growers in Southern Louisiana where Seymour had been born. In 1860, the total southern sugar crop was more than 225 million pounds. By 1870, the number had fallen to less than 90 million pounds.[43]

In St. Mary Parish the sugar crop was 48,779 hogshead in the 1860-61 season, but it had fallen to 16,515 ten years later.[44] The shortage of plantation labor was so acute that 700 formerly enslaved individuals were sent to the parish from border states.[45] White laborers were in even greater demand. A tenant worker could clear upwards of $1,200 a year.[46] This is quite amazing considering the average annual income in the United States was less than five hundred dollars.[47] The "scarcity of negro labor" even forced some plantation to bring workers from Portugal and Spain.[48]

Without slave labor, the size of farms in Louisiana was radically reduced. In 1860, the average farm was 536 acres.[49] One decade later, the size declined to only 247 acres. Owners of large plantations were forced to sell. In St. Mary Parish in 1860, there were ninety landowners who enslaved more than fifty people. By 1877, only twenty-five of these still held their farms.[50]

Another example of the excessive cost of the war is the value of farms and equipment. In 1860, Louisiana farms were valued at $248 million; thirty years later, their value was only slightly more than $110 million. Farm equipment valued at $18 million before the war was worth only $7 million in 1890.[51]

The southern infrastructure was all but destroyed. Roads were in total disrepair, and bridges were either burned or washed away. Riverboats had been captured by the Union or destroyed, and most railroads were in ruin. Further, mules, horses, wagons, and carriages were extremely scarce.[52]

The poor economy hit emancipated Black people (also known as "freedmen") the hardest. In three years following the war, the United States government, through the Freedman's Bureau, distributed 15 million rations to former slaves.[53] Even this did not keep many from starving. It is estimated that in 1865 alone, 100,000 Black people died from starvation or disease.[54]

Black people who found field work in St. Mary Parish in 1866 were paid only $20 a month. Their meager salary was supplemented with a cabin (usually deplorable), rations, and fuel.[55]

Before and after the war, white people imposed legal restrictions on former slaves by using black codes. In Louisiana a Black man was required to choose his employer for an entire year by the first ten days of January. If he did not fulfill the contract, for example by voluntarily leaving after several months, he would forfeit wages for the entire year.[56] Black people who did not find work could be arrested for vagrancy and given fines that the courts knew they could not pay. They were then forced to work for the government or hire themselves out to other employers for a period of up to twelve months.[57] This system was not much different from slavery.

In 1865 St. Landry Parish instituted an even more restrictive version of "The Black Code." Among other things, it required all Black people to be employed by a white man. Black people were not allowed to rent or own a house and had a nightly curfew of ten o'clock. They could not even pass through the parish without a written permit. Black people could only assemble for meetings during the daylight hours, unless of course they were attending a church service conducted by a white man. Black ministers could not preach without a special permit.[58]

In 1866 Congress passed a Civil Rights Act that gave citizenship to all African Americans born in the United States. The legislation gave Black people "full and equal benefit of all laws…as is enjoyed by white citizens."[59] Someone must have failed to inform the white people of Louisiana.

During most of the war and during reconstruction, much of southern Louisiana, including St. Mary Parish, was under the supervision of federal troops, commanded by General Philip Sheridan. General Shepley, a subordinate to Sheridan, referred to Seymour's boyhood home as "the obstinate proslavery parish of St. Mary."[60] Violence against Black people led another of Sheridan's officers to dispatch a detachment of soldiers to Franklin in 1876.[61]

The federal government attempted to impose some justice for freedmen through its ill-fated Reconstruction fiasco. It seemed progress was being made. Newly franchised Black people elected men of their race to high government positions in Louisiana. A new constitution was adopted in 1868. It guaranteed many rights that had been denied to former slaves, including the guarantee of integrated public education.[62]

In 1874 the "white people of Louisiana, embracing the Democratic party" issued their political platform. They mocked the federal government, claiming the congress could not enact laws "to force the two races into social union or equality." They further asserted that necessary reform in the state could only be accomplished by electing "white men of known capacity and integrity."[63]

Unfortunately, Federal troops left Louisiana in 1877, when Seymour was only seven. All hopes for equality under the law were lost. In an address to the people of Louisiana, Governor William P. Kellogg described the acts of white people against freedmen as "public disorders" and "sentiments of ostracism and antagonism" and said they were a "standing menace."[64]

Little has been written about life in St. Mary Parish during the years of Seymour's youth. One small glimpse comes in 1881, when Seymour was eleven. The report came in *The Weekly Louisianan*, a New Orleans newspaper published by and for Black people. Harsh weather had played "havoc" with the parish. Planting had been delayed, and roads throughout the parish were almost impassable. Crops were "large and the hopes for next year buoyant."

There were fewer "colored planters" in the parish than any of the other wealthy parishes. However, there were eight or ten Black men who were successful merchants.

There was no public school in the parish. The schools, it appears, were hamstrung by bickering over political appointments. One citizen complained that the "dear children" were being "illtreated [sic] and ruined by the class of ignoramuses appointed over them as teachers."[65]

Because of the poor educational environment, residents refused to pay the obligatory "poll tax" to finance the schools. Only a fraction of the budget had been met, and the editor of *The Weekly Louisianan* lamented, "Only one colored man not owning property had paid his poll tax." "This," he wrote, "is a very bad showing for the colored men of St. Mary's."[66]

In the area around the village of Pattersonville[67] the citizenry had been without law enforcement for nearly two months, and not one crime had been committed by Black or white people. The peace and security were credited to "plenty of money and bad whiskey free."[68]

The tranquility would soon be interrupted. By 1898, white people had regained control of the state government and ordered a new constitutional convention. The theme of the convention can be summed up in the words of Thomas J. Semmes, former president of the American Bar Association: "We [meet] here to establish the supremacy of the white race...."[69]

Groups similar to the Ku Klux Klan terrorized Southern Black people, raping, beating, and lynching them. The White League was a white militia composed mostly of former Confederate soldiers. They numbered in the thousands in Louisiana. During the Reconstruction period, members of the White League murdered 10 percent of the Black men in Caddo Parish.[70]

The "most important, secret" organization in Louisiana was the Knights of the White Camellia, patterned after the Klan. The terrorist group was born in St. Mary Parish in 1867.[71]

The White League was organized in St. Mary parish in 1874. Their platform made their intentions clear: "We enter into and form this League for the protection of our own race against the daily increasing encroachments of the negro...." Taking racial hatred to the extreme, they continued,

> We own the soil of Louisiana, by virtue of our endeavor, as a heritage from our ancestors, and it is ours and ours alone. Science, literature, history, art, civilization, and law belong alone to us, and not to the negroes. They have no record but barbarism and idolatry, nothing since the war but that of error, incapacity, beastliness, voudouism [sic], and crime.[72]

Another group that harassed Black people and their sympathizers in Franklin was paradoxically known as "Seymour's Knights." This group was formed to support the presidential candidacy of Horatio Seymour. Like the Klan members, they wore uniforms and marched throughout the city streets.[73]

In contrast, Black men and women were largely good citizens. One government official reported to Washington, "The freedmen will not engage in any insurrection against the State, or any portion of it.... The colored population live much under the control of the Christian religion, and they have no disposition to murder or destroy. They are peaceable, forgiving, merciful...."[74]

White people who could no longer "own" freedmen were determined to deprive and control them. In Franklin, laws were passed that prohibited freedmen from entering the town without permission of their employer. Additionally, freedmen could not sell goods, own firearms, or preach without a license.[75]

In 1867, Franklin's *Planter's Banner* reported, "We don't think the Negroes are fools enough to risk an open issue with the white people of this parish. There are too many among them who know what would be the terrible consequences to men of their race were such an issue brought about. But it will have a good effect for all white men to have their arms in working order in case the club meetings, the Diossys and other mean white men should directly or indirectly bring about a collision of the races in this parish." The paper further threatened, "Let the Negroes and mean white men beware!"[76]

Unfortunately, Black people found no better refuge in most churches than in society. In 1874, a Catholic publication wrote, "There is but one way now to manage the Negro. He is, as a class, amenable to neither reason nor gratitude. He must be starved into the common perceptions of decency."[77]

One engraving from 1870, the year of Seymour's birth, shows a Black couple with an infant child cowering under a Klansman and a member of the White League. A burning school and lynched Black man are in the background. The captions read, "This is a white man's government," "The lost cause" and "Worse than slavery."[78]

In one particularly calloused outbreak of hostilities in Grant Parish, between one hundred fifty and two hundred Black people were murdered. The atrocities committed against these unfortunate people are almost unspeakable. Nearly all were shot between three and twelve times, many in the back of the head, and the bodies of dozens were burned beyond recognition. A witness says Black people "were shot down like dogs." *Harper's Weekly* reported, "A general feeling of insecurity prevails among the colored people of Louisiana, and hundreds are seeking safety in the swamps and forests."[79]

The Southern outrage against freedmen continued with the enactment of "Jim Crow" laws that essentially denied the vote to Black people through grandfather clauses, poll taxes, and literacy tests. Public transportation and accommodations were segregated, with Black people almost always having far less than equal facilities. An American historian describing the plight of Southern freedmen said, "Forgotten in the North, manipulated and then callously rejected by the South, rebuffed by the Supreme Court, voiceless in national affairs, he and his descendants were condemned in the interests of sectional harmony to lives of poverty, indignity, and little hope."[80]

As the nineteenth century faded into history, the grand promises of change for freedmen proved elusive, and the threat of violence, injustice, and death was ever present. One newspaper editor wrote, "The lynching spirit is stalking abroad, and nearly every day records its victim."[81] Dick Coleman, a Black man in Maysville, Kentucky, was burned to death by "a mob of savages" while awaiting trial for murder. "He was tortured in the most brutal manner."[82]

In Arkansas, seven Black men were shot and hanged by a "white mob." Although their bodies were "full of bullet holes" and the "mark of the rope" was on their neck, a coroner's jury ruled they had "frozen to death."[83]

Samuel Hose was chained to a tree and burned to death in Newman, Georgia. His lips, ears, fingers, and other body parts were cut off before he was set aflame. After his demise, men scrambled "like mad for bits of the charred remains to exhibit as relics of the ghastly scene." An eyewitness said, "Shouts of joy like demonic laughter rent the air."[84]

At nineteen years of age, a Black man named Ed Aikens was walking down a path when a white girl approached him. The two were never less than ten feet apart, but she was "afraid and ran." A Georgia judge sentenced Aikens to ten years on a chain gang. He said he wanted to make an example of him "so that young darkies would get out of the path when they saw white girls coming."[85]

Indeed, life was inhumane for a poor Black man growing up in Southern Louisiana. This was the only life William Seymour knew. He must have lived every day wondering if he would be the next victim. Perhaps the fear of the crazed mob was worse than the mob itself. Young William Seymour adapted to his harsh environment. He was a survivor.

3

THE ROOTS:
THE SEYMOUR FAMILY

William Seymour's parents were Simon Seymour, also known as Simon Simon (pronounced See-mone), and Phillis Salabar Seymour.[86] They were both former slaves, the children of slaves and at least second-generation Louisianans.[87]

Simon was biracial and was born in St. Mary Parish, Louisiana.[88] The exact date of his birth is not known but it was probably around 1841.[89] The identity of his white master is also unknown.[90] Simon seemed to be a common name for slaves in the parish.[91] At age twenty-one, Simon was five feet eight inches tall and had a dark complexion, black hair, and black eyes.[92]

He was one of the first Black Americans to serve in an all-Black regiment of the United States Army. Early in the Civil War, President Lincoln had resisted the idea of enlisting Black soldiers, especially slaves. However, pressure was building to use the "contrabands" in the military. This was particularly true in Louisiana, where a regiment of freedmen had served in the Native Guard, supporting the Confederate forces.[93] One soldier wrote cynically, "What's the use to have men from Maine, Vermont, and Massachusetts dying down here in these swamps. You can't replace these men, but if a n----- dies, all you have to do is to send out and get another one."[94]

With the Emancipation Proclamation freeing all slaves held by the rebels on January 1, 1863, former slaves "of suitable condition" were actively recruited as volunteer soldiers.[95] This declaration forever changed not only the country but also the Union army. Before the end of the conflict, more than 170,000 Black soldiers served.[96]

General Benjamin F. Butler, who organized the first Black regiment in Louisiana, reported, "Better soldiers never shouldered a musket."[97] Not every white soldier, however, was so proud to serve with Black troops, and prejudice continued throughout the war.

Simon enlisted as a private in the Union Army on October 10, 1863. His unit, the 25th Regiment Infantry, was organized in New Iberia on November 21, 1863, and he was one of the original volunteers. Seymour, who enlisted for three years, was recruited by James Blanchard. The 25th was attached to the 1st Brigade, 2nd Division, Corps d'Afrique, Department of the Gulf. The regiment saw duty at New Iberia, Franklin, and Brashear City.

In April 1864, the designation of the unit was changed to the 93rd Regiment Infantry, United States Colored Troops. The new regiment was attached to the 2nd Brigade, the District of LaFourche and Department of the Gulf. The soldiers were involved in a skirmish with the Confederates at Lake Fausse Point on November 18, 1864. This appeared to be the only battle in which Seymour's unit participated. Afterward, the troops continued to see duty in south Louisiana until they were broken up on June 23, 1865.

When the 93rd was dissolved, Seymour was in the General Hospital in New Orleans, where he had been admitted on June 16, 1865. On July 14, he was transferred to the 82nd Regiment Infantry but was not released from the hospital until October 31.[98] On two occasions, Seymour suffered from fever, once he had rheumatism and bronchitis. More important, he contracted chronic diarrhea, a problem that plagued him for the rest of his life.[99] It seems likely that he acquired a fever or parasite while marching in the swamps of Louisiana and Florida.

When Simon returned to duty, his unit was stationed at Apalachicola in the District of Florida. He served there until he was mustered out when the regiment disbanded in Barrancas, Florida, on September 7, 1866. Seymour never rose above the rank of private but was always present for duty and faithfully served his country.[100]

After his release from the military, Simon moved to Bayou Sale, where he met Phillis Salabar, his bride-to-be.[101] The couple became acquainted in January, about six months before their wedding.[102]

Phillis, a Black woman, was born on November 23, 1844, on the Adelard Carlin (pronounced Car-line) plantation on Bayou Sale near Berwick City, St. Mary Parish.[103] More than likely, her parents were Michael and Lucy Sweet Salabar of Centerville. After emancipation, both parents were farm laborers.[104]

Carlin, born in 1800, and his wife, Carmelite, were very affluent planters. They probably raised rice, the principal crop of the region. In 1860, his real estate was valued at $150,000; his personal property, $160,000. He owned 112 slaves, including Phillis, accounting for much of his great wealth.[105] The latter reported that Carlin was "the only master I ever had."[106]

Phillis had several siblings, including Polly, Antirnette, Adaline and Michael.[107] Harriet Bedford, another slave on the Carlin plantation, helped with Phillis's childhood care.[108] Like most slave children, Phillis could neither read nor write and "never had the advantages of an education."[109]

Phillis and Simon were married in Franklin on July 27, 1867. Simon needed Washington Mitchell to help him with the hundred-dollar bond the parish required for the license.[110] The ceremony was performed by R. K. Diossy, a Methodist minister.[111] Diossy performed ceremonies for dozens of freedmen when marriage became legal for the former slaves.[112] His fraternizing with Black people earned him the scorn of his white brothers. The Franklin newspaper said he and his companions "stir up the worst spirit among the Negroes. What little talent they have is in the service of Satan."[113]

The legal witnesses to the wedding were Michael Salabar, Jefferson Ellis, and Charles Brown.[114] Morris Bowens, another observer at the wedding, said that following the ceremony, they "repaired" to the Carlin plantation, where a "dinner and supper were given to celebrate the said marriage."[115] For a short time, at least, the couple must have remained in Carlin's employ.

Carlin's plantation home still stands just south of Centerville on what is now Highway 317. It lacks the grandeur of many plantation homes. North of the white frame home is a small house that was once quarters for slaves. Phillis and Simon likely spent their wedding night in this house or a similar one located on the same property.

Because slaves had not been allowed the privilege of matrimony, Phillis was married before her parents. Michael and Lucy were united on September 19, 1868. Simon was a witness.[116]

On September 4, 1870, Simon and Phillis brought their infant son, William, to the Church of the Assumption, a Roman Catholic church in Franklin, Louisiana, for Christian baptism. It is likely that he was born in the slave house near Centerville. He was christened "William Simon" by Father M. Harnais. Charles Morette and Azelie Peter were godparents.[117] William's middle name, Joseph, must have been added later, perhaps at the time of his conversion.

Simon Seymour was employed as a brickmaker or brickmolder, the same vocation he had had before entering the army.[118] He could read but could not write. He could, however, scribble his own name.[119]

Almost nothing is known of Seymour's childhood or adolescence. His parents had a large family, but most of their children did not live to adulthood. Rosalie, an older sister born in 1869, died before 1880. Simon Jr., was born May 29, 1872; John Emmuas, March 2, 1874; Benjamin, June 4 or 5, 1875; Amos, probably 1876; Andrew, February 11, 1879; Julia, May 11, 1880; Caleb, October 13, 1882; Jacob, June 7, 1885; and Isaac, March 31, 1887.[120]

John died before 1880. Benjamin died on June 10, 1875; Andrew, July 10, 1879; and, Caleb, September 1883. None of the latter three children reached their first birthday.[121] There was also another daughter, Emma, although nothing of her birth and death dates can be established.[122] Illness and bereavement were a constant presence in the Seymour home.

Life in the parish was difficult. One resident said the area was "not prosperous." An outbreak of yellow fever brought a quarantine to the county. A report to the newspaper said forty people were murdered in five years. A school with a Black teacher had been "broken up." Printing offices were destroyed, riots raged, and officers were assassinated.[123] A hurricane blew through the parish, destroying buildings and decimating crops. All of this was before Seymour was nine years old.[124]

In 1880, William, ten years old, was attending school. He could read but had not yet learned to write. In fact, his deprived surroundings afforded little opportunity for formal education. Political disagreements with the school board closed the public schools in the parish when he was eleven.[125] It is reported that even as an adult he had difficulty reading, and what reading he did was confined primarily to the Bible.[126]

Only one anecdote from Seymour's childhood remains, and apparently it made a real impact on his life, as he shared it with participants of the revival. The youngster was walking home late one night and took a shortcut through a cemetery. To his absolute horror he saw a headless man advancing slowly toward him. Even given the terror and intimidation he must have faced every day, the awful sight caused him to freeze in his tracks. As the monstrosity came closer, his little heart pounded harder. Finally, the creature raised itself, and William realized it was only an unhobbled horse peacefully grazing its way through the graveyard.[127]

On August 8, 1883, when William was thirteen, his father purchased a four-acre farm bordering the beautiful Bayou Teche. Located just east of Centerville in the tiny village of Verdunville, the new home must have provided a wonderful place for an adolescent boy to fish, hunt, and reflect on the wonders of God's creation. The property cost Simon one hundred and twenty-five dollars.[128]

Near the end of the decade of the 1880s, Simon Seymour became extremely ill. His condition was described as "weak and feeble" and "hardly conscious."[129] In 1890, he requested a permanent disability or invalid pension from the military. He suffered from dysentery, chronic diarrhea, rheumatism, and affliction of the eyes.[130] On July 16, 1891, he was examined by a physician in New Orleans. The doctor recommended a limited pension because of piles but said Seymour's general appearance was "healthy."[131]

Without any evidence, one is left to guess about the fairness and willingness of a Southern doctor to assist an emancipated slave who had served the Union forces and helped put down the former's rebellion.

During the night of November 14, 1891, Simon Seymour died, suffering from severe chills. A doctor was called but did not respond. The Reverend Valsin Hernandez was also summoned, but Seymour had passed away before he arrived.[132] Phillis lovingly nursed him to the end, then closed his eyes in death and dressed him for burial.[133]

The next day, Hernandez officiated at the obsequies, which were held at the home. Seymour was buried in an unmarked grave in the New Providence Baptist Church cemetery.[134] His request for a disability pension was officially denied two weeks after his death.[135]

Three children under sixteen years of age were left in the Seymour home at the time of Simon's death. From all the evidence available it appears that William, Simon Jr., and Amos had left home to find employment elsewhere.[136] Phillis reported she had "no means of income whatsoever" and she supported her family by her own "manual labor."[137] A neighbor reported that Phillis had no income from her land but sustained herself and the children with a vegetable garden, corn, and potatoes.[138]

Phillis was impoverished. She lived in a small cabin without a chimney. The family farm was assessed at only $100.[139] Her personal property consisted of "one old bedstead, one old chair and one old mattress." The total value of all her belongings was "about fifty-five cents."[140]

With hungry children to feed, in 1894 Phillis sold one half of the farm for only thirty dollars.[141] The struggling family continued to live on what was left of the farm in Verdunville.

For more than a year, Phillis tried to draw a widow's pension from the government. On June 6, 1893, she was finally able to qualify for eight dollars a month plus two dollars each for her three minor children.[142] With this meager sum, she was forced to continue rearing her family in abject poverty.

The family's limited resources were further strained in 1894, when Phillis spent four months in the charity hospital in New Orleans. She was suffering from a carbuncle.[143]

Although the church was called upon at times of transition, such as weddings, births, and deaths, the depths of the Seymours' faith is not known. Traditions say that William Seymour's early religious training was as a Baptist.[144] This seems somewhat suspect, considering the family's Roman Catholic tradition.[145] If he was a Baptist, he was yet unconverted. From his youth, however, he was reported to have had "visions" and held a strong premillennialist view of unfulfilled prophecy.[146]

4

THE SOJOURN BEGINS: SEYMOUR HEADS NORTH

The crises of racial oppression, segregationist laws, familial instability, and economic hardship would force Seymour to leave southern Louisiana at an early age. He was one of a growing number of Black people fleeing the South for greater opportunities in the North. One writer stated, "The Negroes are 'wild to come Norf.'"[147]

The editor of a Black newspaper wrote, "The race troubles which have occurred in the South have driven a great many colored people away from there, and they are starting North with a decided eastward drift...." He continued, "At the rate the colored people are moving northward...the North will be their haven."[148]

One Louisiana newspaper reported that freedmen had "Kansas fever." The writer couldn't quite understand why they were fleeing the parish "with the advantages the colored population have here," but, he argued, "one might as well attempt to cure typhoid fever in a white man with reason, as to cure the Kansas fever in a Black man by that process."[149]

Desiring to migrate to the North and arriving there were two different matters. Some Black people could pay their own way after a prosperous year of work, but this was very challenging for anyone in Seymour's economic class. Those relying on assistance from others often received help from their families and friends, Northern employers, or employment agencies that brought Black people north with the promise of work.[150]

Despite the challenges of these circumstances, William Seymour left his family and all that was familiar to him and headed north. His journey took him from city to city, trying to find the northern "promised land." Specific circumstances, timing, and experiences of that journey are not known.

What we know for sure is that Seymour lived a few years in both Indianapolis and Cincinnati. The details about the rest of his sojourn are speculative. With previously known information, along with census records and city directories, this author theorizes on Seymour's route to economic freedom.[151]

Perhaps Seymour headed first for Memphis, Tennessee, in 1891. (It is impossible, with the evidence now available, to definitively say that the William Seymour in Memphis was W. J. Seymour.)[152] For centuries, Memphis, on a cliff eighty feet above the Mississippi River, had been the site of forts for the French, Spanish, and Americans. The city itself, however, was designed and named in 1819. The fledgling city prospered during the Civil War but faced numerous challenges in the decades that followed. A severe outbreak of cholera and yellow fever in the city prompted non-residents to suggest burning the entire city. By the time Seymour arrived, residents had begun a revitalization that included the digging of hundreds of miles of ditches to drain mosquito breeding areas.[153]

How Seymour traveled from southern Louisiana to Memphis is still unknown. It is possible that he traveled by railroad. The tracks through Centerville had been laid when Seymour was eight.[154] It is also possible, and even likely, that Seymour traveled the Mississippi River on a steamboat from New Orleans or Baton Rouge, which would have been an attractive option for someone of Seymour's economic standing.

Travelers who could not afford a cabin could obtain deck passage at a discount of up to 80 percent. Working with the steamboat's crew could bring a further reduction in the fare. Although the "deckers" were often exposed to the elements, had to supply their own meager rations, and were subjected to a very dangerous journey, thousands chose this method of transportation. Unfortunately, a lack of accommodations and poor sanitation often forced deckers to travel in "filth," while diseases (especially cholera) were prevalent.[155]

In Memphis, Seymour boarded with Henry S. and Lydia Seymour, who were residents at 94 Pontotoc. Perhaps the couple were relatives of the traveler. Not only do they share the same name, but Simon Seymour was a brickmaker and Henry was a bricklayer. On July 19, 1891, during the two years that William was in Memphis, Henry died prematurely at the age of forty-three.[156]

Seymour had two jobs in Memphis. First, he worked as a porter for Joseph Celle, who had a barber shop and grocery store at 32 Jefferson.[157] In 1892, he worked as a driver for the Tennessee Paper Co.[158]

The migrant possibly left Memphis in 1893 and headed up the Mississippi River to St. Louis. For the next several years, he would visit a few cities, like Memphis and St. Louis, that were famous to Black people who had fled slavery during the days of the "underground railroad."[159]

From 1880 to 1900, the Black population in St. Louis exploded. The large cities in Missouri had a 78 percent increase in Black residents in this period.[160] Many of the newcomers were forced to live in conditions described as "grimy and foul beyond our powers of description," "wretched" and "sinks of iniquity." Four out of five St. Louis residents lived in tenement houses, where "Black and white people are mixed up promiscuously."[161]

Seymour lived near the downtown area, boarding at 205 N. 12th and 820 Market. Still unconverted, he worked as a bartender in one of St. Louis's almost 1,500 saloons. On 12th Street alone, there were four saloons within two blocks of Seymour's home.[162] Just over a mile from Seymour's Market Street home was the Rosebud Bar, a nationally known center for ragtime music. It was advertised as a "headquarters for colored professionals."[163]

Seymour moved to Indianapolis, Indiana, at the age of twenty-five.[164] Indianapolis at the time had several very successful Black businesses and professional men. One gentleman, Mr. Puryear, was also a member of the city council.[165] By 1900, the city had a Black community of 16,000, about 9 percent of the entire population.[166]

Indianapolis even had *The Indianapolis Recorder*, "A Negro Newspaper Devoted to the Best Interest of the Colored People of Indiana." The paper claiming to be the best newspaper in Indiana and "the newest, spiciest and best edited journal in the state" carried news and advertisements of special interest to the Black community. News of horrible injustices against Black people and horrific lynchings were interspersed with local news about church events, weddings, and funerals. The weekly newspaper claimed a circulation of 20,000.[167]

Seymour's homes in Indianapolis were at 127 1/2 Indiana Avenue and later 309 Bird Street.[168] The neighborhood wasn't the best or the safest. A few doors down a neighbor killed his wife after he found her in "company with another man." Another neighbor lady was found unconscious after being struck by her husband.[169]

He found employment as a waiter in some of the city's finest hotels.[170] The enterprising young man worked at the Bates Hotel at the corners of Illinois and Washington, the Denison at Pennsylvania and Ohio, and the Grand at Illinois and Maryland.[171] The Grand Hotel Cafe, where Seymour served, was called "Indianapolis' best cafe."[172]

Being a waiter in a fine hotel was one of the best jobs available to a Black man. At a convention for Black waiters, a keynote speaker said:

> No class of man in the employ of the service of men should be less capable of thinking rightly upon the topics of the day than the Negro waiter of America. For none have greater opportunities than he. He is permitted by his daily vocation, to stand at the table of priest, minister, layman, philosopher, student contractor, mechanic, laborer, statesman, dignitaries, potentates, President of these United States of America, and representatives of kings and queens.[173]

Waiters in Indianapolis's "first-class houses" were described as "men of neat appearance, with bright, clean costumes, freshly shaven, close cut fingernails, snowy linen, shoes in good repair (if old and easy); men of pleasant countenance, willing and sprightly."[174]

In December 1899 the Bethel A.M.E. Church in the city hosted a special night to honor Black waiters. Seymour may well have been in attendance. The largest audience in the church's history gathered for the celebration. Showering praise on the profession, the pastor said:

> And gentlemen right there I want to drive a nail in a sure place regarding the relationship between the hotel waiters and the church. The church, above all other classes has always been the hotel waiters' friend, because the waiters have always been first, last and all time the churches' friend. There is no class of people who are in deeper sympathy with all of the churchs' [sic] movements and progress than hotel waiters. No class of people in the main attend church better [sic] hotel men. No class of men are more constant and liberal in their giving than hotel men. No class of men are more genteel in their appearance at church than hotel men....[175]

More than likely, Seymour would have joined a secret Black trade union, the Knights of Industry of the Hotel Brotherhood. The organization was founded in 1885 by H. J. Poe.[176] A person working as a waiter could earn two to five times as much in a northern city than similar employment would pay in the South.[177]

Conditions in the North, however, were not always as good as Southern myth had portrayed them. One contemporary wrote that "difficulty in obtaining a suitable place to live meets the Negro who comes to a large northern city." Many houses and apartments were simply not available to Blacks at any price. When they found quarters, Blacks could be expected to pay more than people of any other race.[178]

While in Indianapolis, Seymour was converted and joined the all-Black Simpson Chapel Methodist Episcopal Church.[179] This life-changing encounter with Jesus Christ marked the beginning of a new pilgrimage for Seymour. Like Nicodemus in the New Testament, he was born again. The old things of his life passed away, and all things became new. (See 2 Corinthians 5:17.) It was the most important event in Seymour's already eventful life. He traded sin for salvation, disgrace for God's grace, and doubts for shouts.

It is easy to understand why Seymour would have found in a Methodist church. Methodist minister R. K. Diossy had married his parents and was also chairman of the Committee on Freedman's Aid Society.[180] Like many Methodist preachers, he was a friend to the Black community and well-known in St. Mary Parish.

The American Missionary Association (AMA) established more than five hundred schools and colleges to teach freed slaves and their children.[181] Seymour might well have attended one of the schools and been taught by a Methodist teacher.

Methodists in the north were much more benevolent to Blacks than their counterparts in the south. The Methodist Episcopal Church South had split from the northern group over the issue of slavery.[182] As early as 1864, Northern Methodists formed African American conferences that ordained Black preachers and allowed them to lead Black churches.[183] About one-fourth of Northern Methodists were Black.[184]

Seymour's life had a newfound purpose after he found salvation. He was no longer traveling from place to place just to escape the poverty and oppression of the South. Now he was a spiritual pilgrim heading for the celestial city on high.

During the time Seymour was in Indianapolis, Simpson Chapel had two pastors: Louis M. Hagood and George A. Sissle. The church was also located in two different facilities: first, at Howard and Second Streets; then, in July 1899, at Missouri and Eleventh.[185]

Church membership in the life of Blacks of this period was more than just a religious experience. According to a contemporaneous survey, the Black church was...

> ...the center of the social life and efforts of the people. What the church sanctions and supports is of the first importance and what it fails to support, and sanction is more than apt to fail. The Negro church historically, as to numbers and reach of influence and dominion, is the strongest factor in the community life of the colored people. Aside from the ordinary functions of preaching, prayer, class meetings and Sunday school, the church is regarded by the masses as a sort of tribune of all of their civic and social interests. Thousands of Negroes know and care for no other entertainment than that furnished by the church.[186]

Still, there was another element to religion in the life of Black Americans. It can be illustrated in an anecdote from the life of abolitionist Frederick Douglass. On one occasion, Douglass was so depressed by the cruelties of slavery that he told an audience, "Oh, God surely must be dead; He does not answer our prayers." In the audience, Sojourner Truth stood to her feet and replied, "Fred Douglass, God is not dead! To your knees, oh ye benighted sons of Africa; to your knees; and remain there. There, if nowhere else, the colored man can meet the white man as an equal and be heard."[187] Seymour, oppressed and abused because of his race, found his equality in the courtroom of God.

As the Methodists drifted toward the left, many conservative members left their ranks, starting a national Holiness movement. Seymour felt especially alienated since the Methodists did not endorse his premillennialist views or his fascination with "special revelations."[188] In only a few years, he found a new church home among the stricter Holiness sects. In fact, several prominent leaders in the early Pentecostal movement moved first from Methodism to Holiness and then to the Apostolic Faith.

Indianapolis was the "gateway" for many Blacks on their way to Chicago and other large cities.[189] Seymour was no exception. Chicago, Illinois, became Seymour's home in 1900. With a population of two million, it was the largest city he had ever lived in.[190] Of all the cities of the north, it is reported that Chicago offered "the largest liberty to citizens of all colors...." When Seymour arrived in Chicago, the Black population of the city was slightly more than thirty thousand. With the influx of Seymour's fellow Southerners, this population had grown by 1,000 percent in thirty years; in another five years, it had swollen to over fifty thousand.[191]

Finding employment in Chicago at the turn of the century was particularly challenging for a Black man. In 1905, Fannie Williams wrote, "The colored people of Chicago have lost in the last ten years nearly every occupation of which they once had almost a monopoly." Williams continued, "White men and women have supplanted colored men in nearly all the first-class hotels and restaurants."[192] Despite the hardship, Seymour once again found work as a waiter.[193]

Housing was also a problem in Chicago. Black Americans were not welcome in white residential areas, and most were crowded into the "Black

Belt," a "forbidding and demoralizing" place in the south division along Clark and Dearborn streets.[194] Seymour boarded with seven other people in a boardinghouse at 2329 Dearborn. His fellow boarders were laborers, porters, and cooks.[195]

Apparently, Seymour stayed in Chicago for a very short time.[196] Still it is unlikely that he could have lived in Chicago at all without encountering the ministry of John Alexander Dowie, faith healer and founder of the Christian Catholic Church. Most converts to Dowie's church came from Methodism.[197] His churches across Chicago seated almost ten thousand. Dowie also had a dozen or more institutions throughout the city, including Zion Divine Healing Home, Home of Hope, a junior school, and a college. In early 1900, the church pledged, "Zion will reach every home in Chicago."[198]

Dowie's position on racial integration was radical for his time. He insisted on integrated seating in his facilities and promised that at least one Black man would serve on his board of twelve apostles.[199] In his periodical, *The Leaves of Healing*, Dowie argued the "the whiter you are, the less strong you are." He wrote, "The time has come for this horrible so-called 'race prejudice' to be wiped out," and "There is only one race—the children of Adam and Eve."[200]

If Seymour encountered Dowie, even causally, he caught a glimpse of a world that did not hold black and white in stark contrast. Even a hint of racial equality would have been more than he ever experienced in his childhood and early adulthood in Louisiana.

In some ways, Charles F. Parham emulated the ministry of Dowie and hoped to be his successor.[201] The latter's racial tolerance was a notable exception. Parham was especially interested in Dowie's emphasis on prayer for the sick. Later, Seymour, too, adopted a strong theology of divine healing.

Continuing to move east, Seymour located to Cincinnati, Ohio, in 1901. He worked as a waiter and roomed at 23 Longworth and 437 Carlisle Avenue.[202]

5

THE SANCTIFIED LIFE: THE SAINTS AND THE REVIVALISTS

Whorile in either Indianapolis or Cincinnati, Seymour was "sanctified," a spiritual experience claimed by Holiness people especially in the century following the American Civil War.[203] Sanctification was considered "an instantaneous work of God wrought in the soul of a regenerated man or woman in answer to perfect consecration, unswerving faith, and importunate prayer.... That work, which cleanses the heart from *all* sin, no matter how preceded by mortification of spirit and crucifying of the flesh, is done in a moment, in the twinkling of an eye, by the mighty power of God."[204]

It is reported that Seymour made a "second" trip to the altar and "prayed until he testified to being wholly sanctified."[205] At the time of his sanctification, Seymour affiliated with the Church of God reformation movement with headquarters in Anderson, Indiana. Emma Cotton claimed that both his conversion and sanctification came while worshipping with the Church of God.[206] It is possible that he attended the Methodist church and the Church of God concurrently for a very short time.

The Church of God was known at the time as the Evening Light Saints or Evening Light Church of God Holiness. The Saints believed that God would send an unprecedented outpouring of the Holy Spirit before Jesus

returned for the church. Their scriptural theme was Zechariah 14:7: "…
but it shall come to pass, that at evening time it shall be light" (KJV).

The Church of God prefers to claim that God, not any man, was the
founder of the group. However, the origins of the movement can be traced
to Daniel S. Warner. Warner, who began his ministry in 1867, was part of
a group known as the Northern Indiana Eldership of the Church of God,
a split from the Winebrennerian Church of God. He was also the editor
of *The Gospel Trumpet,* a Holiness newspaper that carried news and views
of the group.

In 1881, Warner urged the small denomination to separate from the
National Holiness Association. When they refused, he was joined by five
couples who established the first congregation in the Church of God reformation movement, a strictly nonsectarian group.

Warner proposed that all true Christians should abandon denominations and join his group. This gave the Saints the nickname "come-outers,"
which they eagerly embraced. Since the Greek word for "church," *ecclesia,*
means "called out," they claimed that all true Christians were "come-outers"—called not only "out of the world, but out of heathen religions, and all
corrupt and bogus Christianity."[207]

Believing that all denominations were from Satan, Warner taught the
Roman Catholic Church was the beast of Revelation. He further claimed
that all other church groups or sects worshipped the beast by "copying its
standards and doing reverence to a human ecclesiastical system."[208]

Even before the split with the Indiana Holiness group, Warner said,
"The Lord…gave me a new commission to join holiness and all truth
together and build up the apostolic church of the living God." Another
early leader, A. J. Kilpatrick, said that any Christian who was a member of
a denominational church was a member of "two" churches and Jesus "built
only one church."[209]

Although the Church of God has never adopted a statement of faith,
they have always been strong champions of sanctification as a second
work. Warner's first book was *Bible Proofs of a Second Work of Grace.* The
church's doctrinal position on sanctification can be identified in this statement from Anderson College School of Theology: "Persons are sanctified

by the cleansing and empowering work of the Holy Spirit who establishes the lives of believers in perfect love and enables those lives to be lifted above the domination of sin."[210]

The Church of God's view of sanctification was really nothing less than "Christian perfectionism." They believed that this instantaneous work of God's grace restored the soul from "innate depravity and uncleanness" and the "destruction of that carnal element." A sanctified Saint could and would live "victorious over every form of sin." The sanctification event also included an "infilling and indwelling of the Holy Spirit."[211]

The Church of God's strict standards of holy living impacted not only Seymour but the Pentecostal movement in general. Early Saints would not drink tea or coffee. Women could not wear lace or ruffles, men could not wear neckties, and neither gender could wear gold. All professional entertainments were also considered too worldly for the Saints.[212]

Like many other Holiness groups, the Saints also believed in the healing of the physical body through prayer and faith. Warner's diary contained multiple reports of dramatic examples of divine healing.[213]

Warner's followers practiced water baptism by immersion and communion. Both were considered symbolic, and neither was considered a "sacrament" that contained saving grace. Foot washing was also added to their celebrated ordinances.[214]

Seymour would most certainly have received a hand of fellowship from the Saints, a group that welcomed Black people and the poor from its inception. By 1900, there were thirty Black leaders in the movement where whites and Blacks "worked hand in hand." The Saints' teaching on Christian unity not only included breaking down sectarian barriers but also class, gender, and racial barriers. But to the earliest Saints, unity was much more than just a teaching; it was a reality.[215]

The Methodist church welcomed Blacks in their place. The Saints welcomed Blacks in every place. This was perhaps the first place where Seymour experienced the true Christian love that transcended racial barriers.

Whites and Blacks attended the same meetings and often sat together. Racism in any form was labeled a sin. *The Gospel Trumpet* made this clear to any reader, writing:

> There is no room for prejudice of any kind in the hearts of sanctified people. If you, as a white man find any of this in your heart toward the Black man as an individual or toward his people, you need to go to the Lord for cleansing; to the Black brother, I will say the same. All prejudice of every kind is outside the church of God.[216]

If there had been any remaining doubt of where they stood on the race issue, Gospel Trumpet Publishing jumped into the controversy with both feet by courageously releasing William G. Schell's *Is the Negro a Beast?* in 1901. Schell was a prominent voice in the early Church of God.

The previous year, the American Book and Bible House had published a book, *"The Negro a Beast": Or, "In the Image of God"* by Charles Carroll. Carroll had argued that Black people were beasts, less than human, but "created with articulate speech, and hand, that he may be of service to his master—the White man." Carroll argued that his book was based totally on the Bible and science. Instead, it was perhaps the worst example of racial propaganda ever introduced to humanity. Among his nonsensical claims was a foolish theory that if there had been many gods, they would have made many races, but since only one God created man in his image, there could only be one race of man. Carroll tried to compare the physical features of Black people to apes, and his preposterous thesis went downhill from there. All of what he wrote is too ignorant to repeat.[217]

Schell, speaking for the Saints, refuted Carroll point by point, revealing the absurdity of his claims. Describing the progress of the race, he wrote:

> Like the Phoenix in the ancient fables, the Negro race has revived quickly from the tyrannical oppression, ignorance, and superstition to which slavery and bondage had reduced it, and during the short period of thirty-four years has by thrift, industry, sobriety, and Christian piety attained such magnitude, that the world with its crowned heads, nobles, statesmen, and chief dignitaries must acknowledge the greatness of the American Negro.[218]

Seymour seems to have also begun his formal ministry with the Saints and may have had some form of clergy registration with the organization.[219] The credentialing process is vague, and the group apparently did not issue certificates. One segment of the group resolved "that we ignore and abandon the practice of preacher's license as without precept or example in the Word of God, and that we wish to be 'known by our fruits' instead of papers."[220]

By today's standards it may seem strange that he would receive ministerial credentials without receiving formal education, but this was common in the reformation movement. One leader wrote, "All theological institutes and missionary training schools are run too much on the theoretical plan, which is detrimental to spirituality and tends to fill the head and empty the heart."[221]

Warner thought education was "useful" but believed "the spiritual qualification as paramount." Since ministry was God's work, having God working in the minister through "the spiritual anointing" was the key to results.[222]

Several items in the unwritten policies and polity of the reformation movement may have influenced Seymour and his future ministry. First and foremost was the church's view of Christian unity, followed by the doctrines of sanctification, divine healing, an indwelling of the Holy Spirit, and the ordinance of washing feet.

The pattern of ministry established by the Evening Light Saints ministers also had a profound effect on Seymour. Long before the invention of airplanes, reformation pioneers traveled so quickly from place to place, they referred to their work as a "flying ministry." Warner would go weeks without missing a single day of preaching, sometimes preaching up to four times in a day. It was not unusual for him to spend up to eight hours in the pulpit in a single day and then take time for seekers at the altar. Seymour would later follow a similar schedule at the Azusa mission.[223]

Like every northern city he visited, Cincinnati was a major stop on the Underground Railroad. Levi Coffin, the primary organizer of the Underground Railroad, lived in Cincinnati. In this southern Ohio city, Seymour must have encountered many of the prejudices he had known in the South. Most Blacks lived in one of two slum areas known as "Bucktown" and "Little Africa."[224] Late in the nineteenth century, a New

York newspaper carried the story of a public school principal and teacher in Cincinnati who were thrown out of a city restaurant, reporting, "The sole trouble was the fact that they were coloured [sic]."[225]

The motto of the State of Ohio is Matthew 19:26: "*With God all things are possible*" (NIV).[226] A few years later, in Los Angeles, Seymour would learn just how true this passage could be. God used him to do impossible things.

While Seymour was in Cincinnati, Martin Wells Knapp's teachings may have significantly influenced him.[227] Knapp was a Methodist minister who accepted the Holiness experience of sanctification in the early 1880s. Like Warner, he was a "come-outer" (or perhaps a "pushed-outer," since he left the Methodists only after they found him "guilty of imprudent conduct" and "contumacy" for holding an unsanctioned revival meeting in 1898).[228] This created an interesting paradox, since one reason why Wesley started the Methodist movement was his resentment against orders by the Church of England telling him where he could and could not preach.[229]

The censure was eventually overturned, but Knapp was increasingly alarmed by the creep of liberalism, especially in some Methodist seminaries. Eventually he found himself too radical even for the Holiness movement within the denomination.

Knapp was also like Warner in that he promoted equality of the races. Blacks and whites both attended his meetings and were trained in his school. Knapp said that "...throwing stones of criticism and ostracism at saints of God because of caste or color, are among the most stupendous of satan's frauds which curse the earth today."[230]

Although Knapp and Warner were both part of the broader Holiness movement and had several points on which they might agree, they were in totally different lanes. There was little or no fellowship between the Saints and Knapp's followers. Warner saw the Cincinnati revivalist and his disciples in a negative light. Warner accused Knapp of preaching false doctrine and disfellowshipped one of his followers for linking with Knapp.[231] Joining with Knapp would indicate that Seymour had left the Church of God.

The two Holiness leaders would certainly have disagreed on eschatology. Warner was an amillennialist who believed the second coming of

Christ would mark the end of the world. Knapp was premillenialist in his theology, believing that the rapture of the church was eminent and would be followed by the second coming of Christ and a literal one-thousand-year reign of Christ on the earth. In his early ministry, Knapp, like most Methodist ministers, would subscribe to the former position, but in he was converted to the "rapture" and "millennial reign" theology sweeping most independent Holiness groups.

Knapp founded the International Holiness Union and Prayer League and was a predecessor of the Metropolitan Church Association.[232] He was a strong proponent of sanctification, holiness, and divine healing. Like most Holiness preachers, he railed against tobacco use and promoted modest attire. He went so far as to suggest coffee and mince pie might hinder a believer's sanctified walk.[233]

Knapp traveled throughout the country as a popular revival and camp meeting speaker. He was also the author of many bestselling books on the virtues of Holiness, including *Impressions*; *Out of Egypt into Canaan: Lessons in Spiritual Geography*; *Revival Tornadoes: Or, Life and Labors of Rev. Joseph H. Weber*; *The River of Death and Its Branches*; *Pentecostal Preachers*; *The Double Cure*; and several others.

Although student lists do not exist, Seymour may have attended Knapp's ministry training school, God's Revival School. Robeck Jr. believes he was part of the class of 1900.[234]

In July 1901, Knapp was arrested for "disorderly conduct" and required to appear in court. The authorities claimed his meetings were too "noisy." Over one hundred of his students, all dressed in white robes, attended the court hearing as a show of support.

Was Seymour one of the white-robed students? We may never know.

When asked if he had a lawyer, Knapp replied, "God is my attorney, and the Bible my defense." A police officer testified in Knapp's defense, saying, "I was sent to Mount of Blessing to preserve order. I became interested and believed that Rev. Knapp was preaching the true gospel, I joined them. There was no disorder at any time."[235]

Loud meetings were the rule for Knapp. His services were marked by shouting, leaping, and exuberant joy. Once, while preaching, he danced back and forth across the platform, jumped about two feet into the air, and shouted, "Hallelujah."[236] His followers later won the nickname "holy jumpers."[237]

In December 1901, while Seymour was still in Cincinnati, the "revivalist" contracted "malignant typhoid fever" after drinking from a contaminated well. True to his belief that God could heal the sick, he had his followers pray earnestly for him for several days. When a doctor was finally called, it was too late. Not receiving a miracle, Knapp resigned himself to the belief that his death was the will of God. He was only forty-eight years old.[238] His ministry lived on through his wife, his followers, and the institutions he had established.

From Knapp, Seymour would have received teaching on the rapture, the second coming of Christ, and the millennial reign of Jesus on the earth. Knapp would have reinforced Seymour's beliefs in sanctification and divine healing. He would have also introduced Seymour to expressive, demonstrative worship.

After moving to Cincinnati, Seymour contracted smallpox, one of the deadliest diseases of the time. For three weeks he battled the awful plague, clinging to life while threatened by an early grave. Seymour was most likely quarantined with other sufferers in a "pest house, short for 'pestilence house,'"[239] designed for those afflicted with communicable diseases. These houses were necessary at the time, but the adequacy of care was a far cry from modern-day hospital facilities.

Before there was a vaccine, approximately three in ten people with smallpox died from the illness. Death rates were even higher among Black people. The smallpox epidemic that afflicted Seymour most likely had arrived from Honduras and spread rapidly through mining town in nearby Kentucky. The outbreak was a mild variant of the disease and most sickened the "colored" people.[240]

It was not uncommon for smallpox to cause blindness. Before there was an effective vaccine, one third of the blindness in Europe was caused by smallpox. Usually a scar would remain after "acute corneal infection," and the infection "was the most common cause of vision loss in patients with smallpox."[241] The illness left Seymour blind in one eye, and the film from scar tissue is clearly visible in some of his photographs.

Like most survivors of smallpox, Seymour sustained facial scars from the disease. The scarring is generally described as a "distinct cobblestone appearance."[242] To hide the ugly scars, Seymour grew a full beard that he wore for the rest of his life.

Contemplating the ravages of the disease and his mortality, Seymour yielded to what he felt was a divine call to the ministry—a call that he had resisted until afflicted and near death.[243]

Daily newspapers would have been a staple in the nice hotel cafés where Seymour was employed. If he had read the papers (which seems quite possible) on January 20, 1901, he certainly would not have missed the beautifully illustrated half-page spread in the *Cincinnati Commercial Tribune*. The article "A Modern Babel of Tongues in Kansas" told the story of Charles F. Parham and the revival at Stone's Mansion in Topeka, Kansas.[244] Considering Seymour's keen interest in spiritual matters, the article, if he saw it, would have most certainly piqued his curiosity and maybe even whetted his appetite for more of God. In just four short years and through a series of divine connections, the lives of Parham and Seymour would be changed forever after they met face-to-face.

It is not clear where Seymour traveled after 1902, when he disappeared from Cincinnati records, until he reappeared, in Houston in 1905. He may have remained in Cincinnati.[245]

It is also possible that he lived in Columbus, Ohio. Columbus, the capital city of the "Buckeye State," was described as "a neighborly place," with "quiet streets under arching trees" and "people sitting on front porches." Unlike some of the busy metropolitan areas where Seymour had lived previously, in Columbus, "well before midnight, the downtown streets were silent and empty."[246]

In 1904 and 1905, a man named "William J. Seymour" lived at 439 King and 315 West Eighth. His occupations were listed as "salesman" and "commercial traveler."[247] Working as a traveling salesman would have allowed Seymour to make several trips to the South, including Jackson, Mississippi, and Houston, Texas. What he encountered on these journeys, like his experiences of salvation and sanctification, would dramatically change his life and spiritual pilgrimage.

6

THE DIVINE
APPOINTMENT:
PARHAM AND SEYMOUR

In the winter of 1904–1905, Seymour traveled by "special revelation" to Jackson, Mississippi. He received spiritual advice and training from Charles P. Jones.[248]

Jones had been raised as a Baptist, graduated from Arkansas Baptist College, and pastored several Baptist churches in Arkansas, Alabama, and Mississippi. He was introduced to the Holiness doctrine of sanctification as a second work of God's grace, which he defined as "that act of Divine grace whereby we are made holy. In justification, the guilt of sin is removed; in sanctification, the inclination to sin is removed. Sanctification must be definitely experienced to fit us to see the Lord."[249] In 1894, he claimed to have had the experience. The Baptist church forced him out for embracing and preaching the sanctification doctrine.[250]

After a period of fasting and prayer, in 1894, Jones hosted the first of a series of annual Holiness conventions in Jackson. These were attended by Charles H. Mason, J. A. Jeter, and other Black leaders. A nondenominational fellowship, Christ's Association of Mississippi of Baptized Believers, resulted from the conventions. Later the Church of God in Christ, an important player in the early Pentecostal revival, was born from this association.[251] Jones parted with Mason over the tongues issue in 1907 and founded the Church of Christ Holiness.[252] From the beginning, Jones wanted to establish a new faith that would make him "one of wisdom's true sons, and like Abraham, 'a friend of God.'"[253]

According to Shumway, after the visit with Jones, Seymour was more firmly grounded in his already strongly held premillennialist views.[254] One of the tenets of Jones's church was, "We believe that the Lord Jesus Christ will return to judge the quick and the dead; and that we who are alive at His coming shall not precede them that are asleep in Christ Jesus."[255]

William J. Seymour journeyed from Ohio to Texas to search for family members who had been lost to him because of slavery and Reconstruction.[256] He found relatives in or around Houston and made a temporary home there.[257] Seymour also supported himself, once again working as a waiter.[258] During his time in the Houston area, Seymour visited Christ Holy Sanctified Church in Lake Charles, Louisiana. He also attended a Black Holiness church pastored by Lucy F. Farrow.[259]

Lucy Farrow was born in Virginia in August 1851. As a young girl she was sold as a slave, perhaps with other family members, and sent further south.[260] Farrow was the niece of the famous abolitionist and leader of the Underground Railroad, Frederick Douglass.[261] Charles F. Parham described her as a "very light colored woman."[262] She was married to William Pointer, who was born in North Carolina. It is assumed that Pointer died, and she married a man named Farrow.[263]

In 1871, Farrow lived in Mississippi, but she migrated to Texas before 1900. By then, she was widowed again and the mother of seven children. Only two of her offspring survived until 1900. In Houston, she lived in the home of her twenty-nine-year-old son, James Pointer, and his wife, Florence. Pointer was a switchman for the railroad, employed by the H. & T. C. Yards.[264] The family was very mobile, living at 1806 Clay, 1626 Winter, 1717 Edwards, and 1606 Dart.

Seymour became the interim pastor of Farrow's church when she left the "Lone Star State" to serve as governess and cook for another Holiness preacher in Kansas City. Her new employer was the Apostolic Faith evangelist Charles F. Parham.[265] The Parhams, either with affection or patronage, referred to Farrow as "Auntie."[266]

Apparently, the church was either not large enough or affluent enough to support a full-time pastor, and Farrow was forced to rely on secular employment.

Late in the fall of 1905, Farrow returned to Houston with the news that while in Parham's home in Kansas, she had been baptized in the Holy Ghost, evidenced by speaking in tongues.[267] The Lord's handmaiden became a powerful worker. A teenager in Houston testified that her parents had attended Farrow's meetings in Houston. The girl's mother had a broken ankle. Lucy prayed for her with the laying on of hands, and the woman was "reclaimed, sanctified, and baptized with the Holy Spirit, and spoke in tongues and was healed instantly."[268]

Farrow shared the message with Seymour, who had some initial resistance to the teaching, believing, like most Holiness people, that he had received the Holy Ghost when he was sanctified. The Evening Light Saints taught that speaking in other tongues could be restored to the church in the last days, but they labeled the experience of Parham's group a "counterfeit" and a "pretension." An article in *The Gospel Trumpet*, official organ for the Saints, ridiculed the group's tongues speaking, saying the students at Topeka "chattered an incomprehensible jargon."[269]

After a period of prayer and honest searching of the Word of God, Seymour asked God to "empty him of his false ideas." The Lord revealed to him that he had been mistaken in his doctrinal position, and, as a result, he accepted the idea that the Holy Spirit baptism was a third work of grace.[270]

Later that year, Parham moved his ministry headquarters to Houston and held services in Bryan Hall. He also established a short-term Bible college like the one where the Holy Spirit fell in Topeka. Apparently, the school, which opened in late December, was first conducted at Caledonia Hall on Texas Avenue near Main Street, and then it moved to a three-story home at 503 Rusk Avenue on the corner of Brazos Street. Classes were offered in several theological subjects, including "conviction, repentance, conversion, consecration, sanctification, healing, the Holy Spirit in His different operations, prophecies, the book of Revelation and other practical subjects."[271]

Farrow and Seymour both attended Parham's services. A worker in Houston recalled that they "seldom missed a service. They were hungry for all of God's blessings."[272]

Seymour also enrolled in Parham's daily Bible school classes. Mrs. Parham said he "faithfully" attended the classes.[273] Howard A. Goss, a Parham associate, vividly remembered Seymour attending the nine o'clock morning meetings.[274] Goss also recalled the daily activities of the students, saying, "We were given a thorough workout and a rigid training in prayer, fastings, consecration, Bible study and evangelistic work. Our week day schedule consisted of Bible Study in the morning, shop and jail meetings at noon, house to house visitations in the afternoon, and a six o'clock street meeting followed by an evening evangelistic service at seven thirty or eight o'clock."[275]

Warren Faye Carothers and Parham taught Seymour the "doctrines held by the movement."[276] The common perception is that because of the Jim Crow segregation laws, Seymour was not allowed in the classroom but listened to the lectures from the hallway through an open door.[277] There is considerable evidence that this was not the case. Sarah Parham seems to suggest that Parham rejected the "Jim Crow" segregation laws and gave Seymour "a place in the class."[278] A. C. Valdez said that Seymour humbly suggested that he sit outside the door, but Parham welcomed him "inside" the school.[279] Another witness said Seymour was "a regular attendant, taking his seat in the classes."[280] The exact arrangement may never be known.

Because of his race, Seymour was not allowed to tarry at the altar with whites and, therefore, did not have liberty to seek the Holy Spirit baptism. Although these circumstances prevented him from immediately receiving the experience, he accepted without further reservations the Pentecostal doctrine that speaking in tongues was the evidence of the Holy Ghost baptism. He and Parham preached side by side but only to segregated crowds in Black neighborhoods.[281]

Despite the limitations imposed upon him due to his race and his lack of formal education, Seymour's deep hunger for the things of God and keen intellect allowed him to excel in the Bible school studies. Later, he would be able to recite Parham's teachings "word for word."[282] Seymour, already trained in sound Holiness doctrines, rejected Parham's more extreme teachings such as the annihilation of the wicked and an eighth-day creation.[283]

Parham originally hoped to send Seymour to minister to his "own color" elsewhere in Texas.[284] But God willed something better for His humble servant, and He was soon to set those grand plans in motion.

7

THE CALL:
SEYMOUR GOES WEST

The Houston church that Seymour pastored was visited by Josephine "Neely" Terry from Los Angeles.[285] Terry's husband, Mason D. Terry, was a day laborer who worked for the street department.[286] The two were married in Houston in 1879.[287]

Josephine Terry received her Pentecostal baptism while in Houston.[288] Returning to California, she rejoined the Holiness church she formerly attended with her family. Like many in the small congregation, she and Mason were both born in Texas. She told Julia Hutchins, the pastor of the church, about the remarkable preacher she had met in Houston.[289]

The congregation summoned the zealous Seymour to the West Coast to "take charge" of the mission.[290] No doubt, Seymour was anxious to go west, not only to spread the gospel but also to find the "promised land" of racial equality he had not found in his northern sojourns and certainly had not found in Texas.

In addition to his plans for Seymour, Parham did not want him to leave for California until he received his Holy Spirit baptism.[291] Carothers admitted that when Seymour "suddenly announced that he was called of God to go to California," the Texas workers were "disappointed somewhat." However, with high hopes that the Apostolic Faith message would spread to a new region of the country, and with Seymour feeling "it was the leading of the Lord," Parham and his students helped Seymour raise the rest of his expenses for the trip west and wished him "God-speed." They hoped that he would soon return to help with the "important work" in Texas.[292]

One of the students who had been baptized in the Holy Spirit in Topeka was Opal Stauffer Wiley. Wiley, originally from Joplin, Missouri, had traveled with the Apostolic band to Houston. According to Wiley family members, she prayed with Seymour on more than one occasion to receive the Holy Spirit baptism. She laid her hands on him and prayed for his success as he left to preach in Los Angeles.[293]

By the time Seymour left for California, he was already an experienced traveler. He knew what it meant to travel as a Black man in Jim Crow America. He encountered indignity long before he boarded the train. Black people were not allowed to enter the terminal through the same door as white people. The ticket counter would have offered separate lines for Blacks and whites. Black passengers often waited until all the white passengers had bought their tickets. Frequently, the delay would cause Black passengers to miss their train. Black passengers would also be sent to a segregated waiting room. Black academic William Scarborough said, "The negro-waiting room is a dirty, filthy place, with here or there a broken chair or a few benches."[294]

Black passengers would also travel in separate coaches, dirtier and less appointed than the cars designated for white passengers. Often the train would stop in a place that left the "colored cars" outside the shelter of the terminal, forcing Black passengers to board in heat, cold, rain, or other inclement weather conditions. The climate was unlikely to improve once on the train. It was common for the "colored" coach to have no fire even on the "coldest days."

On the train, the dining car was often closed to Black passengers. If it was available, they would have to wait in a queue outside the car until all the white diners had finished, or they might be seated in a separate section behind a curtain. Traveling as a Black man or woman was not just and inconvenience, it was humiliating and extremely burdensome. Martin Luther King Jr. lamented the awful state of affairs in his autobiography, saying, "I could never adjust to the separate waiting rooms, separate eating places, separate restrooms, partly because the separate was always unequal, and partly because the very idea of separation did something to my sense of dignity and self-respect."[295]

On his way to the coast, it is believed that Seymour visited some well-known Holiness missions, including Alma White's Pillar of Fire Church in Denver. It is most often said that Seymour stopped in Denver because White offered free accommodations for traveling clergy. This doesn't seem reasonable considering how far he would have to travel off his route.

By this time, the Southern Pacific offered a "Sunset Limited" route that went directly from Houston to Los Angeles in only two and a half days' time. Going through Denver, Seymour would have had to change trains in Ennis, Texas, and Pueblo, Colorado. This segment of the journey would have taken forty-two hours. Getting to Los Angeles from Denver would have been more difficult. Depending on the route, the trip could have taken from fifty to seventy-four hours. The threat of snow covering the tracks while traveling through the Rockies would stop transportation for days, if not weeks.

Going through Denver would have added hundreds of miles and many hours to his journey. Since train fares were determined on a per-mile basis, it would also have been much more expensive to go through Denver. With Seymour depending on others for his fare, it seems he would not have taken the longer journey without a worthwhile justification.[296]

It is reasonable to conclude that the evangelist stopped in Denver because he already knew Alma White. According to a book she wrote in 1902, White had met Martin W. Knapp at a Holiness convention in Chicago in 1901. That summer, she stayed several days at God's Bible School in Cincinnati. Seymour would have been living in the city and perhaps even attending the school at the time of her visit.[297]

It seems odd that she would not have mentioned previously having met Seymour. However, it is also strange that when she revised the book in 1910, she removed any mention of Knapp and the school in Cincinnati.[298] Both anomalies can be understood in the light of an ugly schism that separated Alma from the Burning Bush organization in 1905.[299]

Another mystery is why Seymour would want to visit White even if he knew her, knowing she was a racist. This is a complicated question. Alma did believe in white supremacy and was a strong supporter of the Ku Klux Klan. Her Pillar of Fire organization was said to be as close to the KKK as "a bee is to a honey barrel."[300] Susie Stanley argues that it was anti-Catholicism and patriotism that attracted White to the Klan, not prejudice against Black people.[301]

There is some evidence for this. In her earliest biography she speaks of her experience as a teacher when she was required to teach two Black students. She said she had been taught that it was "a disgrace to teach colored people." She later wrote it was a pleasure to teach the children and that "all things were working for my good, and that in this the Lord was breaking down my prejudices."[302]

White also spoke contemptuously about a group of white men that closed one of her meetings over racial prejudice. Black people had attended the segregated meeting and were invited to the altar to pray after the white congregation was dismissed. She sympathetically referred to the Black attendees as a "down-trodden" race.[303]

White also traveled with and worked with Black evangelists. She spoke in the most glowing terms about "Aunt Rebecca" Grant, a Black preacher who camped with her and worked in her mission in Denver. White called her "a mighty instrument of prayer" and boasted of the work she accomplished. She eulogized the dear saint, saying that "only eternity will reveal" all she did for the Lord.[304] White also traveled with "Black Susan" Fogg, an evangelist with the Burning Bush.[305] These incidents are not indicative of a woman who hated Black people. Perhaps her prejudices grew stronger as she grew older, or perhaps they are mischaracterized.

One thing is certain: White became one of the bitterest opponents of Pentecost. In her writings she criticized Seymour's appearance and demeanor, even suggesting he had "demons." Her disparagement established an unfair pattern of biased stereotypes against the preacher that continue even today.[306]

8

THE CITY:
LOS ANGELES, CALIFORNIA

When William Seymour arrived in Los Angeles, he came to a relatively new city. One writer said it was a "city without a past. It has no memories, because it has nothing to remember."[307] In some ways, that was correct, yet the environs and the geographical area had a rich and colorful history.

Two hundred and twenty-five years ago, the area now known as Los Angeles was inhabited by the Gabrielino tribe. These generally peaceful and affable people had held the land virtually undisturbed for centuries.[308] They called their little village of three hundred inhabitants "Yang-na."[309]

The Spaniards first visited the area in 1542. More than two centuries later, on August 6, 1771, a group of soldiers, sailors, and missionaries established San Gabriel, the first European mission, near present-day Los Angeles.

When the company arrived at the site, they were immediately surrounded by an armed party of indigenous people whom they assumed to be hostile. Fearing the loss of life, a priest unveiled a canvas with a painting of Mary, the mother of Jesus. The natives were "subdued" by the image, threw down their bows and arrows, and laid their beads and other trinkets at the feet of the painting. The incident changed the attitude of the Native Americans, who then welcomed the European guests to their area.[310]

By decree of California's Spanish Governor Don Felipe de Neve on September 4, 1781, the first settlement was established in the area. The founding name was El Pueblo de Nuestra Señora la Reina de los Ángeles, or, in English, The Town of Our Lady the Queen of the Angels. The original party of settlers comprised eleven men from multiethnic backgrounds: three of Spanish descent, two Blacks, two of biracial descent, and four Native Americans. Included in the settlers' party were their families.[311]

Heads of households were required to be "a man of the soil, *labrador de exercicio*, healthy, robust and without known vice or defect." Three families left within six months, leaving the town with a starting population of only thirty-two.[312] It is not often reported that twenty-six of the founders of Los Angeles were Black.[313]

By 1790, the city had grown considerably, with a total population of 141, eighty of whom were under sixteen years of age. Although no Black people were listed, the group included twenty-two biracial people, one European, seventy-two Spaniards, seven Native Americans Indians, and thirty Mestizos.[314] Because Spanish soldiers were sent to the area to retire, more than one tenth of the population was over ninety.[315] The area provided a pleasant climate, adequate water, and good soil. The colony grew beyond all expectations.

In 1822, the inhabitants of California learned that Mexico had successfully overthrown Spanish rule and the region was now part of the Mexican empire.[316] By 1830, the population reached 1,000, making Los Angeles the largest settlement in California.[317]

In 1846, the United States gained control of California through the Treaty of Guadalupe Hidalgo. On September 9, 1850, the territory became the thirty-first state to join the Union.[318] At statehood, Los Angeles was a humble agricultural village with only 1,610 people. The town had no railroads, no natural harbor, and very few streets.[319]

However, in 1848, the gold rush started a great migration to northern California and prompted a higher demand for cattle raised on the ranches around Los Angeles. One observer noted, "Everybody in Los Angeles seemed rich, everybody was rich, and money was more plentiful at that time, than in any other place of like size, I venture to say, in the whole world."[320]

Despite this widespread prosperity, the ensuing decades were "the darkest chapter in the history of Los Angeles." The gold rush had attracted people from all walks of life to the state, regardless of their social status or background—"the bad as well as the good."[321] For twenty years, the city was called the "toughest town of the entire nation," rife with "fights, murders, lynchings, and robberies."[322] It was a city in need of God.

From 1850 to 1860, the population of Los Angeles grew by 172 percent to 4,385. In the next decade they had a 27 percent growth to 5,728.[323] The result of this growth was a great deal of social unrest. Under Spanish rule, law and order were easily maintained by the church and the strong Catholic family. That was rapidly changing.

One traveling preacher observed, "The name of this city is in Spanish the city of Angels, but with much more truth might it be called at present the city of demons." Taking note that there was not a Protestant church or minister in the city in 1856, the Star reported that the situation "presents a case of destitution, we are certain, without precedent in the state."[324]

Spanish/Mexican California was almost totally Catholic, but Protestant Christianity made some early inroads into the state. In 1826, the first person to arrive in California by traveling overland was Jedediah Strong Smith, known as the "Bible toter."[325] His guide was Jim Beckworth, a Black trapper and trader.[326]

The president of Harvard, the Reverend Edward Everett, exhorted miners to go to the West Coast "with the Bible in one hand and your New England civilization in the other and make your mark on the people and the country."[327] The Los Angeles press also appealed for missionary assistance.[328]

The California Conference of the African Methodist Episcopal Church organized on April 6, 1865. California had over 4,000 "free people of color" at the time. The first African Methodist Episcopal church in the state had been dedicated in San Francisco more than a decade earlier, on February 22, 1852. The Episcopal Church and African Methodist

Episcopal Zion church were also involved in early missionary work among California's Black population.[329]

It can be argued that, even though it went through many changes, Los Angeles essentially remained a Mexican pueblo until the 1880s. Beginning in 1887, competition between railroads led to a rate war, causing the city to grow dramatically. Los Angeles experienced a real estate boom and completed the transition from pueblo to American city.

In 1880, the census showed 11,183 inhabitants. Because Los Angeles had a population of less than ten thousand before this time, governance of the city had been controlled by acts of the state legislature. By 1889, the city had drawn up its own charter and began self government. A mayor, nine councilmen, and a board of education were elected.[330] By 1885, the population grew to about 20,000.[331] This was just the beginning of Los Angeles's phenomenal growth.

The city had grown to 50,000 by 1890. A small percentage of the city, 1,250 people, were Black, many of whom had fled the oppression of the southern states.[332] In another ten years, the city's population exceeded 100,000. By 1910 the number was 319,000, and 7,599 were Black.[333]

When the revival started on Azusa Street in April 1906, there were approximately 228,298 residents in Los Angeles. This was more than double the figures from the federal census taken only six years previously. Los Angeles was the seventeenth-largest city in the United States.[334] The population of the city tells only one part of the multifaceted story of a growing metropolis. Ralph Bunche, a Black native of Los Angeles who later worked for the Department of State and United Nations, illustrated the social and economic condition of Blacks in his city with a story of a Black man from Texas who visited California. In Texas, the man had been in quasi-slavery, subservient to his white "boss."

After his trip west, he refused to go back to his old job. The master approached him, saying, "Sam, you'd better come on back on the job. We've just killed a new batch of hogs, and I've got some mighty fine hog jowls for you."

Sam shook his head and replied, "Uh uh boss. You ain't talkin' to me, no suh. I've been to Los Angeles, and I don' want yo' old hog-jowls, cuz I'm eatin' high on up on de hog now!"[335]

A contrasting anecdote was created when a white man from Texas applied for a job at *The Eagle*, a Los Angeles newspaper serving the Black community. The man told the Black editor, "I am from Texas and down there whites never address Negroes as 'Mr.' and 'Mrs.' So, if you please, I would like to know your first name." The editor informed the stranger that he did not allow employees to become so familiar. The Texan had traveled more than a thousand miles to receive his first lesson in "racial tolerance."[336]

Unfortunately, this perception of Los Angeles as a promised land for Blacks was part reality and part myth. It is true that the city offered more opportunities and equality for Blacks than anywhere in the deep south. Nevertheless, Blacks in Los Angeles did not have the privileges for advancement available to whites. For example, in 1930, Blacks made up less than 4 percent of the total population, but more than 72 percent of the city's porters were Black, as were 31 percent of janitors. Blacks comprised less than one-half percent of doctors and less than 2 percent of lawyers in Los Angeles. A de facto segregation pervaded the city, and Blacks and other non-whites were often refused "food in restaurants, rooms in hotels, tickets at theaters, rides in jitneys, and other services in public accommodation. They were also denied communion by religious congregations, brotherhood by fraternal orders, affiliations by commercial organizations, and membership in the metropolis' other voluntary associations."[337]

Charlotta Bass described the situation of her Black kinsmen with eloquence:

> The Negro people understood clearly why they had come to what they considered the Promised Land. They came believing that their economic status would change from poverty in ghettoes to a better standard of living in better homes and communities. They came hoping also that they were leaving behind that peculiar American brand of discrimination practiced against them in their old home, humiliated them and reduced their status to second class citizenship. When the first breath of race hate poison was blown in their

faces, they became aware that although they had left Texas, Jim Crow had followed close on their heels to their new home.[338]

Los Angeles's newspapers were filled with advertisements and cartoons that were insulting and demeaning to Black people. There was definite racial tension in the city.

On April 6, 1906, just days before the Holy Ghost revival began in Los Angeles, John Davis, a Black man, was taken into custody for a "statutory offense." The authorities had chased him for nearly a mile. Fearing that Davis would be lynched, "a mob of nearly a hundred Negroes" tried to prevent him from being arrested by a police detective.[339]

To this city of mixed signals, God would send William J. Seymour, a humble servant who in so many ways proved that he was ahead of his time and bigger than his environment.

9

THE PREPARATION: HUNGER FOR GOD

The Azusa Street revival, like every great move of God, was not born in a vacuum. In 1916, Frank Bartleman, a Holiness evangelist and Los Angeles participant, wrote, "It would be a great mistake to attempt to attribute the Pentecostal beginning in Los Angeles to any one man, either in prayer or in preaching… 'Pentecost' did not drop suddenly out of heaven. God was with us in large measure for a long time before the final outpouring. It was not a mushroom of a night by any means."[340]

As 1906 drew near, Los Angeles was ripe for a spiritual awakening. Several churches in the area had been praying for a revisiting of the first-century Pentecost. Frank Bartleman was busy stirring the city with tracts and calls for revival. He said, "Day and night the Spirit was heavy upon me…until it seemed I must die."[341]

Born in Carversville, Pennsylvania, on December 14, 1871, Bartleman was the son of immigrants. After a difficult childhood, he found Christ on October 15, 1893. He testified, "He entered powerfully into my soul." Soon, Bartleman accepted a call to the ministry.[342]

In his lifetime, he preached, first as a Baptist, then as a Methodist, next as a cadet in the Salvation Army, and afterward with the Free Methodists, Wesleyans, and Holiness movement. He closed his ministry as a nonaligned independent. While living in Chicago, Bartleman was privileged to meet the great evangelist D. L. Moody, one of the many men who influenced his life.

Evangelizing in the South, Bartleman witnessed the ill-treatment of Black people. He said, "There seemed little justice for the man whom God had made with the black skin." He developed a love for Black people and other marginalized individuals, commenting, "They needed our help the most."[343]

Bartleman lived by "faith," which often meant subsisting on the verge of poverty and starvation. His family endured tremendous hardships as they traveled across the country, arriving in Los Angeles on December 20, 1901. He said, "The Spirit had led us to Los Angeles for the 'Latter Rain' outpouring."[344]

Joseph Smale was also making an important spiritual contribution in Los Angeles. Smale was born in England on July 7, 1867, and was educated at Spurgeon College in London. He started his public ministry as a street preacher in England's capital city. Afterward he pastored a church in Great Britain for three years. Resigning from his church, Smale immigrated to the United States and assumed the pastorate of the Baptist Church in Prescott, Arizona.[345]

Smale left Arizona and moved to southern California, where he became the pastor of the prestigious First Baptist Church in Los Angeles on January 22, 1898. From the beginning, Smale had problems at the church with 10 percent voting against his election. The following comments from the new pastor were an indicator of his hunger for God and a predictor of his stormy relationship with the more traditional First Baptist congregants: "Reformation is not the first need of humanity, but regeneration. If you would have pure politics, clean government, a moral society with peace and contentment reigning, men must have new hearts, and they must let God work through them as they seek to do his will."[346]

Smale led the church through a successful building program, but he was always "an evangelist at heart." Evening services at First Baptist were always directed toward the lost. Famed evangelist D. L. Moody was a guest in the church's pulpit.

A group of lay leaders within the church asked for Smale's resignation in 1902. During three business meetings, one of which lasted eleven hours, the disgruntled members called Smale "unfriendly," "injudicious," "arbitrary," "arrogant," "dictatorial," and more. The church minutes reported, "While our pastor was speaking the weight of the complaints had been almost perceptibly vanishing and the turning of sympathy toward him could well nigh be felt."[347]

Smale's first wife died from complications following the delivery of a child who also died. Smale married again, but the couple soon separated and finally divorced. Grief and loneliness were his companions.[348]

In 1905, Smale preached a series entitled "Is There Eternal Punishment for Those Who Die Christless?" The weight of the messages, the problems at First Baptist, and the personal tragedies had taken a toll on Smale's health.[349]

He requested a sabbatical, during which he visited Greece, Egypt, the Holy Land, and Great Britain. While in Wales he visited Evan Roberts, leader of a mighty outpouring of the Holy Spirit. When he returned to the United States, Smale hoped for an identical outpouring in Los Angeles. His first Sunday sermon was called "The Great Welsh Revival." The service lasted from eleven in the morning until quarter past two that afternoon.[350]

On Monday and Tuesday, he continued sermons on the subject, and he would have presented the same topic on Wednesday, "but the Spirit led the meeting" and there was no chance to preach. It was reported, "The Spirit has come upon some of the members in a remarkable way."[351]

On the following Sunday morning, the clerk reported, "At the close of the first hymn...one member remained standing and witnessed that she had been filled with the Spirit. Then followed testimony, prayer, and praise until about 1:30. The Pastor had no opportunity to preach." That evening, evangelist A. P. Graves asked Smale to forgive him for an offense the evangelist had caused. This, too, was interpreted as sign of revival—that the Holy Spirit was "making clean the House of God."[352]

For fifteen weeks, revival services continued at First Baptist. Hungry people from all over the city gathered twice each day at two thirty in the afternoon and quarter to eight in the evening to believe God for revival.

The slogan for the meetings was, "Pentecost has not yet come, but it is coming."[353]

Smale spoke often about Pentecost and a Holy Spirit baptism subsequent to salvation. In a sermon he entitled "The Explanation," he said, "It is God the Holy Ghost who creates and sustains a Christian, and also who creates and sustains a church."[354]

In another message he called "The Pentecostal Blessing," he continued his emphasis on the Holy Spirit:

> The Holy Ghost! The Holy Ghost! The Holy Ghost!!!—Oh I wish I could ring the truth into every preacher's ear, and into the ears of every church member throughout the world—The Holy Ghost, not our genius; The Holy Ghost, not our culture; The Holy Ghost, not our money; The Holy Ghost, and not man. The Holy Ghost is the sum and substance of our need; for Christ having died and risen again, all that is now needed is the power of the Holy Ghost to deliver souls from death and bondage, and to defeat the devil, and to bring the religion of heaven upon the earth.[355]

Smale was convinced that a Pentecostal baptism required a "second work of grace." He told his audience, "In the advocacy of Pentecostal Blessing we maintain that the blessing known in conversion is not the blessing known in Pentecost."[356] He urged the people to go deeper in God, saying, "Oh, believer, be ever going in for more and more, and more, and more."[357] It seemed a great revival was breaking forth.

Then, members of First Baptist began to complain that church activities were being neglected. The usual method of receiving finances through pledges was replaced by freewill offerings. Church finances declined and the choir director was released.

The "church dignitaries" could not tolerate this new emphasis on revival, and some called on the pastor to desist or "get out." Professor Melville Dozier, a deacon, and his wife, Barton, who served as church collector, took the side of the dismissed choir director and complained that there was too much noise and confusion in the meetings. Dozier also suggested that visitors should be asked to stay away from First Baptist on

Wednesday nights so the church could be left to its own members for at least one night each week.[358]

Following the Sunday morning service, the church voted to give Dozier a dismissal letter. He refused to accept the letter unless it was voted on by all the members at a called meeting. That night, Smale resigned, and a majority of the church voted to accept. The clerk closed the minutes of the meeting by writing, "May God have mercy on this church for rejecting His anointed."[359]

Bartleman, who had been attending the revival meetings, lamented, "What an awful position for a church to take, to throw God out."[360]

Within two weeks, 190 members had requested transfers of membership. Smale started the First New Testament Church located in Burbank Hall, next to the Burbank Theater on Main Street. Bartleman was one of the charter members, as were many of the former leaders and members of First Baptist Church. The prayer for revival continued.[361]

While Smale's group was in a spiritual battle for Los Angeles, Elmer K. Fisher, pastor of First Baptist Church in nearby Glendale, was waging a similar assault on his city. The spiritually hungry pastor often went to his church and prayed throughout the night. After he preached a series of sermons on the need for revival and the Holy Spirit, his deacons also informed him they did not want that kind of preaching in their church. Fisher was quick to offer his resignation and then joined Smale at the First New Testament Church.[362]

It is also significant that the English preacher F. B. Meyer conducted meetings in Los Angeles in the spring of 1905. Meyer was a "deeper life" evangelist, pastor, and author associated with the Keswick movement. He spoke warmly of the revival in Wales, where he had recently visited. Robert Anderson says that Meyer spoke to "large" crowds.[363] Meyer's preaching made a deep impact on Bartleman, who wrote, "My soul was stirred to its depths."[364]

Bartleman continued to work hard for revival, praying, preaching, writing, and distributing G. Campbell Morgan's tract "Revival in Wales" and S. B. Shaw's book *The Great Revival in Wales*. He had also begun written correspondence with Evan Roberts in Wales. The Welsh revivalist responded, "Congregate the people who are willing to make a total surrender. Pray and wait. Believe God's promises. Hold daily meetings. May God bless you is my earnest prayer."[365]

The Methodist churches in Los Angeles were also eager for spiritual awakening. From March 11 to 21, 1906, a "'ten days' Pentecostal convention" was held at the First Methodist Church located at Sixth and Hill streets. The meetings, sponsored by a group called the Pacific Pentecostal Association, were held each day at half past ten in the morning and seven o'clock in the evening. Joseph Smith, a Methodist, and E. F. Walker, a Presbyterian, were the featured speakers.[366]

At 919 Boston Street a group of Armenian immigrants met for services in the home of Demos and Goolisar Shakarian, the grandparents of Demos Shakarian, who would found the Full Gospel Business Men's Fellowship International. The family had recently moved from their homeland of Armenia to escape Turkish persecution. The problems in Armenia had been anticipated by a prophecy that warned the Shakarians and others to flee.

Six years earlier, Grandfather Demos and other family members had spoken in tongues after receiving prayer from Russian missionaries. They were seeking a similar experience in Los Angeles.[367]

The Shakarians were not the only ones in the city who had experienced glossolalia. Early testimonies tell of one lady in Los Angeles who spoke in tongues several months before the Azusa Street revival and another person who had had the experience thirty-five years earlier.[368] Mrs. Elmer Fisher also had a "wonderful" experience with the Holy Spirit when she spoke in tongues and prophesied several years before the Azusa Street revival. As we shall see, what happened to these individuals, although very real to them, was quite different from the Pentecostal outpouring on Azusa Street. None of them realized that speaking in tongues was the unique initial, physical evidence of a New Testament Holy Spirit baptism.

Hundreds more, no doubt, were seeking a revival in their city. Among them were Louis and Cena Osterberg and their son A. G. Osterberg, the young pastor of the Full Gospel Assembly at 68th and Denver. The senior Osterbergs were also newcomers to the City of Angels, arriving from

Michigan and having previously lived in Chicago, where they had met William H. Durham, pastor of the North Avenue Mission.[369]

Other pastors who had a deep hunger for more of God and would eventually be receptive to a new Pentecost included A. G. Garr at the Burning Bush Mission; Thomas G. Atteberry, pastor of People's Church; William Manley of the Household of Faith; William Pendleton, a Holiness preacher; and Ansel H. Post, another Baptist. One young observer said, "For a long time people had been crying out for a deeper walk with God."[370]

A small Holiness sect with a couple dozen churches located mostly in the Los Angeles area held a camp meeting near Downey, California, in August of every year. In 1905, the theme of the meeting was God's desire to send an outpouring of His Holy Spirit. The message was straightforward: if the Holiness people did not "dig in" and get the blessing, God was going to pass them by and "raise up a people who would."[371]

At about the same time as these prophetic words were being preached at the camp meeting, God was at work, gathering the group that would receive Pentecost when it came to Los Angeles. The series of events that brought them together began at the Second Baptist Church. Founded in 1885, Second Baptist was Los Angeles's first Black Baptist church and the second Black congregation in the city.[372] C. H. Anderson served as pastor of the church from 1888 until December 1907.[373]

Mrs. Julia Hutchins, a member of the church, had been teaching sanctification as a second work of God's grace. Hutchins was born in Georgia in 1867. Her birth name was Frances Julia Woods. Sometimes she was referred to as "Fannie." In 1894, she married Willis Hutchins. Willis held lots of jobs, mostly as an unskilled laborer. He could neither read nor write. The couple had three children who died before their fifth birthday, leaving them with one son, Jethro. Julia was born again in 1901, but the circumstances of her conversion are not known. Willis and Julia were newcomers to Los Angeles.[374] Like so many others, they hoped to find a better life on the West Coast.

Hutchins's emphasis on sanctification caused quite a disturbance in the Baptist church, and Pastor Anderson and his congregation could not tolerate this deviation from traditional Baptist doctrine. Mrs. Hutchins and eight families were expelled from Second Baptist.[375]

Looking for a church home, the estranged group of Black believers temporarily joined William Manley, the white pastor of the Household of Faith mission meeting, in a tent near 1st and Bonnie Brae streets. The groups soon divided along color lines, with Hutchins's group moving into another tent near 7th and Broadway.[376]

As winter approached and, with it, the threat of rains, the saints moved their services into the 214 Bonnie Brae Street home of Richard and Ruth (Penn) Asbery, one of the participating families. The Asberys lived in a middle-class Black neighborhood with comfortable but not wealthy homes.[377] The couple had married in Texas in 1885 and had lived there prior to their move to California. In 1900, they were living in the same neighborhood, but at 222 Bonnie Brae. Richard was working as a porter on a train.[378]

By the middle of the decade, Richard had found employment as a janitor in an office building. He was forty years of age and was a native of Baton Rouge, Louisiana. Ruth, born in Virginia, was forty-seven. The Asberys had nine children; only six survived until 1910. Four children, Willie Ella (also called Willella), Robert, Morton, and Richard were living in the home.[379]

On Monday nights, the group would hold a gospel concert in front of the house, attracting curious families from the neighborhood. As the crowd grew, they would be invited inside for an evangelistic service. Among those won to Christ through these efforts was Jennie Evans Moore, who lived with other family members across the street from the Asberys at 217 Bonnie Brae.[380] Miss Moore was employed as a cook by an influential white family.[381]

Jennie Moore was born in Austin, Texas, on March 10, 1874, to Jackson and Eliza Moore.[382] Before moving to Bonnie Brae, Miss Moore had lived on Grand Avenue, where she was a servant in the home of Walter B. Cline.[383] Cline lived at 2530 Figueroa Street and was the president of the Los Angeles Gas and Electric Company.[384]

For more than a year these humble saints had been praying for "more power with God for the salvation of lost and suffering humanity."[385] In God's perfect timing, He was about ready to answer their prayers.

10

THE UNEXPECTED RECEPTION: REJECTED IN LOS ANGELES

Although the home at 214 Bonnie Brae was not small and had a double parlor, by February of 1906, it was too crowded for the meetings to continue there. A small building at 9th and Santa Fe was leased for the services.[386]

Hutchins continued to oversee the congregation, with different members sharing leadership duties. The lay ministry model did not work as well as was originally hoped. Bad doctrines were preached, and some people inappropriately tried to gain ascendancy over the others by harsh means. All seemed to sense the need for a man of God to teach them the Word. They prayed that God would send them a "Holiness" man.[387]

Neely Terry, a cousin of the Asberys, had just returned from Houston, Texas, where she had met Parham, received the Holy Spirit baptism, and spoken in tongues.[388] She had also met a Black Holiness pastor, William Joseph Seymour. Since he had impressed her as a "very godly man," she recommended Seymour to the fledgling congregation. After prayer, the church agreed to send Seymour an invitation with his train fare. He agreed to come and "give them some Bible teaching." The Los Angeles group believed Seymour had already received the Holy Spirit baptism, but he, too, was only a seeker.[389]

The Holiness church on Santa Fe in Los Angeles was eager to see the "man of God" they had heard so much about. When Seymour arrived in Los Angeles on February 22, 1906, all the saints were "happy to see him."[390] They believed it was as "truly a call from God as when He sent His holy angels to tell Cornelius to send for Peter."[391]

The young pastor from Louisiana must have been equally excited to be in California. Many African Americans saw the Golden State as a promised land. Segregation was less severe, and though racism and prejudice were present, they were not as pronounced. The opportunity to serve a new church must have been a dream come true and an answered prayer. Add to this that he had been commissioned and sent forth with a new doctrine from a red-hot revival movement that was growing with every month. He was their first ambassador to the west. Things could not have looked better or brighter for the son of formerly enslaved people.

Seymour started services in the Holiness church on February 24.[392] He preached on regeneration, sanctification, and faith healing. As expected, he also preached on the necessity of being baptized in the Holy Spirit and speaking in tongues.[393] Although Seymour admitted that he himself had not had the experience of speaking in tongues, he taught it was a necessary sign of the Holy Spirit baptism and asked the church to meet him that afternoon at three o'clock to pray with him until "all received their Pentecost."[394]

Some of the group believed that since they were sanctified, they already had the Holy Spirit baptism. Others, probably those familiar with Parham's teaching, did not believe they had received it because the New Testament signs were not following them.[395] Pastor Hutchins herself was less than receptive to Seymour's message because of the emphasis on tongues and his strong premillennialist views. After several meetings she did an about-face, rejected Seymour, and locked him and his supporters out of the building![396]

W. H. McGowan, with his family, attended the meetings. He was a rancher and chicken farmer who had moved to Los Angeles from Brown County, Texas.[397] McGowan did not feel Seymour had been treated fairly and insisted he receive a hearing.

A business meeting was called by Dr. J. M. Roberts, the director of the Southern California Holiness Association. Roberts and several other Holiness ministers were brought into the church to discuss Seymour's theology.

Roberts was called "one of the oldest and most highly esteemed citizens of this community" and a man who was known as "an earnest Christian."[398] Roberts was also a captain in the Third Missouri Cavalry.[399] He had pastored Holiness churches in Garvanza, Azusa, and Pasadena. Bivocational, Roberts also was a dentist, practicing at 505 New York Street.[400] He was elected chairman of the Holiness Association in 1903.[401]

The Holiness Church of California was "one of the earliest organized bodies to separate" from the Methodists over holiness and sanctification.[402] Many others followed. The association was made up of thirty-nine churches with "an estimated membership of 1,500".[403] Twice each year they had a large camp meeting on land they owned in the Arroyo Seco Valley. Describing the camp, one reporter said, "The Holiness Church adherents do not believe in hiding their light under a bushel, and the frequent 'Amens' and fervent 'Hallelujahs' with which the meetings are interspersed help to keep things warm."[404] The association published a church paper called "The Pentecost."[405]

Seymour was given a chance to defend himself and his doctrine. According to one witness, Roberts was glad Seymour was seeking the baptism and he hoped the visitor from Texas would soon receive it. However, the Holiness brethren believed they had received the Holy Spirit when they were sanctified and did not need another experience. Roberts did, however, ask Seymour to contact him and let him know when he had received the Spirit baptism.[406]

Regardless, Seymour was asked not to preach the Pentecostal message in the Holiness churches, including the one that had invited him to California. Seymour found himself hundreds of miles from home with no place to preach, no way to fulfill his mission, and more than likely without enough money to return to Houston.

This unfortunate turn of events not only left the pilgrim unemployed and with very little or no money but also without room and board. One can only imagine Seymour's loneliness and disappointment. Surely his heart ached. Life had been tough for the preacher. He had known prejudice of a different kind, but this may have been his first taste of religious prejudice. What could have prepared him for this unkind rejection by his peers in the Holiness movement? His hopes for a new life in a new land had been crushed under the heavy foot of sectarianism.

The displaced preacher found harbor in the small home of Edward S. Lee. Lee had merely invited Seymour home for lunch. Fortunately for Seymour and later for Lee, the hospitable host would not allow the guest from Texas to be turned out into the street.

11

THE UNSUNG LEADER: EDWARD S. LEE

Edward Spencer Lee, the unexpected host to William Seymour, played a pivotal but sometimes neglected role in the birth of the revival. Perhaps no person but Seymour was more important in the earliest days of the outpouring.[407]

According to census records Lee was born in Dorchester County, Maryland, in December 1859. He was the son of Richard and Ellen (Elanor) Lee. He had one older sister and six younger siblings: three brothers and three sisters. The Lee family worked a small farm near Dorchester, Maryland.[408] In 1860, Lee's real estate was valued at $2,500 and his personal property, $500.[409] The Lee's holdings were well above the 1860 median property wealth of less than $1,200. A farm laborer in Maryland in 1860 earned only about $184 per year.[410]

On November 1, 1864, slavery was abolished in Maryland under Article 24 of the Declaration of Rights of the Maryland Constitution of 1864. President Lincoln had carved out the state when he issued the Emancipation Proclamation in 1863.[411] However, every indication is that Richard Lee was a free Black man, and that Edward was born free. By 1860, Maryland had the highest number of free Black people in the country, with nearly 84,000 non-enslaved individuals.[412]

In Dorchester County 80 percent of the Black populace with the sur-name "Lee" were freemen. Richard is listed as a farmer in the censuses of 1850 and 1860 before the Emancipation Proclamation. Hannah Lane, archivist at the Maryland State Archives, says the listing in the 1860 census "suggests that Edward Lee was born to a free Black family."[413]

Richard is on none of the county's slave rolls, but a man named Richard Lee is on the list of former slaves. He was manumitted by his owner, Samuel Cook, on October 12, 1855.[414]

Court records show that Richard lived in a house owned by James and Elizabeth Thompson. After their deaths, their son conveyed a parcel of land to William Lee, "a free colored man." William was a next-door neigh-bor to Richard and most likely a close relative.[415]

At the time of the federal census in 1880, Edward was still living at home, working on the family farm. The death of his father in April 1880 disrupted his life.[416] His father's death may have forced him to leave the security of home and begin a westward migration.

Little is known of Lee's activities over the next twenty years. In 1888, he registered to vote in Alameda, California, and worked as a porter. In 1892, he worked as a butler in San Francisco. He registered to vote in Fresno in 1898, citing his occupation as a "preacher." Apart from these small bits of information, his travels, conversion to Christ, and early spiri-tual journey are currently a mystery.[417]

In 1900, Lee was still living in Fresno, California, and was working as a hostler, caring for the horses of Charles B. Shaver, the owner of a local lumber mill. At forty years of age, Lee was still single.

Lee was also the pastor of an African Methodist Episcopal Church in Fresno. He had led the congregation for about four years.[418] The circum-stances that brought him to this ministry are unknown and may never be known. The ministry did not support him financially, and he held numer-ous personal service positions common for Black men of the period.

Lee attended the annual conferences and served on the Children's Day Money Committee in 1898. That same year he was recommended to the "second year's class." On Sunday, August 21, the Tabernacle Baptist Church, an African American congregation in Los Angeles, appointed Lee to speak at their morning service.[419]

In 1901, Lee left the pastorate in Fresno and moved to Los Angeles. He was still a Methodist minister in good standing with the Stephens A.M.E. Church. He was itinerating as an evangelist and preaching revivals in nearby churches. He had also established an unaffiliated benevolence ministry located in a storefront building at Mateo and East Seventh streets.

Lee called the new ministry the Home Mission. He partnered with Rev. and Mrs. John Hayes, pastor of the People's Church, a congregation in fellowship with the local Holiness Association. The Hayeses were white.

The Home Mission had services every night of the week and held classes for children on Saturday and Sunday afternoons. The underprivileged children in the neighborhood were not only taught the Bible but practical skills like sewing and cooking.

The work requested but did not receive the blessing or support of the Merchants and Manufacturers' Association and, therefore, had limited resources, depending only on the generosity of individuals and their free-will offerings. They were part of no denomination and claimed no particular doctrines. They were interested in helping people from all churches as well as those with no church.

Lee said, "The beauty of our mission is that while we are in perfect harmony with all the churches we do not teach any particular brand of religion. All we want is to save souls and prepare sinners to join the church of their choice." According to Lee the work was a great success, and he boasted that four people had been converted one night. [420]

Lee said a Congregational church was the only other place in the city that was carrying on a similar work—with one notable exception: "they draw the color line."[421]

The Home Mission had no "color line." People of all nationalities, ages, and previous conditions were welcome. Their congregation was about half Black and half white. The Los Angeles Times reported there were no "race wars" on record.[422]

It is significant that five years before the color line was washed away at 312 Azusa Street, Edward Lee joined with a white couple and was leading a fully integrated work in Los Angeles. Under his shepherding, Black and white people worked and worshipped together for the good of the community and the kingdom. He was a forerunner.[423]

In the next few years, Lee found love and married Mattie Wiley.[424] There was an age gap of over twenty years between the couple.[425] In 1900, Mattie had been living at home with her parents, Peter and Mary Wiley, in Santa Rosa. She was a music teacher.[426]

Mattie's brother Frank and his wife, Ophelia, made headlines in 1905 when Ophelia was "sanctified" and "joined the Holiness Band." Seeking a divorce, Frank complained that his wife was neglecting him and giving all her time and attention to church work. He said she was giving his hard-earned money to the church like "throwing water down a rat hole." At night Ophelia would go in the front yard to "sing, pray and shout," while she would get the "jumps." Staying up at night to prevent her from disturbing the neighbors was disturbing his sleep, and he "could not efficiently face the next day's work." For Frank, all of these "exaggerated religious ideas" amounted to "extreme cruelty" and warranted a divorce.[427]

By 1906, Edward and Mattie joined the Holiness movement, attending the Peniel Mission. Founded as a rescue mission in 1896, Peniel built a large sanctuary in 1894. The primary funding for the new building was provided by British philanthropist and famed cricket player George Studd. The mission was nonsectarian and nondenominational but Holiness in their theology. Phineas Bresee, founder of the Church of the Nazarene, was one of their early leaders. Later, many of the participants at the Azusa Street revival would come from Peniel Hall.[428]

The Lees had also joined the faithful at the Asbery House on Bonnie Brae. Lee was employed as a janitor at a bank located at Seventh and Spring streets. Lee, "a much esteemed saint," and his young wife, Mattie, lived at 114 1/2 South Union Avenue near First Street.[429]

Three years earlier, Lee had met Charles F. Parham and learned about the Holy Spirit baptism evidenced by speaking in tongues. He had been seeking the experience since that time.[430]

Lee would receive the Holy Spirit baptism before Seymour. He would receive before any of the seekers meeting at Bonnie Brae. As the story unfolds, it does so around Edward Lee and his profound hunger for more of God.

12

THE PRAYERS
ANSWERED: HOLY GHOST
OUTPOURING

Lee and Seymour began to pray together each day when the former returned home from work.[431] Soon, cottage prayer meetings began as other spiritually hungry members of the church visited Seymour in the Lees' home. This little group of seekers became determined to receive "their 'Pentecost' at all costs," sometimes praying all night long.[432] Men would also leave their jobs just to spend time in prayer.[433]

With no one to look to but the Lord, Seymour entered an even more intense time of prayer and fasting. Even before he had heard the Pentecostal message, he had a deep desire for more of God. John G. Lake, who later became a friend of Seymour, recalled Seymour's testimony as follows:

> Prior to my meeting with Parham, the Lord had sanctified me from sin, and had led me into a deep life of prayer, assigning five hours out of the twenty-four every day for prayer. This prayer life I continued for three and a half years, when one day as I prayed the Holy Ghost said to me, "There are better things to be had in the spiritual life, but they must be sought out with faith and prayer." This so quickened my soul that I increased my hours of prayer to

seven out of twenty-four and continued to pray on for two years longer, until the baptism fell on us.[434]

Seymour tried to explain what happened when individuals received the Holy Spirit baptism. At times, he said, they would shake under the power and anointing of the Holy Spirit. This seemed like foolishness to some of the people, and Seymour could not explain it adequately to satisfy their curiosity.[435]

In the meantime, the spirit of prayer consumed Lee. At times he would go into the basement of the bank where he was employed and "hide away," spending hours in prayer.[436] One day while seeking the Lord, Lee had a vision. He knew he was awake, because he was praying, but he saw two men come toward him. He knew them to be Peter and John. Both men lifted their hands to heaven, began to shake under the power of God, and spoke in other tongues. The Holy Spirit came upon Lee and he, too, began to shake. The entire experience frightened Lee, as it might have done to almost anyone, and he jumped up, wondering what was happening.[437]

That night, Lee came home and told Seymour, "I know now how people act when they get the Holy Ghost." Lee's hunger was intensified, and he sought God even more earnestly.[438]

Jennie Moore, who had never had such an experience in her life, was also given a vision. Moore saw three cards, and each one had two languages written on it. In total, they were French, Spanish, Latin, Greek, Hebrew, and Hindustani.[439] Although blessed by the experience, at the time she had no idea what the vision meant.

One evening when his faith was high, Lee told Seymour, "If you will lay your hands on me, I will receive the baptism." Seymour hesitated, remembering the Bible said to lay hands "suddenly" on no one. Later in the night, feeling it was time, the minister placed his holy hands on the seeker and said, "Brother, I lay my hands on you in Jesus's name."

Lee fell to the floor like a dead man. Mrs. Lee was so scared, she cried, "What did you do to my husband?" Seymour realized that they were too frightened for the Lord to finish His work at that time, so he prayed that Lee would get up. In a "few minutes" Lee got up and sat in a chair, but he had had a touch from heaven and would never be the same. From that day forward, he sought God day and night.[440]

Cottage prayer meetings continued at the Richard Asbery residence.[441] The small group of Black believers waited on God, occasionally joined by a few white visitors, such as the McGowans. Frank Bartleman visited for the first time on March 26.[442] Despite much opposition, special services and serious seeking continued for several weeks.

Concerned that no one had received the baptism, Seymour sent to Houston for two helpers, Joseph A. Warren and Lucy F. Farrow.[443] Farrow, the Houston pastor, was especially gifted to lay hands on people who would then receive the baptism in the Holy Ghost with evidentiary tongues. Howard Goss once saw a line of twenty-five people stand before her for prayer. As she prayed for them, "many began to speak in tongues at once."[444]

Warren was a forty-five-year-old grandfather who had received a miraculous healing from persistent "chills and fever."[445] In Houston, Warren had worked as a drayman or driver for Hugh Waddell, Henke and Pillot, Houston Trunk Factory, and Joseph F. Meyer Company. He had lived at several addresses, including 613 Taylor, 812 Robin, and 509 Henderson.[446] Apparently, he, like Seymour, was an earnest seeker for Pentecost but had not yet received his baptism.[447]

Services on Friday, April 6, lasted far into the night. Seymour encouraged the small group to begin a ten-day fast, trusting God for His blessing. Remarkable services were also held on Saturday and Sunday at Bonnie Brae.[448] Two different but not especially contradictory accounts exist describing what took place on Monday, April 9, the third day of the fast. Emma Cotton, an early participant, remembered Lee asking Farrow to pray for him. Like Seymour, she hesitated at first, but while at dinner, she rose from her chair, went to Lee, and prayed for him. Lee fell from his chair and spoke in tongues for a "few minutes." Lee's wife and brother-in-law thought it strange that God did not do "much" through him.[449]

According to Charles Shumway, who interviewed the participants, Lee became ill after fasting for three days and asked Seymour to pray with him for his healing. At about six in the evening, while Seymour was there, Lee asked the preacher to pray for him that he might receive the Holy Spirit.

As Seymour laid hands on him, Lee was baptized in the Spirit and began speaking in tongues.[450] It is not implausible that both accounts are true, taking place the same evening in the Lee home, the latter experience following Seymour's prayer being more satisfying to Lee.

The weather was fair and warm that evening as Seymour and Lee made their way to the prayer meeting on Bonnie Brae Street.[451] At the start of the service, only Black attendees were present. They sang, prayed three times, and shared personal testimonies. Seymour preached on the Holy Spirit using Acts 2:4 as his text. When he finished, Lee lifted his hands to heaven and began speaking in tongues. Jennie Moore, resting on an organ stool, fell to the floor. She began speaking in tongues immediately, becoming the first woman in Los Angeles to receive the Holy Spirit. As she spoke, she was reminded of her vision. She said it seemed like "a vessel broke within me and water surged up through my being." When this rush reached her mouth, she spoke in all six languages she had seen on the cards in her vision, and after each message in tongues, there was an interpretation in English. After this, Moore, who had never played the piano before that time, went to the keyboard and played the instrument while singing in tongues.[452]

The outpouring that followed must have been wonderful. When Moore fell to the floor, several attendees were also struck down "as by a bolt of lightning from Heaven." Some attendees were in trances for up to five hours. Several, including a Brother Hughes, a Sister Traynor, and her two children, Bud and Sis, were baptized in the Holy Ghost in a few minutes. The Asberys' daughter, Willie Ella, ran in from the kitchen to see what was happening.

The exuberant congregation rushed into the front yard, still speaking in tongues and magnifying God. Bud Traynor stood on the front porch preaching and prophesying. Jennie Moore prophesied in the Hebrew language. The meeting lasted until ten in the evening.[453] Pentecostal revival had arrived in California.

The outpouring of the Spirit on Bonnie Brae did not catch the attention of Los Angeles's newspaper reporters. Instead, on April 10, *The Los Angeles Express* carried the story of the previous evening's service at a revival in Newman Methodist Church. The evangelist, R. S. Marshall, and his work in Los Angeles, although notable, have been long since forgotten. But what happened that night on Bonnie Brae will be remembered as long as church history is recorded and revival fires continue to burn.[454]

Despite the silence from the secular press, by the next morning, there was such a crowd of observers, visitors could not get near the house. Among those who persisted and did get inside, many fell under the power of God when they entered the Asbery home.[455]

Over the next three days, services continued almost day and night. Crowds of both Blacks and whites filled the house and the yard. A writer described it like this: "The porch became the pulpit, and the street became the pews."[456] Hundreds were saved and many healed or baptized in the Holy Spirit. Several "sanctified washwomen" were baptized in the Holy Ghost, and May (Mrs. G. V.) Evans was the first white person to receive the Pentecostal blessing.[457] F. W. Williams, another Black brother who had been attending the meetings, soon received his baptism.[458]

Witnesses said the house literally shook as in the days of the Acts of the Apostles.[459] On one occasion, the porch gave way under the weight of the crowd, but no one was injured, and the porch was quickly repaired.[460]

On the third day after the initial outpouring, Thursday, April 12, Seymour received his Pentecostal baptism.[461] Seymour and a white brother had tarried late, seeking the Holy Spirit. Seymour's companion, weary and discouraged, said, "It is not the time." Seymour, refusing to quit, replied, "Yes, it is. I'm not going to give up." In a short time, he came through to the baptism and spoke in tongues. He testified that it was like a "sphere of fiery, white-hot radiance falling upon him."[462] The Asberys' son, Morton, said Seymour "fell under the power of the Holy Ghost like he was dead, and spoke in unknown tongues."[463] Describing the event later, Seymour said, "We had prayed all night, when at four o'clock in the morning, God came through the window."[464]

During the day on Good Friday, Jennie Moore was assisting her employers and a guest attorney with a dinner party. As the event concluded and her mistress was addressing her, Moore started speaking in tongues. As one can imagine, the mistress was "scared," and all present were concerned. Thinking that something was seriously wrong with Moore and that she might be "losing her reason," the employers insisted, against her protestations, that she take a week off to "rest."[465]

When she heard about the meetings, Cena Osterberg was at the Crocker Street Hospital praying for someone with a broken leg. A Black woman from the Bonnie Brae meetings heard her pray and entered into the intercession. After the joint prayer, she told Cena about the meetings and invited her to attend. When she arrived at her home, she asked Louis, her husband, to attend the meeting with her.[466]

At first, Louis was hesitant; a hardworking carpenter, he was weary from the day's work. Cena, determined not to miss a blessing, went to the meeting alone and was greatly impressed. The following night, she shared her testimony at the Full Gospel Assembly, where her son, A. G., pastored.[467]

Soon A. G. Osterberg and three of his men—Brothers Holler, Dodge, and Weaver—attended the meeting.[468] Before they got to the house, they heard the singing; with some sense of relief they said, "They are singing just like we do."[469] His mother had failed to mention the racial composition of the meeting, and the pastor, having never worshipped with Black people, was not prepared for the interracial audience. Commenting to himself, he said, "What kind of a mess are we getting into here?"[470] All walls were broken down, however, when he heard the Black brothers and sisters testify and then pray "with such earnestness that tears were running down their faces."[471] The people would also tremble and shake under God's power. Osterberg noted that the whole trend of the meeting was, "We are hungry for more of God."[472]

A lady from the congregation spoke in tongues, and Osterberg remembered Paul's writing to the Corinthians. Soon another lady went to the piano and began to play as she sang in tongues. To the curious observer, "It was harmonious and beautiful."[473] Others on their knees began to speak in tongues. When they arose, their faces looked like those of angels. "There was nobody praying for them; nobody laying hands on them; nobody trying to urge them on to something; it was just simply God opening the window of heaven and throwing down upon them, the blessings that they themselves could not contain."[474]

Osterberg did not get into a mess, but something got into him. Remembering the meeting, he recalled, "We got humble pretty quick or we didn't get very far."[475]

It was evident that the news of Pentecostal revival was rapidly spreading through all quarters of the city.

13

THE PLACE: "OLD AZUSA"

Seymour and his followers searched for any facility large enough to accommodate the growing revival. They found a vacated African Methodist Episcopal (AME) church building at 312 Azusa Street. The forty-by-sixty-foot structure was just off San Pedro near downtown Los Angeles. Azusa Street was a two-block-long dirt lane originally called "Second Street" or "Old Second Street."[476] The Los Angeles River and a freight terminal for the railroad split Azusa Street into two separate blocks; the mission was near a dead-end of the western side of Azusa Street. The legal description of the property was "lots seven and eight of Orange Tract, City of Los Angeles, County of Los Angeles, State of California."[477]

Bridget "Biddy" Mason was the previous owner of the property obtained by the church. Mason was born a slave in Georgia. She never knew the names of her parents. She was brought to California from Hancock County, Mississippi, via Salt Lake City, Utah. Her master decided to leave California and move to Texas. When they stopped in Los Angeles County, the news spread that Mason and others were being taken to Texas and back into slavery. The county sheriff issued a writ preventing the owner from taking the slaves out of California.

After a long and sometimes disappointing attempt to flee slavery, Mason won her freedom in the California courts on January 19, 1854. Trained as a nurse on a Southern plantation, she became a successful midwife and invested her earnings wisely, becoming one of the wealthiest and most respected women in the city. By the 1870s, she owned a large acreage in the area that would become downtown Los Angeles, including what we know as 312 Azusa Street. The AME church was started in the bedroom of Mason's home on Spring Street between Third and Fourth.[478]

The church was originally established as Stevens AME in 1872. Some of the Bonnie Brae attendees had been members of the church when it was first built.[479] There was a cottage on the front end of the property that was moved to the back of the lot so the church could be built where it had stood.[480] The original structure had a sharp pitched roof and decorative Gothic windows and doors. The sanctuary was upstairs, accessible from both sides via A-framed stairs on the front of the building.[481] Apparently the unfinished lower floor, called the basement, was used to stable horses, one of which strayed from its owner in 1899.[482]

Stevens AME (now First AME[483]) was the oldest Black church in Los Angeles. It was started with a "small membership and labored under many disadvantages to pay for the old church property on Azusa Street." Under the capable leadership of Pastor J. E. Edwards, the debt was paid in 1902.[484]

In the years following 1888, Azusa Street began to change as large warehouses were built near the church. Disturbed by the decline of the area, in 1903 the congregation moved into more comfortable facilities and a better neighborhood at Eighth Street and Towne Avenue.

After the congregation moved out, the function of the building at Azusa Street was changed. The former upstairs sanctuary was partitioned and converted into living quarters for renters. Little is known of the clientele, though the newspaper reported when two of the boarders died.[485]

In early March 1904, an arsonist began to set fires in Los Angeles. After midnight on March 6, a secondhand store was torched, and an upstairs boarder barely escaped with her life. On March 10, at almost the same time, a fire started at the Olive Stables. Thirty-two horses perished in their stalls, and almost as many rigs were lost. While firefighters were battling the blaze, another fire started at a feed mill on San Pedro Street. A third fire burned the old AME church on Azusa Street. Fortunately, the building was unoccupied; the only loss was the structure. News reports said that "repairing it will probably be impossible." Nevertheless, it was repaired, at least to some extent. The structure lost its aesthetic appeal when a flat asphalt roof replaced the pitched church roof.[486] Formerly a picturesque chapel, it now resembled a burned-out box. In 1906, the deteriorating two-story structure was being used by a contractor as a warehouse for construction materials and a stable for hay and stock.[487]

The windows were broken out of the old building and the exterior stairs were removed. The only reminder that the building had once served as a house of worship was the former upstairs entrance, which retained the shape of a Gothic window.[488]

The structure, as dilapidated as it must have appeared, fit well into the neighborhood. Azusa Street itself was said to be similar to "a back alley" in an Eastern city.[489] One writer described the surrounding area as a "slum."[490] Stables, wholesale houses, lumberyards, and a tombstone shop surrounded the old church building. Saloons in the locale and other unwholesome establishments gave the district a "skid row flavor."[491]

Seymour was able to rent the building, still marked with a large "For Sale" sign, for only eight dollars a month.[492] Sawdust was scattered on the dirt floor of the large barn-like room downstairs. Straw matting was placed around the altars. The ceiling was low, and the joists were exposed. The walls were unfinished but had been whitewashed. Fire damage was still visible on the walls and ceiling, and cobwebs had collected in the joists and windows. The building had no indoor plumbing, and a smelly outhouse behind the building was the only available restroom.[493]

Skeptical visitors on a wet night in December 1906 were not impressed with the edifice. They gave this unflattering appraisal:

> The building was a humble one, and the so-called "saints" were meeting in the basement. It had been raining considerably. There were no sidewalks to step upon and we had to wade through the mud at the danger of slipping constantly, and this would give a little idea of what we saw inside. On entering the building, we found the surroundings unfit for public gatherings.... The hall is a very plain, unplastered room that would be far more suitable as a place for "assembling" horses, than people.[494]

Even an avid follower, Clara Lum, wrote, "It was the most humble place I was ever in for a meeting."[495] Other, more sympathetic visitors compared the rough quarters to Bethlehem's manger.[496]

There was no raised platform, and seating was arranged in a square around the makeshift pulpit fashioned from two wooden shoe crates stacked one on top of the other and covered with a cotton cloth. According to one attendee, a junkman would value the lectern at about "fifteen cents."[497] Seymour sat behind these boxes with his head bent low in prayer. He did not sit with a shoebox on his head, as some have falsely reported.[498]

Arthur G. Osterberg, who also worked as a "straw boss" for a major construction company, was working on the gas building next to the Huntington Building at Sixth and Main streets. He asked three of the men on his crew if they wanted some overtime and hired them to help clean and renovate the building. They worked for almost a week on the run-down structure.[499] The men brought in nail kegs and rough wooden planks for benches and added some mismatched chairs.[500]

J. A. Warren and some other worshippers built an altar, but Osterberg said it was too flimsy. He approached his employer, a successful builder named J. B. McNeil, and asked for some two-by-sixteen-inch pieces of lumber, saying he would replace them if they were needed. A friend of the pastor/builder with a long "express" truck carried the planks to the mission, and Osterberg built the altar. When Osterberg went to pay McNeil, who had once been a student for the priesthood, McNeil replied, "Well, I would be a poor former Roman Catholic priest that couldn't do that much for some colored religious folks."[501] Most worshippers never knew they were kneeling at a "Roman Catholic" altar.

The second floor of the building provided an apartment for Seymour and other church workers. Another long narrow room upstairs that stretched the length of the building would become the Pentecostal upper room. A sign would be placed in the room that read, "No talking above a whisper."[502]

Almost a year before the revival began, Frank Bartleman had prophesied, "Los Angeles is a veritable Jerusalem. Just the place for a mighty work to begin. I have been expecting just such a display of divine power for some time. Have felt it might break out any hour. Also that it was liable to come where least expected, that God might get the glory." God found that "least expected" place at 312 Azusa Street.[503]

14

THE BEGINNING: THE FIRST WEEKS OF REVIVAL

The first service in the mission was likely held on Saturday, April 14, 1906, the day before Easter. According to one early participant, the building could provide seating for no more than a few dozen seekers.[504] Approximately a dozen saints gathered for daily services, as evening services continued for a few nights at Bonnie Brae.[505]

On Easter Sunday, Jennie Moore attended Pastor Smale's First New Testament Church, which still worshipped at Burbank Hall. At the service's close, attendees were invited to share their testimonies. Moore told about the prayer meetings at Bonnie Brae and her experience with tongues speaking. She said that Baptists were receiving the Pentecostal baptism. Following her testimony, she gave a long utterance in tongues. Ruth Asbery followed with the English interpretation, saying, "This is that prophesied by Joel." The effect on the congregation was varied. Some shouted, others spoke in tongues, and some ran into the street in fear. After the benediction, many from the congregation stood on the sidewalk discussing the significance of what had occurred.[506]

That Sunday afternoon, services were held at Bonnie Brae, where God was "working mightily."[507] Mack E. Jonas attended the Azusa Street

Mission for the first time that evening. He said afterward, "I had never been in a meeting like that before."[508] The news continued to spread.

On Tuesday, April 17, the *Los Angeles Daily Times* sent a reporter to the mission. His article, although very critical, could not have been timelier. The piece appeared on page one of section two on Wednesday, April 18, under "Weird Babel of Tongues." He described the congregation as "colored people and a sprinkling of whites," and Seymour as an "old exhorter" who cried, "Let tongues come forth." The reporter's assessment of the meeting can be summarized as "pandemonium."[509]

At 5:12 a.m. the same morning, most of California was shaken by a deadly magnitude 7.8 earthquake that all but destroyed San Francisco. "In the city and surrounding region, at least 700 people were killed and losses totaled more than $400 million (1906 dollars)."[510] Author Jack London described the devastation: "Not in history has a modern imperial city been so completely destroyed. San Francisco is gone."[511]

Shortly before noon on April 18, two earthquakes shook Los Angeles within ten minutes of each other. People had gathered to read telegraphic dispatches of the disaster in San Francisco when the ground trembled beneath their feet. "Thousands ran in panic when the earthquakes struck."[512]

No one should underestimate the impact of this seismic activity on the Azusa revival. Frank Bartleman wrote concerning the earthquake, "It had a very close connection with the Pentecostal outpouring.... Men began to fear God....This paved the way for the revival."[513]

On April 20, the *Los Angeles Express* published a cartoon depicting the Grim Reaper with his sickle of death poised over San Francisco. The caption read, "Ye Know Not What a Moment May Bring Forth."[514] This poignant message in a secular medium was a shocking reminder of the brevity of life.

Bartleman immediately published a widely read tract about the earthquake. Forty thousand copies were distributed in Los Angeles alone in a matter of weeks.[515]

A. G. Garr wrote to his Burning Bush colleagues and reported:

How much this makes me think of the coming of Jesus! No one was looking for this awful disaster, but today on our streets you can hear nothing but the "renewed horrors" coming on the cities around San Francisco as well as Frisco itself. It seems the fires of Hell were fanned by the festivities of sin until the iniquity of this great city reached the throne of God, and now they have reaped the reckless wrath of eternal justice.[516]

On the night after the earthquake, only "about a dozen" Black and white worshippers were at the mission, but they quickly provided additional seats as more seekers gathered. Although Rachel Sizelove says there were only about a dozen present for an afternoon meeting in June, there must have been much larger crowds at night.[517] A. G. Osterberg said one hundred were present at his first mission visit—which probably occurred in the evening, since he worked by day for McNeil Construction Company.

For three years, the Apostolic Faith Mission held services three times a day—morning afternoon, and night—seven days a week.[518] More often than not, the services had no break, with people staying all day and sometimes until dawn. Lawrence Catley, an early attendee, said the services lasted from "can to can't."[519] Another observer said, "The place was never empty. The people came to meet God. He was always there."[520]

The atmosphere was so charged with God's Holy Spirit that people would worship all day without thoughts of food. The Osterberg family habitually gathered around their table for coffee and Sunday lunch at two o'clock in the morning after a full day and night at Azusa. The spiritual bread served at God's table was better than anything waiting at home.[521]

The services were dynamic. Everything was spontaneous. There were many prayers, hymns, songs sung in tongues, testimonies, Scripture readings, and sermons being preached. People shouted, shook, prophesied, and spoke in tongues. At times, men would fall all over the house, like an army slain on the battlefield, or they might "rush for the altar en masse."[522] Jennie Moore led the singing, and some favorite hymns included "Under the Blood" and the most popular one, "The Comforter Has Come."[523]

It was not uncommon for worshippers to see bands of angels. Sarah H. Payne received the Holy Spirit baptism at the mission when she heard "the real message of His soon coming." A few nights later, she heard a legion of angels singing, "Behold, I come quickly." The heavenly visitors sang unbroken verses from the final chapter of Revelation and a few lines from other parts of the Bible.[524] Others reported seeing the "glory over the building."[525]

Prayer was a central part of the meeting. During a typical service, the congregation would be down on their knees six or eight times, praying for special requests.[526]

Seymour and others would often prophesy, as was the case on March 2, 1907, when William Durham received the Holy Spirit baptism. Seymour had retired to his apartment to rest, but the Lord spoke to him, saying, "Brother Durham will get the baptism tonight." He returned to the altar in time to hear Durham speaking in tongues. Seymour raised his hand and prophesied that wherever Durham preached, the Holy Spirit would fall on the people.[527]

Testimonies often lasted for hours "as so many had so much to tell of God's blessings." One night, little Ruth Fisher stood for a "long time," waiting her turn to testify. When the leader, presumably Brother Seymour, said, "All right, little girl," her courage failed her. She "became frightened and sat down."[528]

When proud men would come into the building, the Spirit would arrest them and humble them before the congregation. Bartleman said, "The breath would be taken from them. Their minds would wander, their brains reel. Things would turn black before their eyes. They could not go on." The church would pray, and God would do the rest.[529]

Despite the small beginnings in a humble barn, Osterberg's report continued that within thirty days, "The meetings were attended by people of every group on the face of the earth."[530]

15

THE REVIVAL: HEAVEN ON EARTH

Osterberg reported that after only a few months of being open, the mission saw approximately 1,300 people attend the services: up to 800 crowded into the building, and the rest stood on the boardwalk outside observing through the low windows and open doors. Every inch big enough for a chair was "jammed full."[531]

The *Los Angeles Daily Times* reported, "The room was crowded almost to suffocation. Many were seated in the windows and scores who could not enter crowded around the lobby and struggled for a view."[532]

Many were surprised, if not perplexed, by God's choice of instruments and locations, but no serious seeker could doubt that God was sending revival. When Dr. J. G. Speicher left Zion, Illinois, for Los Angeles, he was a skeptic and a critic. He described himself as "bitter and opposing all these things." He "abominated" the Pentecostal movement. However, upon arriving at Azusa, he testified, "I soon lost sight of the human in the more marvelous manifestations of the divine." Speicher said, "I saw and heard things that broke down my prejudice completely for I became convinced that it was none other than the wonderful power of the Holy Spirit that was working through this people."[533]

William Manley, pastor of an "un-denominational" mission in Oakland and editor of the *Household of God*, visited Azusa Street for the first time in August of 1906. He said, "God had full control from first to last." The Holiness editor was so touched by the Holy Spirit that he told his readers, "This is the most heavenly place I ever was in. My soul is charmed and filled, and is dancing for joy."[534]

When Pastor William Durham of Chicago arrived in February of 1907, he said, "As soon as I entered the place, I saw that God was there."[535] Clara Lum reported that Azusa "was the most humble place I was ever in for a meeting," but she added, "But have never seen the power of God manifest in so many people, nor have I ever seen such manifestations of his power."[536]

Los Angeles was a very cosmopolitan city at the time of the revival. One resident said, "I suppose there is not a tongue or people on earth not represented here, more or less."[537] Many times, foreign residents or visitors in Los Angeles would come to the mission and hear people speaking in their native language. This phenomenon convinced and converted many skeptics who had visited the mission out of curiosity or criticism.

The mission was visited by a Muslim from the country of Sudan. He worked as an interpreter and spoke sixteen languages. While in the service, he heard messages in tongues directed to him that no one else could understand. He identified the languages and wrote them down.[538]

On another occasion, Anna Hall visited a Russian church in Los Angeles and was able to speak to the congregants in their native tongue. Hall had no knowledge of the language. Later, a group of Russians visited at Azusa Street, and when Irish Lee spoke and sang in tongues, they understood him to be speaking to them in their language. *The Apostolic Faith* reported that it was a "holy sight" to see one of the Russians embrace Lee.[539]

It is impossible to know how many were saved at the mission. Bartleman wrote that such instances were "too numerous to take space to mention."[540] Witnessing these miracles not only convinced many of the authenticity of the gift but led multitudes to salvation.[541]

The first person saved was a Hispanic worker whom A. G. Osterberg had hired to help clean and prepare the building for the first services. Some Black women from the Bonnie Brae prayer group were already at work in the mission, but when the new crew of workers arrived, they immediately announced a prayer meeting. One of the ladies began witnessing to one of the workers, a Roman Catholic. Initially, he resisted her witness, even trying to insult her with "smart" talk. She replied, "Don't you start to give me that kind of language. I want you to listen to me because you are going to have to give an account of yourself to Almighty God on the day of judgment." Soon he was off in a corner on his knees, weeping, praying and being born again.[542]

The first Black man saved in the mission was Mack E. Jonas. His conversion occurred on April 20, 1906, less than a week after the mission opened for the first service.[543]

If each individual testimony of the converted could be known and recorded, they would fill volumes. Bridget Welch, a drug addict who had been in and out of prison for twenty years, was among the converts. Another attendee with a morphine addiction was saved and "has no more desire for the stuff." A nonbeliever who was twice committed to an asylum for the mentally ill, and who went from place to place denying Christ, was saved and was working to win others.

One man testified, "Last week I came in a backslider and half drunk and the Lord forgave my backsliding right in my seat and in a few days afterward, He sanctified me and baptized me with the Holy Ghost." A burglar who had been plotting to rob a house came to the altar at Azusa. He left his skeleton keys under the altar, was saved, and was baptized in the Spirit.[544]

Late in the summer of 1906, the mission sponsored a water baptism service to immerse many of the new converts. About five hundred "singing, shouting, joyful" pilgrims made the trip to Terminal Island, a beach near Los Angeles. The group spent all day worshipping the Lord and baptizing new converts. On this day alone, Seymour baptized 106 people in the Pacific Ocean.[545]

Seymour would lead the service seated behind a makeshift shoe-box pulpit. Often, he would bow low with his head inside the crates or leaning against their side, praying as the services progressed.[546] Witnesses remembered him as "very prayerful, a very quiet man."[547] The Azusa leader believed, "Our highest place is low at His feet."[548]

A holy awe filled the mission. When worshipers arrived, they wanted to meet God "first." Attendees did not salute each other or even shake hands with each other. Instead, they knelt by their chairs, which would be wet with tears, or they put their head under a bench or in a corner. They met men in the Spirit, not the flesh.

To avoid the gratification of the "flesh," songs and singers went unannounced; performances received no applause. No one would stand to sing or testify unless they knew God had moved on them. Seymour said, "Dear loved ones, these meetings are different from any you ever saw in all your born days. These are Holy Ghost meetings, and no flesh can glory in the presence of our God."[549]

Those anointed with the message would stand and deliver it. It might be a man, woman, or child. The message could come from the back row or front row. A participant said, "It made no difference," and the official newspaper reported, "No instrument that God can use is rejected on account of color or dress or lack of education."[550]

It was wonderful when God moved on someone in the audience. One such time, a little Black girl rose to her feet and sang unto the Lord while tears coursed down her cheeks. Another leader in the mission announced to the participants, "God can use any member of the body, and He often gives the more abundant honor to the weaker members."[551]

One of the most remarkable features of the meetings was the "heavenly choir." As few as one or two or as many as twenty men and women would spontaneously join in an anthem, all in harmony and different pitches, each singing in a language unknown to them. An observer described the manifestation by saying, "This singing service was literally inspired by the Holy Ghost. It was mostly in known tunes, but the words were chosen by the Holy Ghost."[552] Another source reported, "It was not a something that could be repeated at will, but supernaturally given for each special occasion and was one of the most indisputable evidences of the presence of the power of God."[553] Bartleman said it was "beyond description...the very foretaste of the rapture."[554] Williams reported, "It would sweep over the congregation, no words, just worshiping, intoning in the Spirit."[555] Many skeptics were convinced of the authenticity of Pentecost when they saw and heard this demonstration.

At times the meetings would become so boisterous that the police were called. On at least one occasion they were sent by the ministerial association. When the police interviewed neighbors and received no objections to the endless noise, they withdrew without hindering the meeting.[556]

With all the demonstrations of the Holy Spirit, some argued that the Azusa group was out of order. Nothing is further from the truth. Brother Seymour kept a constant rein on the services, even if it was a loose rein. *The Apostolic Faith* reported, "This gospel cost us too much to run off into fanaticism."[557]

In West Africa, there is a parable comparing discernment and holding an egg. If you hold it too loosely, you could drop and break it. If you squeeze it too tightly, you could crush and break it. You must hold it very carefully. Del Tarr noted that this same careful balance is needed while handling a move of God.[558] This is the kind of pastoral supervision Seymour gave to the Azusa revival.

Seymour himself described the decorum of the service: "Often when God sends a blessed wave upon us, we all may speak in tongues for awhile, but we will not keep it up while preaching service is going on, for we want to be obedient to the Word, that everything may be done decently and in order and without confusion."[559] He also told the congregation, "Now don't go from this meeting and talk about tongues, but try to get people saved."[560]

The wise pastor counseled the church against "unbecoming and fleshly demonstrations." If someone would get too loud, pounding his or her seat, Seymour would tap that person on the shoulder and say, "Brother, that is the flesh." While services were conducted downstairs, Bible study and prayer often continued upstairs. If the pastor was in the upper room and things got too boisterous while someone else was leading the services in the modest sanctuary, he would stomp on the floor or call out, "Hey!....,
Hah!..., Hey!...Hah!" signaling a call to order.[561] Azusa Mission was not a place to blow off steam. Men did not "fly to their lungs," they flew to the mercy seat.[562]

John G. Lake recalled a service when one man insisted on "getting up and talking every little while." Seymour endured the long-winded fellow for a long time but finally ran out of patience with his disorderly conduct. Pointing his finger at the man, he said, "In the name of Jesus Christ, sit down." Lake said the man did not sit down, he fell down and was carried out of the service.[563]

Clara Lum, who later left the mission, said Seymour had "true wisdom and gentleness in conducting the meetings. All realize that he is called of God and anointed for the work."[564]

Elmer Fisher, another minister who led the services one night in 1908, announced to the congregation, "We have no planned program, nor are we afraid of anarchy or crooked spirits. God, the Holy Spirit, is able to control and protect His own work. If strange manifestations come, trust the Holy Spirit, keep in prayer, and you will see the word of wisdom go forth, a rebuke, an exhortation that will close the door on the enemy and show the victory won."[565]

When asked about the physical demonstrations and manifestations, E. S. Williams recalled, "I think there was perfect liberty, far as I seen, never pressure put on anybody for or against."[566]

If a gentle rebuke was not enough to guarantee order, the elders employed a more active strategy. A visitor stood to testify, and when the audience did not well receive his remarks, he complained, "He picked himself up from the sidewalk." Edward Lee and Elder Kaufman had removed him from the meeting.[567]

As many as one hundred at a time would be in the upper room seeking the Holy Spirit baptism or divine healing.[568] They would pray at three California redwood planks laid end to end on backless chairs.[569] Crutches, canes, pipes, and other trophies of divine deliverance hung on the walls of the upper room.[570] One report said, "People were healed there every day."[571]

Emma Cotton described herself as a "walking drug store." She suffered from weak lungs and cancer. After prayer at Azusa Street, she was instantly healed. For decades she never returned to a doctor. She said, "In those days...when they said God would heal you, you were healed."[572]

A. G. Osterberg witnessed his first miracle during the mission's opening week. He said when people had a request for prayer, Seymour would say, "Let us stand and ask the Lord's help in this matter." Osterberg noticed a Catholic man in the congregation. He would cross himself and watch the others to see how they prayed. Osterberg noticed, as the man came down the aisle with his wife, his face uplifted and clapping his hands, that the man had a club foot. Osterberg further noticed that, after a few minutes of walking back and forth, the man was no longer stumbling as he walked. The man was so deep in the Spirit that he had not seen the difference in his physical condition. When he realized his miraculous healing, he walked to the altar shouting, "Hallelujah."[573]

"I was a wreck in my body," was Florence Crawford's self-diagnosis. She was thin, diseased, and broken down after suffering from spinal meningitis. An early accident had left her with a spinal injury that required her to wear a harness with straps and a metal plate for eleven years. After visiting Azusa, she received complete healing. She testified, "Once diseased from the crown of my head to the soles of my feet, I was made sound and well through the blood of Jesus."[574]

One baby that accidentally swallowed medicine it had found in a closet was miraculously healed. The baby's body was already cold, but the mother cried out to God, "Lord, save my baby."[575]

When Maggie Bowdan first visited the mission, her husband, William, threatened to leave her if she got "mixed up" in the new sect. When Maggie came home baptized in the Holy Ghost, William changed his mind and became a seeker. He received a few nights later when they heard "a sound as a high wind" sweep the building. The Bowdans longed for another child and promised God that if He listened to their prayer, they would give the baby back to Him to preach the gospel. Once again, God came through, and Frank, their miracle baby, was given to God for the ministry.[576]

Rachel Sizelove's daughter, Maud, was afflicted with a kidney stone and had suffered miserably for almost twenty-four hours. According to her sister, Snowdie, she was "writhing in agony." Matt, another of the Sizelove children, was sent to the mission to summon Seymour. Seymour came to the home and approached the suffering child's bed. He opened a bottle of anointing oil, anointed the girl's head, and said, "Little girl, do you believe

God can heal you?" Seymour did not get "excited." He prayed "calmly" and believed in God for healing. Instantly, the girl turned over in the bed and fell into a "peaceful sleep." She slept through the entire night, healed by God's mighty power.[577]

A next-door neighbor was talking over a three-strand barbed-wire fence when Lawrence Catley heard about God's power to heal. The lady said, "They pray and people get well." Catley was suffering from "consumption" and sorely needed a miracle. He asked his mother to take him to the mission. When she did, "God delivered him."[578]

These healing miracles were not the only ways God demonstrated His mighty power at Azusa Street. Demonic spirits were powerless when confronted with God's awesome presence. One young man fell before the altar at the front of the church. He groaned and foamed at the mouth as his body and limbs went through various contortions. Seymour courageously met the challenge and demanded, "Come out of him thou unclean spirit."

After almost three hours of spiritual warfare, the man "turned and writhed on the floor, barking and snarling like a dog when finally the unclean spirit departed." The penitent was immediately baptized in the Holy Ghost and began speaking in tongues.[579]

Financial miracles were commonplace at Azusa Street as well. The mission did not take offerings at the beginning of the meetings. A mailbox was placed in the meeting room with a sign above it, "Settle with the Lord." Members and visitors filled the box with their freewill offerings.[580]

As God would speak, people would give. One witness says that Seymour would walk around with five and ten-dollar bills sticking out of his hip pockets without knowing who had placed them there. From day to day, food would arrive from unexpected and anonymous sources to feed the many volunteers who lived or worked at the mission.[581]

One day, a wealthy orange grower resisted God's invitation to give a considerable amount of money to an outgoing missionary. The Spirit shook the man off his chair and onto the floor. No one knew what was happening with him until he later testified, told the whole story, and said, "Yes, Lord."[582]

The revival initially began among a few who were African American by ethnicity, Holiness by doctrine, and were from the lower to middle economic classes. However, eventually, men and women from all ethnicities, creeds, and socioeconomic positions worshipped together in the unassuming little mission. While some intoxicated homeless individuals stumbled into the meeting barely standing on their wobbly legs, the wealthy railroad mogul Collis P. Huntington and his wife arrived in a beautiful buggy drawn by "well-groomed" horses.

When A. W. Orwig arrived for his first service in September, he was surprised by the presence of "so many people from the different churches, not a few of them educated and refined." He saw pastors, evangelists, foreign missionaries and "others of high positions." And yet, "All took part in the services in one way or another."[583] Even a critic of the movement acknowledged that the Pentecostal message had captured the hearts of "some of the brightest and best."[584]

Cecil Polhill, one of the "Cambridge Seven" who left the university to pledge their lives to missionary service, was baptized in the Holy Spirit at Azusa Street.[585] C. T. Studd, another of the seven, had a brother, George, who taught a Bible class at Azusa.[586] Other veteran missionaries who visited and endorsed the work of the mission include Daniel Awrey, Paul Bettex, and Samuel Mead.[587]

One of the best-known attendees was Aldophus S. Worrell, a Baptist scholar and evangelist. Worrell was an extremely colorful character who was a Confederate officer in the Civil War. A graduate of Mercer University, he taught biblical languages in at least three colleges and was the president of at least three others. Worrell wrote at least eight books, translated the New Testament, and edited several periodicals.[588] Concerning the Azusa revival, Worrell wrote, "There are real gifts of tongues here in Los Angeles, and other gifts of the Spirit."[589]

Dr. Henry S. Keyes, the president of the Emergency and General Hospital in Los Angeles and a member of the First New Testament Church, was an early believer. Keyes said he "had been one of the most skeptical...and did not wish to be convinced." Yet, in a short time, he was convinced that the gift was "genuine." When his daughter, Lillian, received the baptism of the Holy Spirit at the First New Testament Church, it was front-page news in Los Angeles.[590]

"Professor" Carpenter, the head of the math department at Los Angeles High School, was also a participant at the meetings.[591] Night after night, he would listen to the exhorting of a spiritual leader with no formal education. The contradiction should be obvious.

A witness said, "Divine love was wonderfully manifest in the meetings. They would not even allow an unkind word said against their opposition, or the churches. The message was the love of God. It was a sort of 'first love' of the early church returned." "We only recognized God...All were equal."[592]

Frank Bartleman observed, "The 'color line' was washed away in the blood."[593] Other participants remembered, "Nobody ever thought of color," and "everybody went to the altar together."[594] A. G. Osterberg remembered, "In the beginning, color meant nothing to us. There were no Blacks and no whites...It was God's Spirit welding us together, and that is a kind of unity that you can't define."[595]

The Apostolic Faith reported, "One token of the Lord's coming is that He is melting all races and nations together, and they are filled with the power and glory of God. He is baptizing by one spirit into one body and making up a people that will be ready to meet Him when He comes."[596]

In this respect, Azusa was fulfilling the New Testament pattern of "*There is neither Jew nor Greek, there is neither bond nor free, there is neither male nor female: for ye are all one in Christ Jesus*" (Galatians 3:28 KJV). Many believe that this unity of the Spirit, more than glossolalia, was Azusa's unique contribution to the Christian church.[597]

What Seymour accomplished was truly phenomenal. In 1906, more Black men were lynched in America than in any other year.[598] Jim Crow laws racially segregated Black and white populations and subjugated Black people under a patronizing false claim of "separate but equal."[599] Racial epithets and slurs filled Los Angeles newspapers. Reporters and cartoonists lampooned Black people.

An editor in Bombay wrote, "Less than fifty years ago Negroes were owned by white people in the United States as slaves. No one but an American can rightly understand how despised the Negro is."[600] Yet, Seymour led an interracial revival that literally changed the world. Frank Ewart said, "His sweet winsome ways broke down all barriers erected by spiritual bigotry, and won the love and trust of the people to such an extent that they forgot their natural animosities."[601]

The Holy Spirit drew people from all over the world to Azusa Street. Pilgrims came from Canada, Africa, China, Japan, and India.[602] Many rode trains for more than three thousand miles to visit the mission.[603] One family rode a horse-drawn wagon for five hundred miles.[604] People gave testimonies saying they felt the power of the revival when their train was still miles out of Los Angeles. Many said the "atmosphere changed" when they got within a few blocks of the meeting, and the Holy Spirit literally "pulled" them along to the mission.[605]

M. L. Ryan said, "Converts from all quarters of the globe are arriving constantly not knowing why they come nor the impelling cause...they are just moved by the Spirit to go to Los Angeles and when there are directed to their destination, the Azusa Street stable."[606]

Bartleman wrote, "Conviction was mightily on the people. They would fly to pieces even on the street, almost without provocation. A very 'dead line' seemed to be drawn around 'Azusa Mission,' by the Spirit. When men came within two or three blocks of the place they were seized with conviction."[607]

Demos Shakarian and his brother-in-law, Magardich Mushegan, were walking on San Pedro Street, looking for a job in the nearby stables, when they heard the familiar sounds of Pentecostal worship. They did not know other people in Los Angeles spoke in tongues. After inquiring at the door, they were welcomed into the mission.[608]

The Apostolic Faith, the periodical published by Seymour and his staff, grew until it had a worldwide circulation of more than fifty thousand.[609] Like Paul, who sent out prayer cloths from his body, the workers would lay their hands on the papers before they were mailed.[610] Many who received the periodical were instantly healed, saved, or received the baptism of the Holy Ghost.

A band of volunteers worked on the paper, answered mail, prayed over the hundreds of letters received in the offices, and oversaw the organization's expansion. Warren and Farrow, who had come from Texas to help Seymour, were regular helpers, but many more were added as the work grew. Glenn A. Cook, a former newspaperman, was the business manager and assistant state manager; Hiram Smith was an associate who, along with Seymour, signed ministerial credentials (he was given the title "deacon"); Jennie Moore and Phoebe Sargent were city missionaries; Florence Crawford was state director; G. W. Evans was field director; and Reuben Clark, a Civil War veteran, served as secretary to the board of trustees. Mary Perkins and many, many more worked as needed.[611]

Clara Lum was the secretary, stenographer, and editor of the paper. Perhaps more than any other individual, she recorded and preserved the authentic story of the Azusa Street Revival. If Lum had not transcribed Seymour's sermons and published them in *The Apostolic Faith*, we would have no examples of his preaching.

Lum was born on April 3, 1869, in Dane County, Wisconsin.[612] She was the daughter of Rev. Charles Lum, a founder of the Methodist seminary in Evansville, Wisconsin.[613] The family moved to Oregon, and Clara moved farther south to California.[614] She graduated from the "normal school" at Occidental College in Los Angeles in 1892.[615] The next year she attended the World's Fair in Chicago.[616] In 1894, she was recommended for a supplemental document equal to an educational diploma.[617] Lum attended the Methodist's Epworth League Convention in Los Gatos in 1895. That in itself is not remarkable, but she received attention for riding a "wheel," or bicycle, twenty miles to the meeting.[618] She served as a public-school teacher in El Toro and Artesia, California.[619]

Charles Haney, founder of the World's Faith Missionary Association in Shenandoah, Iowa, visited the West Coast, and Clara heard him speak. She took a subscription to his publication *The Firebrand* and was even more impressed by his work. Soon she moved to Shenandoah, where she joined the association. She had a life-changing spiritual experience in 1898. Haney called her "one of the Lord's handmaidens especially adapted for this work." Lum began to write for *The Firebrand* and was soon made the associate editor. As new positions and assignments at the WFMA office were multiplying, her health began to fail.[620]

To avoid the severe winters in Iowa, Lum moved back to Oregon, where she continued in the gospel work. By the winter of 1905, she was back in Los Angeles serving as a stenographer for Phineas Bresee, the founder of the Pentecostal Church of the Nazarene. She planned to return to Shenandoah in the spring but instead found her way to the mission on Azusa Street, where she became as a "little child" and received the baptism in the Holy Ghost.[621] Her talents proved to be a blessing to thousands.

Some workers lived in the apartments above the mission, while others lived in a small cottage behind the church building. Meals for the mission workers were also prepared, cooked, and served in the cottage.[622] After returning from a short tenure as a missionary to Africa, Lucy Farrow had a room in the cottage, where God continued to use her to pray for visitors to be healed and baptized in the Holy Spirit.[623]

Many of those baptized in the Spirit at Azusa became Pentecostalism's greatest leaders. Soon, the message of Pentecost spread from Azusa and circled the globe. Phineas Bresee, an early critic, compared the influence of the Azusa Street Revival to a pebble cast into the sea. If such was the case, this small pebble created a spiritual tidal wave.[624]

16

THE WORD:
SEYMOUR'S PREACHING

Like the famed Welsh revivalist Evan Roberts, Seymour did not preach long or often, allowing things to go their own way or, more appropriately, "the Lord's way."[625] E. S. Williams, a regular participant, said, "His preaching was very limited."[626] Yet, when he spoke, he ministered under such an anointing that his words changed the world.

A. G. Osterberg described Seymour the preacher "as a slow speaking, humble, unpretentious, Bible loving, God fearing minister."[627] In another interview, Osterberg said of Seymour and his preaching: "He was meek and plain spoken and no orator. He spoke the common language of the uneducated class. He might preach for three-quarters of an hour with no more emotionalism than that post. He was no arm-waving thunderer, by any stretch of the imagination. The only way to explain the results is this: that his teachings were so simple that people who were opposed to organized religion fell for it. It was the simplicity that attracted them."[628]

After hearing Seymour at the Los Angeles mission, John G. Lake commented:

He had the funniest vocabulary. But I want to tell you, there were doctors, lawyers, and professors listening to marvelous things coming from his lips. It was not what he said in words; it was what he said from his spirit to my heart that showed me he had more of God in his life than any man I had ever met up to that time. It was God in him who was attracting people.[629]

Seymour preached to ten thousand people at John G. Lake's church. Lake said, "God was in him." When the "glory and power of God" was on him, men shook, trembled, and cried out to God.[630]

Tom Hezmalhalch came to Azusa Street after reading about the revival. He said the idea of conscious cleansing became "very real" to him as Seymour taught from John 15:3 (KJV), "*Now ye are clean through the word which I have spoken unto you.*"[631]

When William Manley attended, he described Seymour's sermon as "short" and "fiery." He said, "They speak with the most intense earnestness I have ever seen, and what they say is in the tenderest love. Not a harsh word is spoken. No denunciation of anyone, except in tender love."[632]

Charles H. Mason, a founder of the Church of God in Christ, recalled his visit to Azusa, commenting, "I also thank God for Elder Seymour who came and preached a wonderful sermon. His words were sweet and powerful, and it seems that I can hear them now."[633]

Another witness recalled the response to Seymour's exhorting: "As soon as it is announced that the altar is open for seekers for pardon, sanctification, the baptism with the Holy Ghost, and healing of the body, the people rise and flock to the altar. There is no urging. What kind of preaching is it that brings them? Why, the simple declaring of the Word of God. There is such power in the preaching of the Word in the Spirit that people are shaken on the benches."[634]

It was not the preaching, but one "Hallelujah" that captured Florence Crawford's heart. She said, "It just went through my soul as she thought, 'God, I have heard the voice from Heaven.'"[635]

Almost nothing is known about the resources Seymour used in preparing sermons. Of course, the Bible was his primary source, but whether he had or used commentaries may never be known. The contents of his personal library are unknown except for one title. The book, authored by A. B. Simpson of the Christian and Missionary Alliance was owned and signed by Seymour and now resides at the Flower Pentecostal Heritage Center.

Simpson greatly impacted Seymour's teacher in Cincinnati, Martin W. Knapp. It is also no surprise that the book is *The Holy Spirit or Power from on High*. Seymour read the book carefully, underlining and marking passages that had special meaning to him. It seems his favorite subjects were complete consecration and the indwelling of the Holy Spirit. This paragraph he highlighted can serve as an illustration:

> The Holy Ghost was to become corporately united and identified with the life of the believer, so that He would bring us into direct personal union, and act not upon us, but in us and through us, becoming part of our very life, and controlling every faculty, volition, and power, from the inmost depths of our being. This is the difference between the two classes of Christians we find today; those who have God with them, and those who have Him in them.[636]

Seymour also made handwritten notes in the book. Beneath the table of contents is scrawled, "About the wife, 367." He had also marked the passage:

> You do not marry a wife to do your cooking and ironing...but to be your companion, and to give you the devotion of her heart.[637]

Simpson wrote:

> There is to be no new revelation, no new Bible, no new authoritative voice from heaven. We have it all now in the Holy Scriptures, and all we have to do is "that which we have, hold fast till He comes."

At the end of the sentence, Seymour added, "to the Bible and to faith."[638]

Seymour must have had and used many other books. It seems almost certain that he would have had books by A. S. Worrell, the language scholar who visited and endorsed the revival.

Regardless, with services at the mission held three times a day for several years, he must have prepared and preached hundreds of sermons. Audio recording was quite rare in the first decade of the twentieth century, and we are unable to hear Seymour's voice. Yet, because there was a stenographer in the meetings who transcribed some sermons and published them in *The Apostolic Faith*, we can have a taste of his preaching.

Nineteen sermons are credited to Seymour in *The Apostolic Faith*. Several others without an author listed are consistent with his style and were probably his sermons. He addresses many theological or doctrinal issues such as salvation, sanctification, divine healing, the second coming of Christ, and the baptism in the Holy Spirit. He also proffered advice on practical Christian living, speaking about finances and marriage.[639]

Seymour's preaching is more topical than expository, but it is biblical. The sermons in *The Apostolic Faith* are almost certainly condensed. Yet in the published portions we have, in one single message he quotes twenty-eight different Scripture passages.[640]

Following are some short excerpts from Seymour's sermons:

"The Precious Atonement"—September 1906

Healing of our bodies. Sickness and disease are destroyed through the precious atonement of Jesus. O how we ought to honor the stripes of Jesus, for *"with his stripes we are healed."* How we ought to honor that precious body which the Father sanctified and sent into the world, not simply set apart, but really sanctified, soul, body and spirit, free from sickness, disease and everything of the devil. A body that knew no sin and disease was given for these imperfect bodies of ours. Not only is the atonement for the sanctification of our souls, but for the sanctification of our bodies from inherited disease. It matters not what has been in the blood. Every drop of blood we received from our mother is impure. Sickness is born in a child just as original sin is born in the child. He was manifested to destroy the works of the devil. Every sickness is of the devil.

Man in the Garden of Eden was pure and happy and knew no sickness till that unholy visitor came into the garden, then his whole system was poisoned and it has been flowing in the blood of all the human family down the ages till God spoke to his people and said, *"I am the LORD that healeth thee."*

The children of Israel practiced divine healing. David, after being healed of rheumatism (perhaps contracted in the caves where he hid himself from his pursuers), testified saying, *"Bless the Lord, O my soul: and all that is within me bless his holy name...who forgiveth all thine iniquities; who healeth all thy diseases."* David knew what it was to be healed. Healing continued with God's people till Solomon's heart was turned away by strange wives, and he brought in the black arts and mediums, and they went whoring after familiar spirits. God had been their healer, but after they lost the Spirit, they turned to the arm of flesh to find something to heal their diseases.

Thank God, we have a living Christ among us to heal our diseases. He will heal every case. The prophet had said, *"With his stripes we are healed,"* and it was fulfilled when Jesus came. Also *"He hath borne our griefs"* (which means sickness, as translators tell us). Now if Jesus bore our sicknesses, why should we bear them? So we get full salvation through the atonement of Jesus.[641]

"In Money Matters"—November 1906.

God does not expect all to sell out for He says in 1 Cor. 16:1, *"Now concerning the collection for the saints,* [the text is abbreviated] *upon the first day of the week let every one of you lay by him in store, as God hath prospered him."* It does not mean for you to have great real estate and money banked up while your brothers and sisters are suffering. He means for you to turn loose because all that money is soon going to be thrown to the moles and bats. So it is better to spread the Gospel and get stars in your crown than to be holding it. But for us to go and tell you to do it, pick out somebody that has money and read the Word to them, would not be the Spirit of the Lord. The Spirit will tell you what to do. He makes you do it. When He wakes you up at night and tells you what to do you cannot sleep till you obey. He says everyone shall be taught of God from the least to the greatest. God wants a free giver.[642]

"The Baptism with the Holy Ghost"—February–March 1907

"And there appeared unto them cloven tongues like as of fire." Beloved, when we receive the baptism with the Holy Ghost and fire, we

surely will speak in tongues as the Spirit gives utterance. We are not seeking for tongues, but we are seeking the baptism with the Holy Ghost and fire. And when we receive it, we shall be so filled with the Holy Ghost, that He Himself will speak in the power of the Spirit.

"And they were all filled with the Holy Ghost, and began to speak with other tongues, as the Spirit gave them utterance." Now, beloved, do not be too concerned about your speaking in tongues, but let the Holy Ghost give you utterance, and it will come just as freely as the air we breathe. It is nothing worked up, but it comes from the heart. *"With the heart man believeth unto righteousness; and with the mouth, confession is made unto salvation."* So when the Holy Ghost life comes in, the mouth opens, through the power of the Spirit in the heart. Glory to God![643]

"Behold the Bridegroom Cometh"—January 1907

May God fit every one of us for the coming of the Lord, that we may come back with him on white horses and help Him to execute judgment on the earth and make way for the millennial kingdom, when He shall reign from shore to shore, and righteousness shall cover the earth as waters cover the sea.[644]

17

THE PILGRIMS: WILLIAMS, MASON, AND CASHWELL

Thousands of people from all over the world visited the Azusa Street Mission from April 1906 through 1908. Most left with a burning fire that brought light to the world around them. It would be impossible to tell each of their stories, even if volumes were to be written. However, the visits of three men—Ernest Swing Williams, Charles Harrison Mason, and Gaston B. Cashwell—were especially important because of the role they played in the nation's major Pentecostal denominations.

ERNEST S. WILLIAMS

E. S. Williams was born in 1885 in San Bernardino, California. Williams's parents were common people who could not provide him with many material things or even a good education. Yet, they gave him something much richer: a godly heritage. Williams testified, "It was my happy lot to be taught principles of righteousness."[645]

The Williams family were charter members of the first Holiness church in Southern California. They proudly named their son "Swing" after the founding president of the Southern California and Arizona Holiness Association, James R. Swing.

At the age of nineteen, Williams became "greatly concerned" about his soul.[646] He was born again at a Free Methodist meeting.[647] In 1905, he and a friend decided to travel to Chicago to attend Bible school. Their poorly planned adventure ended prematurely in Colorado where, hoping to earn enough money to return to California, both young men found employment on a ranch near Denver.[648] Williams said, "Conscious of the presence and fellowship of the Lord whom I loved, I was yet conscious that there was something still lacking in my experience. But those among whom I worshipped seemed not to shed further light on my pathway than I was walking in."[649]

During the spring of 1906, Williams's mother began to write about what was happening at Azusa Street. She told about his "old acquaintances" receiving the Holy Spirit baptism and speaking in tongues. One letter told how his father had been so touched by God at the meetings that he would break down and weep when he returned thanks at the dining room table. This made "a definite impression" on Williams's heart. He said, "I felt this must be none other than a work of God if it bore such fruits of righteousness and tenderness."

Soon, Williams received a copy of *The Apostolic Faith*. He said, "It would be hard to describe how the Spirit witnessed to my heart…it felt… something like the soft, warm, dripping of pleasant waters."[650]

That September, Williams and his companion returned to their home in Los Angeles. On his first Sunday back, Williams had his initial taste of Pentecost. He attended the morning worship service at Bartleman's mission at Eighth Street and Maple Street. After the service, he walked to Azusa Street, where the altar service was in progress. He said, "I wish I could describe what I saw. Prayer and worship were everywhere. The altar area was filled with seekers; some were kneeling; others were prone on the floor; some were speaking in tongues. Everyone was doing something; all seemingly were lost in God. I simply stood and looked, for I had never seen anything like it."[651] Williams said that, had it not been for his deep hunger for God, he "might have turned away, for I had been taught that entire sanctification and the baptism with the Holy Spirit were one."[652]

Before seeking the baptism, Williams spent a short time studying his Bible, seeking Scripture which might teach an experience subsequent to the experience of sanctification. He said, "I did not wish to be led into anything unscriptural; however much the Azusa Street worshipers might seem divinely blessed. Then the Lord prompted me and I felt I must seek, as my heart was extremely hungry."[653]

Still not rushing into the experience, Williams, who had not been able to regularly attend worship while working in Colorado, prayed that he might be cleansed. A young man met Williams at the altar and told him that, if he would praise the Lord, he would be filled. Williams's interest, however, was *"Search me, O God, and know my heart; try me, and know my thoughts: and see if there be any wicked way in me"* (Psalm 139:23–24 KJV). [654]

Finally assured of his salvation and sanctification, he began to seek the Holy Spirit baptism. Late in September, Williams had a remarkable experience while praising and worshiping God at the mission. It was late in the evening, and only he and two other seekers remained. He said it seemed that the Lord was dealing with his "very physical flesh." A woman, unknown to him, came near and said, "Lord, give this young brother rest." He said he experienced a rest he had never expected to know "this side of heaven."

At about midnight, Williams got up from the altar and said, "I have gotten something, what is it?" He was told, "You have received the anointing." Williams said he left the mission and walked in "undisturbed spiritual peace," feeling as though he was protected from any invasion by "the hills of God" that rose on both sides of him.[655]

On October 2, Williams received his Holy Spirit baptism. A young man who had received the experience the previous night prayed with Williams and encouraged him to pray with his "mind stayed on Christ." Although he spoke in tongues that night, Williams did not receive the "ecstasy" he expected. The next morning, however, in a grove of eucalyptus trees, the "glory met" him. The Holy Spirit not only took his tongue, but his whole being. Williams said that "language after language" rolled from his lips.[656] Soon, Williams entered the ministry, but not without some struggle. Paul Bettex once told him, "I never pitied a young man more than I pitied you when you started out. You seemed so limited in possibilities."[657] Williams, however, resisted discouragement and persisted.

Ordained by Seymour, he traveled as an evangelist and pastored several churches before being chosen as the General Superintendent of the General Council of the Assemblies of God in 1929. He successfully held the post for twenty years and led the organization in the powerful, yet gentle, spirit of Azusa.[658]

Williams never retired from ministry. Upon resigning from the leadership of the Assemblies, he joined the faculty of Central Bible College. After leaving that position, he became an "unofficial" chaplain at Maranatha Village, the Assemblies of God retirement community. Williams received his heavenly promotion on October 25, 1981.[659]

C. H. MASON

Charles Harrison Mason received news of the revival at Azusa Street when F. W. Williams visited Mississippi in 1906. Undoubtedly, he also read about the meeting in many of the Holiness papers that were circulating at the time. Mason said, "I saw that I was not above my Master. If He needed the Holy Ghost, I needed it to do the will of God."

Mason was born September 8, 1866, on a farm near Memphis, Tennessee. Mason's parents were members of the Missionary Baptist Church, and he followed them in the faith. At the age of twelve, he accepted Christ as his Savior following a series of visions of heaven and hell. In fact, Mason had many dreams and visions in his youth.[660] The young man prayed that God would give him "a religion like the one he had heard about from the old slaves and had seen demonstrated in their lives."[661]

In 1879, the Masons moved to Arkansas and worked on a plantation, hoping to avoid the yellow fever epidemic in Memphis. Their plans to escape the ravages of the disease were unsuccessful, and Mason's father succumbed to the affliction in 1879.[662] The next year, suffering from fever and chills, Mason, too, was facing death before his fourteenth birthday. However, on September 5, 1880, the "glory of God" appeared to Mason, and he was instantly and completely healed.

More committed to Jesus Christ than ever before, Mason was baptized at Mount Olive Baptist Church near Plummersville, Arkansas, by Pastor I. S. Nelson, his brother-in-law. Young Mason, still only a layman, traveled Southern Arkansas sharing his testimony and working the altars at summer camp meetings.[663]

Following a call to the ministry, Mason was given a license to preach by Mount Gale Missionary Baptist Church in 1893. He attended Arkansas Baptist College for only three months before leaving, convinced that there was "no salvation in schools and colleges."[664]

Soon after his ordination, Mason read the autobiography of Amanda Smith, an outstanding Black Holiness evangelist. He was deeply impacted.[665] In 1894, he accepted the Holiness doctrine of sanctification and preached the "second work" in Arkansas, Alabama, and Mississippi. The following year, Mason met C. P. Jones in Jackson, Mississippi. The two became fast friends and colleagues in ministry. Their Holiness message, however, was strongly opposed by Mason's former Baptist colleagues. Following a convention in 1897, Mason, Jones, and others founded a new sect, the Church of God in Christ.[666]

Before visiting Azusa Street, Mason, "hungry and thirsty," began preaching the Holy Ghost baptism to his congregation. Late in 1906, according to his own testimony, he was "led by the Spirit to go to Los Angeles, California." J. A. Jeter and D. J. Young accompanied Mason on his spiritual pilgrimage.[667]

When he arrived at the mission, Mason was forty years old. He was a mature believer and seasoned minister of the gospel. After his first service in the mission, Mason said, "I sat by myself, away from those who went with me. I saw and heard some things that did not seem scriptural to me, but at this I did not stumble. I began to thank God in my heart for all things, for when I heard some speak in tongues, I knew it was right."[668]

The cautious but curious preacher remembered Seymour and the role he had played in his Holy Spirit baptism: "When he closed his sermon, he said, 'All those that want to be sanctified or baptized with the Holy Ghost, go to the upper room, and all those that want to be healed, go to the prayer room, and all those that want to be justified, come to the altar.' I said that (the altar) is the place for me, for it may be that I am not converted and if not, God knows it and can convert me."

Mason and his friends were called from the altar to Seymour's upstairs room in the mission. The pastor welcomed the brethren from the South and told them that God would do great things for them. He also cautioned them not to run around the city looking for worldly pleasures, but to "seek the pleasure of the Lord."

Satan used several people to hinder Mason. Jeter had some doubts about the meeting and criticized what was going on. When Mason met one lady whom he had known previously, he had to apologize for bad thoughts he had had about her.

Despite numerous temptations, Mason pressed on to the baptism. Finally, he said,

> The sound of a mighty wind was in me, and my soul cried, "Jesus, only, one like you." My soul cried and soon I began to die. It seemed that I heard the groanings of Christ on the cross dying for me. All of the work was in me until I died out of the old man. The sound stopped for a little while. My soul cried, "Oh, God, finish your work in me." Then the sound broke out in me again. Then I felt something raising me out of my seat without any effort of my own. I said, "It may be imagination." Then I looked down to see if it was really so. I saw that I was rising. Then I gave up for the Lord to have His way within me. So there came a wave of glory into me, and all of my being was filled with the glory of the Lord. So when I had gotten myself straight on my feet there came a light which enveloped my entire being above the brightness of the sun. When I opened my mouth to say, "Glory," a flame touched my tongue then ran down to me. My language changed and no word could I speak in my own tongue. Oh, I was filled with the glory of my Lord. My soul was then satisfied.[669]

Now baptized in the Holy Spirit, Mason sang in tongues, spoke in tongues, and even preached in tongues. The gestures of his hands and the movement of his body were totally yielded to God.[670]

Five weeks after his first service at Old Azusa, Mason and his friends returned to Memphis. Glenn Cook had already arrived in Tennessee, and the "fire had fallen." For weeks, Mason held services in a small frame church on Wellington Street. The highly successful meetings often lasted from seven thirty in the evening until six thirty the next morning.[671]

Although C. P. Jones had encouraged Mason to go to Los Angeles and seek the baptism of the Holy Spirit, the two parted fellowship over the necessity of evidentiary tongues. Mason continued to lead the Church of God in Christ until his death. Under his capable leadership, the Church of God in Christ became the largest Pentecostal denomination in the United States. He left his mark on all it has accomplished. Mason lived to the ripe old age of ninety-five, passing away on November 17, 1961.[672]

GASTON B. CASHWELL

Gaston B. Cashwell read about the Azusa Street revival in *The Way of Faith*, a Holiness periodical published in Columbia, South Carolina. Frank Bartleman had contributed news of the revival to this and many other Holiness papers. These testimonies created an intense hunger in Cashwell's heart. He reported that "the Spirit led him more and more to seek Pentecost." He spent many days weeping and praying as God prepared him for a Pentecostal ministry.[673]

Cashwell was born in Sampson County, North Carolina, in 1862.[674] Early in life, Cashwell was a "prodigal son" who "raised his share of 'hell.'" According to members of his family, he "was an unlikely prospect for a future preacher, much less one that would ever amount to anything."

On one sojourn in Georgia, Cashwell, always a prankster, had another man write a letter to his grandfather saying he was dead. The trick contained more truth than Cashwell could have realized. He encountered a Georgia evangelist and was converted. Indeed, the "old" Gaston Cashwell died in Georgia—and a new man was born. When he returned to North Carolina, some joked that the "dead man had come back to life again."[675]

Cashwell entered the ministry soon after his conversion. He was credentialed by the North Carolina Conference of the Methodist Episcopal Church, South.[676]

While working in the Methodist Church, Cashwell came under the influence of Abner B. Crumpler, an attorney and evangelist. Crumpler had left Methodism after adopting the doctrine of sanctification as a second work of God's grace. In 1897, he founded the North Carolina Holiness Association, and in 1900, the Pentecostal Holiness Church.[677] In 1903, Cashwell joined Crumpler in the new denomination.

Longing to be in Los Angeles, Cashwell borrowed money and made the western pilgrimage in November of 1906. He rode a train three thousand miles to receive the baptism in the Holy Spirit. The six-day journey was a time for Cashwell to fast and pray continually.[678]

As Cashwell left for California, members of the Pentecostal Holiness Church were meeting for their annual convention. When Cashwell's non-attendance was noted, Crumpler read a letter in which the absentee stated he had received a new consecration to God. He also apologized to anyone he had offended and announced he was off to Los Angeles, "where I shall seek for the baptism of the Holy Ghost."[679]

Arriving at Azusa Street, Cashwell had mixed feelings about the meeting. He thought some things were "fanatical" but believed that, by and large, "God was in it." The main problem for Cashwell, a proud Southerner, was the mixing of the races. He said it caused "chills to go down my spine" when he thought of Black people laying hands on him and praying for him. For five days he wrestled with this as he sought God in the upper room of the mission.

Finally, in his hotel room, Cashwell experienced a "crucifixion" of his prejudice. He went to the mission and asked Seymour and several Black boys to lay hands on him. Returning to the service on the ground floor, he listened as Clara Lum read testimonies from T. B. Barratt and others who had received their Pentecost. Cashwell wrote,

> Before I knew it, I began to speak in tongues and praise God...He filled me with His Spirit and love, and I am feasting and drinking at the fountain continually and speak as the Spirit gives utterance both in my own language and in the unknown tongue...The Lord also healed my body. I had been afflicted with rheumatism for years, and at a healing service held here, I was anointed and prayed for and was immediately healed of rheumatism and catarrh and have a sound body and clothed in a right mind.[680]

The good folks at Azusa Street bought Cashwell a new suit and a train ticket back to North Carolina. On December 31, 1906, he started a meeting in his hometown of Dunn. The meeting, held in a three-story tobacco warehouse, lasted a full month and was phenomenal. Over a thousand people, including dozens of Holiness ministers, attended. People came from all over the South to attend the Spirit-filled meetings. The revival has been called "Azusa Street East."

As a direct result of this meeting, the Pentecostal Holiness Church, the Fire Baptized Holiness Church, and the Pentecostal Free Will Baptist Church all came into the Pentecostal movement. Later, while Cashwell was preaching in Birmingham, Alabama, M. M. Pinson, and H. G. Rodgers, instrumental in the founding of the Assemblies of God, were Spirit-baptized.[681]

In 1907, Cashwell began publishing *The Bridegroom's Messenger*,[682] a monthly Pentecostal periodical. The paper carried news about the Pentecostal revival at Azusa Street, in the South, and around the world.

A. J. Tomlinson, General Overseer of the Church of God, invited Cashwell to Cleveland, Tennessee, in January of 1908. Tomlinson said, "By the close of the year, I was so hungry for the Holy Ghost that I scarcely cared for food, friendship, or anything else. I wanted one thing—the baptism with the Holy Ghost." On Sunday, January 12, while Cashwell preached, Tomlinson received the Holy Spirit and spoke in ten languages that were unknown to him. He testified, "A peculiar sensation took hold of me, and almost unconsciously I slipped off my chair in a heap on the rostrum at Brother Cashwell's feet. I did not know what such an experience meant…As I lay there, great joy flooded on my soul. The happiest moment I had ever known up to that time. I never knew what real joy was before."[683]

In only a year, God had used G. B. Cashwell to bring four Holiness denominations into the Pentecostal movement and had seen the conversion to the faith of future leaders of a fifth, not yet established, denomination, the Assemblies of God.

Cashwell continued to spread Pentecost, especially in the South, until his homegoing on March 4, 1916.[684]

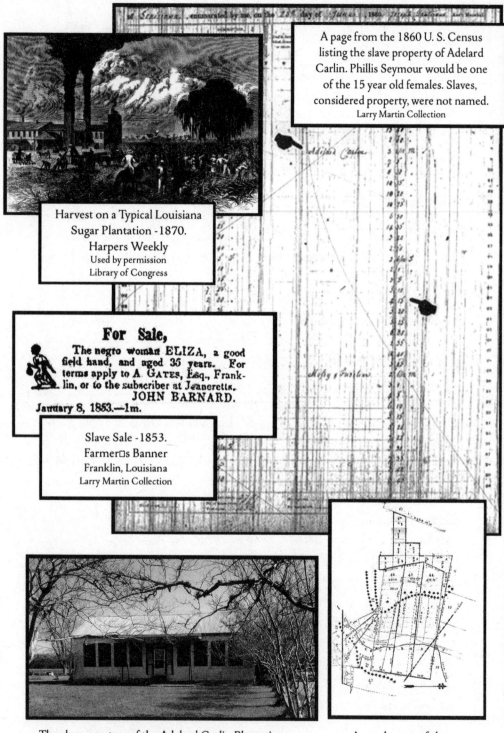

A page from the 1860 U. S. Census listing the slave property of Adelard Carlin. Phillis Seymour would be one of the 15 year old females. Slaves, considered property, were not named.
Larry Martin Collection

Harvest on a Typical Louisiana Sugar Plantation - 1870.
Harpers Weekly
Used by permission
Library of Congress

For Sale,
The negro woman ELIZA, a good field hand, and aged 35 years. For terms apply to A. GATES, Esq., Franklin, or to the subscriber at Jeanerette.
JOHN BARNARD.
January 8, 1853.—1m.

Slave Sale - 1853.
Farmer□s Banner
Franklin, Louisiana
Larry Martin Collection

The slave quarters of the Adelard Carlin Plantation. Phillis and William Seymour were born in this house or a similar one very nearby.
Centerville, Louisiana
Larry Martin Collection

An early map of the Adelard Carlin Plantation.
Centerville, Louisiana
Larry Martin Collection

L | 93 | U.S.C.T.

Simon Seymour

, Co. B , 93 Reg't U. S. Col'd Inf.

Appears on

Company Descriptive Book

of the organization named above.

DESCRIPTION.

Age 21 years; height 5 feet 8 inches.

Complexion Dark

Eyes Black ; hair Black

Where born St mary Parish La

Occupation Brick Moulder

ENLISTMENT.

When Oct 10 , 1863 .

Where New Iberia La

By whom Jn Blanchard , term 3 y'rs.

Remarks:

Hadfield

(383g)   Copyist.

Top: U. S. Colored Troops in Louisiana
Larry Martin Collection

Left: Simon Seymour's military
service record
Larry Martin Collection

Below: Members of the
Corps de Afrique
Port Hudson, Louisiana
Photo used by permission The National Archives

Above:
Confederate money
issued in Centerville, LA.
Larry Martin Collection
Below:
Centerville, LA -1881.
(Notice the troops and
cannons in the streets.)
Larry Martin Collection

MARRIAGE CERTIFICATE.

no 174

State of Louisiana,
Parish of St Marys } This is to Certify, That Rev R. K. Dossy

an ordained minister of the Gospel, by virtue of the license required by Law, did on this 27th

day of July A.D. 1867. unite in MARRIAGE Simon Simon

and Phillis Sellaba (their mutual consent being first obtained,) of the Parish

of St Marys State of Louisiana.

In Testimony Whereof, I have caused the said parties, with myself and three legal witnesses,

to sign these presents, this 27th day of July A.D. 1867

Witnesses: Simon X Simon
                                                    his mark
Charles X Brown   Phillis X Sellaba
        mark   her mark
Jefferson X Ellis
        mark   R. K. Dossy
Michel X Noloha   Minister.
        his mark

Marriage license - Simon Simon and Phillis Salabar
Larry Martin Collection

The Catholic Church in
Franklin, Louisiana
Larry Martin Collection

Baptismal record
William Simon (Seymour).
Larry Martin Collection

Although this is not the Seymour family,
this 1902 postcard is typical of the
way they lived.
Larry Martin Collection

The Verdunville home of Seymour's
brother Jacob. His mother died here.
Larry Martin Collection

Black men freed from enslavement
hide in the swamps of Louisiana, fearing for
their lives.
Used by permission of Library of Congress

This engraving from 1870, the year of
Seymour's birth, shows a Black
family much like his and demonstrates
his difficult circumstances.
Used by permission Library of Congress

Left: The Apostolic Faith Church of God claim this is an early photo of Seymour.
Larry Martin Collection
Courtesy of Oree Keyes

Bottom: This syndicated cartoon from 1901 shows a sterotypical caricature. of a Black waiter.
Larry Martin Collection
From the *Joplin Globe*

Grand Hotel - Indianapolis
This is one of the three hotels where Seymour worked as a waiter.
Used by permission
Bass Photo Company Collection
Indiana State Historical Society

Grand Hotel Cafe
When Seymour served diners.
Larry Martin Collection
from the Indianapolis Star

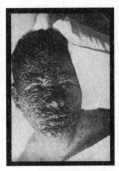

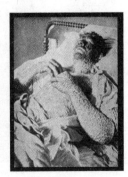

Smallpox victims - 1901-1902
Used by permiossion Kentuky Board of Health

An eye blinded by smallpox.
Vascularized staphlyoma of the cornea.
Larry Martin Collection
Courtesy of Dean McGee Eye Institute
Lawton, Oklahoma

Daniel S. Warner   Martin W. Knapp   Charles P. Jones

Seymour's early spiritual enfluencers.

Larry Martin Collection

The Bible Training School in Houston.

Charles F. Parham and Warren F. Carothers, Seymour's instructors.

Courtesy of the *Apostolic Faith Report*

Alma White
Larry Martin Collection

Joseph Smale
Courtesy of First Baptist Church
Los Angeles

Frank Bartleman
Used by permission
Flower Pentecostal Heritage Center

Below: The AME church choir.

Above: The City of Los Angeles in 1895. The AME Church at 312 Azusa Street is in the backgrond and the insert .

Photos used by permission
Miriam Matthews photograph collection, Library Special Collections, Charles E. Young Research Library, UCLA

Above: Richard and Ruth Asbery
Larry Martin Collection

Above: 214 Bonnie Brae Street
Used by permission
Flower Pentecostal Heritage Center

Left and below:
The first newspaper article.
Los Angeles DailyTimes
April 18, 1906
Larry Martin Collection

Above:
The San Francisco Earthquake
Photo used by permission
National Information Service for
Earthquake Engineering
University of California, Berkeley

Left:
Frank Bartleman's
earthquake tract
Photo used by permission
Flower Pentecostal Heritage Center

THE APOSTOLIC FAITH

Above:
The Leadership Team
Standing from left to right:
Phoebe Sargent, G.W. Evans
Jennie Evans Moore,
Glenn A. Cook, Florence
Louise Crawford,
Thomas Junk, Sister Prince.
Sitting from left to right:
May Evans, Hiram W. Smith
Mildred Crawford in lap,
William J. Seymour, Clara Lu
Used by permission
Flower Pentecostal Heritage Cente
Left:
The first edition of
The Apostolic Faith
Below
The first Azusa letterhead
The Larry Martin Collection

Pentecost Has Come

Los Angeles Being Visited by a Revival of Bible Salvation and Pentecost as Recorded in the Book of Acts

" Go ye, therefore, and teach all nations, baptizing them in the name of the Father, and of the Son, and of the Holy Ghost; teaching them to observe all things whatsoever I have commanded you."—Matt. 28: 19, 20.

The Apostolic Faith Movement

CHAS. F. PARHAM, PROJECTOR

W. J. SEYMOUR, Pastor

312 AZUSA STREET

Los Angeles, Cal., Sept 28 1906

Left:
Cartoons
in Los Angeles
newspapers
stereotyping and
mocking
African Americans.
Larry Martin Collection

Right:
A cartoon from the
Los Angeles Daily Express
lampooning the
demonstrative worship
at Azusa Street.
Larry Martin Collection

A cartoon from the *Indianapolis Star* ridiculing Seymour and a baptismal service.
Larry Martin Collection

Cartoons from the
Burning Bush
(a Holiness publication)
attacking Seymour, Parham
and Pentecostalism.
Larry Martin Collection

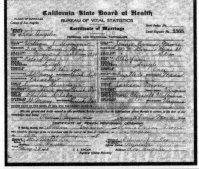

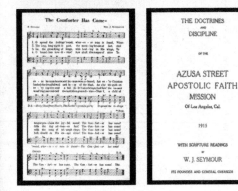

The favorite hymn and
Seymour's *Doctrine and Discipline*
Larry Martin Collection

Above:
Standing from left, John A. D. Adams,
F. F. Bosworth, Tom Hezmalhalch
Seated, From Left:
William J. Seymour and John G Lake.
Perhaps on Seymour's trip to Chicago.

Right:
S. D. Page and F. M. Britton
standing at the door to the
Mission.
Both photos used by permission
Flower Pentecostal Heritage Center.

G. B. Cashwell [4]

Ernest S. Williams [2]

Charles H. Mason [2]

Rachel Sizelove [2]

William H. Durham [1]

Mother Emma Cotton [2]

Glenn A. Cook [1]

A. C. Valdez [2]

A. G. Garr [1]

Elmer T. Fischer [7]

Arthur G. Osterberg [6]

Owen "Irish" Lee [6]

Daniel Awrey [1]

Lucy Leatherman [1]

Frank Bowden [3]

George B. Studd [2]

Ansel H. Post [2]

Samuel J. Mead [1]

R. J. Scott [1]

M. L. Ryan [5]

Photo Credits: 1) Larry Martin Collection 2) Flower Pentecostal Heritage Center, 3) Historical Center, United Pentecosatl Church International 4) Archives and Research Center, Internatinonal Pentecoatal Holiness Church 5) *Grace and Glory* 6) Dean Osterberg 7) Lloyd Colbough.

Above:
William Seymour's grave marker.
Larry Martin Collection
Policemen locked the Mission doors
for the first time.
This photo appeared in
The Los Angeles Daily News
January 5, 1931.
Right:
The last known photo of William Seymour.
Photo used by permission
Dixon Pentecostal Research Center
Below
Julia Seymour Porter Farris
California State Archives, Board of Cosmetology Records
Office of the Secretary of State, Sacramento, CA

The lost boys of Azusa Street
Robert Asbery, Richard Asbery Jr. and Jethro Hutchins
California State Archives, Inmate History Register
Office of the Secretary of State, Sacramento, CA

The California Eagle,
Los Angeles prominent African-American newspaper

The only known photo of the
interior of the mission.
Jennie Seymour and Rupert Griffith both try
to lead the service.
This photo appeared in *The Los Angeles Daily News*
January 5, 1931.
and the *California Eagle*, January 9, 1931.

18

THE COMMISSION:
INTO ALL THE WORLD

O spread the tidings 'round,

Wherever man is found,

Wherever human hearts

And human woes abound;

Let ev'ry Christian tongue

Proclaim the joyful sound;

The Comforter has come![685]

Early in the first year of the revival, a visiting preacher said, "The Lord has shown me that this movement will soon blow over."[686] If there is any element of truth in his lame prophecy, it is the fact that the breath of God soon blew the movement all over the globe.

The world-wide missionary outreach from Azusa was almost unbeliev-able. First, workers began to go out in the area surrounding Los Angeles. Then they branched out further and further until many were ready and willing to take the message all the way around the globe.

Miss Nancy Starret of Cincinnati, Ohio, visited a friend, Clara Pierce, in Los Angeles. Both received the Holy Spirit baptism and returned to Cincinnati with the Pentecostal message. Two thirds of Starret's home church, Christian Assembly, received the baptism.[687] Lucy Farrow took the message to Portsmouth, Virginia, where 150 received the Holy Ghost.[688]

After receiving the baptism in Los Angeles, Edward Vinton and his wife started a mission in Cambridge, Massachusetts. God gave Mrs. Vinton a vision of the building they were to use for services. Following the leadership of the Holy Spirit, they secured a former Presbyterian church on Hampshire Street and began preaching Pentecost.[689]

Miss Iva Campbell took Pentecost to Akron, Cleveland, and Alliance, Ohio. A Los Angeles newspaper called her "the 'gift of tongues' missionary." She caused such a stir in Akron that the ministers of the city passed resolutions "denouncing her."[690]

Adolpha de Rosa and Harmon Clifford went to Oakland. Ophelia Wiley, Lulu Miller, Florence Crawford, C. W. Solkeld and G. W. Evans, Thomas Junk, and their wives went to Oregon.[691] Wiley and Miller were Black, and the others in the party were white, demonstrating attempts to export the racial unity that characterized the Azusa Street services.[692] Wiley, a leader in the group, was a preacher, singer, and songwriter.[693]

Ansel Post went to Santa Barbara; Brigido Perez, to San Diego; Tom Hezmalhalch, to Denver; and Elsie Robinson, to Onawa, Michigan.[694]

When Aldopha de Rosa and Lucy Leatherman preached in Greenwich, Connecticut, in August of 1907, they met fierce opposition, even being accused of witchcraft and hypnotism. A member of an angry mob threw an acid bomb into their tent, which injured de Rosa and "almost suffocated those present." The next night, the ruffians tore down the missionaries' tent and set a torch to it. Following Jesus's admonition to shake the dust off their feet (see Matthew 10:14), Leatherman said, "We will not continue our work further in this locality."[695]

On another occasion, Ophelia Wiley went to Seattle. She "knew no one" in the city, but the Holy Spirit led her to a particular house. When she rang the doorbell, a woman answered and said she had been praying that

God would send someone to her home. Wiley responded, "I'm a missionary, and the Holy Ghost sent me to Seattle."[696]

Lee Hall had ridden to California on a wagon train. To pay his fare, he served the travelers as assistant cook and rode the jenny in front of the chuck wagon to look for holes and obstructions that might hurt the horses that followed. He had been working on a ranch in Hanford when he heard about the revival at the mission. He took a train to Los Angeles, where he was saved and baptized in the Holy Ghost. Hall returned to his native Ozarks and, with two other young men, shared the Pentecostal message in northern Arkansas.[697]

F. W. Williams was saved, and Spirit baptized at the Bonnie Brae meetings. He traveled throughout the South, preaching and planting churches. His first stop was in Jackson, Mississippi. He had little success there, but he was introduced to Charles H. Mason and shared the Pentecostal message with him. The first church he organized, following a tent revival, was in Mobile, Alabama. Returning to Jackson, he preached at Primitive Baptist Church, where the entire congregation adopted Pentecost. Williams established other churches in Birmingham, Alabama; Century, Florida; and even as far away as Chicago, Illinois.

At times, Williams faced blistering opposition. He described his work in Mobile as "a hard battle." Once, in Century, opponents cut his tent down and accused him of casting spells on people. The faithful put the tent up again and continued the services.[698]

This kind of persecution was often the norm for Azusa evangelists. In Salem, Oregon, the violence was so severe that the Pentecostals had to ask for police protection.[699] Saints in Indianapolis, Indiana, faced the same problem as hoodlums disturbed their meetings.[700] Juvenile authorities in Portland, Oregon, tried to take Florence Crawford's daughter, Mildred, away from her mother. "In this instance, we can see that the persecution workers faced was at times driven by objections to Azusa's racial unity; the authorities seeking to separate Crawford from her daughter complained that nine-year-old Mildred was "permitted to roll around on the floor among Negroes and white men for a couple of hours every night."[701]

The press, too, was no friendlier to Azusa missionaries than they had been to the home church in Los Angeles. In Salem, Oregon, the newspaper ridiculed the missionaries by writing, "Perhaps some of the 'Tongues of Fire' people who think they are inspired merely have twinges of the dyspepsia, or plain belly ache."[702] The paper also implied that speaking in tongues was "pigs squeak."[703]

Pentecostalism was mockingly called a "padded cell religion" in Portland. The press quoted an angry neighbor who complained, "For the most part, they are ignorant and feeble-minded persons who have gone insane on the subject. The place is worse than a madhouse when they get to going head on." Services were disparagingly described as "orgies."[704]

Despite such objections, the stories of traveling ambassadors going out from Azusa to spread the flame of Pentecost could go on and on. Their tales of hardship, persecution, and success are almost innumerable. The testimonies of thousands are known only in heaven, but those which are known would also number in the thousands.

Sometimes an experience at Azusa would start a chain reaction with tremendous results. When Harry Van Loon and Louis Osterberg received the baptism at Azusa, they persuaded William H. Durham from Chicago to come and seek at the mission. Durham came to Los Angeles, was baptized in the Holy Ghost, as previously noted, and returned home to bring his North Avenue Mission into the Pentecostal movement.

Pastor Owen Adams from Monrovia, California, also received the baptism at Azusa. He shared the message with Robert Semple, who received the baptism in the Holy Ghost in Chicago at Durham's mission. He shared the message with his bride-to-be, Aimee Kennedy, who also received.

Robert and Aimee answered the call to be Pentecostal missionaries in China. Unfortunately, Mr. Semple contracted malaria and died in Hong Kong. His young widow returned to the United States and married Harold McPherson. Aimee Semple McPherson was the founder of the International Church of the Foursquare Gospel and one of the Full Gospel's most ardent proponents. In one of her meetings, Dr. Charles S. Price received the Holy Spirit and also became a national Pentecostal leader.[705]

The first missionary to leave the mission for overseas was Andrew G. Johnson. He ministered in Colorado, Illinois, and New York before departing for Spain, Jerusalem, and then Sweden. He was followed by dozens of God-called workers who were willing to give their all for Christ and the Pentecostal message.[706] Seymour said missionaries "are going almost every day."[707]

On June 16, 1906, A. G. Garr, a Los Angeles pastor, received the Holy Spirit. One week later, he was called to be a missionary to India. He had no money and no sponsors. By faith, he stood in the mission and said, "Friends, I believe God wants me to go to India with the message." Almost instantly, a man stood and offered $500 for the trip. A woman then gave $200, and another man gave $100. Within fifteen minutes, and without Garr's mentioning an offering, the money was raised to send five people to India. Three weeks after he received the baptism, Garr left Los Angeles, heading east on his way to India.[708]

By October of 1906, eight foreign missionaries and thirty home missionaries had been sent out from the mission.[709] Yet Florence Crawford could not have been more correct when she shared a vision that God had given her that fall. She saw a "beautiful bouquet of flowers" still in the bud. God spoke to her and said, "This movement is just in the bud."[710]

Julia Hutchins, who had received her baptism, her recently converted husband, and Lucy Farrow led a large group on a short-term mission to Liberia, West Africa.[711] Lucy M. Leatherman, the widow of a medical doctor, went to Jerusalem to minister to the Arabic population.

A. G. Garr left India to work in China in the fall of 1907. He arrived in Hong Kong on October 9. M. L. Ryan had also led a party of fifteen or more to the Far East. In his group were two single women, May Law and Rosa Pittman, headed for China. The duo arrived just three days after the Garrs. After losing a child to the plague, the Garrs returned to the United States in 1908.

Two other members of Ryan's party, Bertha Milligan and Cora Fritsch, left their work in Japan to join Law and Pittman. They were soon joined in China by Thomas Junk, Brent Berntsen, Roy Hess, Hector, Sigrid McClean, and several more Azusa Street veterans.[712]

Within two years, the Pentecostal message had spread around the globe as a host of missionaries left for the foreign field. This is not to say that Azusa's missionaries did not face serious setbacks. Charles Parham originally believed that the gift of tongues would allow Spirit baptized missionaries to preach in foreign countries without learning the native language. Scholars call this *xenoglossy* (also written as *xenoglossia*). Seymour, following Parham's lead, preached the same thing at Azusa Street. Faith in this phenomenon increased as many visitors at the mission testified that men and women spoke in their native tongue.

Samuel K. and Ardel Mead, well-known pioneer Methodist missionaries to Africa, visited the mission, and both received the Holy Ghost baptism. They documented many examples of people speaking in African dialects.[713] Although there were a few remarkable instances where this also took place on the mission field, for the most part, the gift of tongues was of little xenoglossic value.

The inability to communicate with the nationals was not the only challenge faced by these missionaries. Many faced such desperate circumstances as famine, disease, and hostility. Not a few died and were buried in the land of their labors. Of the group that accompanied Lucy Farrow and Julia Hutchins to Liberia, seven perished, apparently from black fever. Those who gave their lives for the gospel included the entire family of G. W. Batman: his wife and their three children.[714]

Paul Bettex left Los Angeles for China in 1910. He had no promised support. His only "outfit" was a Bible and a songbook. His wife, Nellie, died in 1912 after two years of malnutrition and near starvation. Bettex was martyred in 1916, his bullet-riddled body found in a shallow grave.[715]

Despite the hardships, the seeds of Pentecost were received into fertile soil almost everywhere the message was preached. Within two and a half years, Pentecost had been established in fifty countries.[716]

When the mission started publishing *The Apostolic Faith* in September of 1906, it also went around the world as a Pentecostal catalyst. M. L. Ryan, the editor of a religious periodical in Salem, Oregon, said that after he received the paper for the first time, "I fell on my knees and agonized Godward a bursting soul of appreciation; a great and blessed conviction seized me, and I rushed out of the office shouting and praising God. The fire had struck my soul."[717]

A lady in New York wrote, "As soon as I began to read your paper, I began to shout and praise God and began to shake so I could not read for some time." She also testified of a wonderful experience in the Holy Spirit, although she was still tarrying for tongues.[718]

A. W. Orwig received a paper and was convinced that the work was of God. He told his wife, "I am going to Azusa Street Mission on Sunday and see and hear for myself." On the first day, he stayed for six hours and left even more convinced. Soon he adopted the faith.[719]

When E. S. Hanson of Dallas, Oregon, received the paper, he carefully read it and then said, "The Spirit testified with my spirit that it was the true teaching of the gospel." After examining the Scriptures, he began to seek God for the Pentecostal gift. In a short time, and after Hanson had received prayer from Pentecostal workers, the Holy Spirit came upon him. He said the Holy Ghost "took possession of my face and jaws and began moving them sideways, back and forth, and I began to speak in other tongues, as the Spirit gave utterance, saying only a few words in each, and then began to chant in the Spirit." He described the moment as a "wonderful thrilling of joy sweeping all over me of such a sweetness of love that it is impossible for tongue to describe it."[720]

Thomas Ball Barratt was a very successful Methodist pastor, publisher, and church leader in Oslo, Norway. He visited the United States on a fundraising mission in 1906. Barratt had hoped to secure enough monetary support to build a "City Mission" upon his return. He went back to Norway without the finances he had hoped for, but in the good economy of God, he had received something much better. He described it as "a blessing of greater worth than every cent in America!"

In September of 1906, Barratt, who had always stood for "holiness and the baptism of the Holy Ghost," read about the Los Angeles revival in *The Apostolic Faith*. A great hunger entered his heart, and he began written communications with the workers in Los Angeles. Mrs. I. May Throop wrote him from the mission encouraging him to stay in a "receptive attitude." She shared some secrets about receiving the baptism, such as, "Be nothing, that He may be all in all." Finally, she closed, "When we have this baptism, we are very different from what we were before—and we would do nothing to lose it…May God bestow the wonderful baptism upon you most speedily is our earnest prayer."

The fire of God fell on Barratt's soul on October 7, 1906. He continued to seek the fullness of God and corresponded with Glenn A. Cook at Azusa. Cook wrote, "The speaking in tongues should follow the baptism." In a later letter, Cook said, "The more earnestly we covet a gift from God and the more we sacrifice to obtain it, the more highly we will prize it when it is obtained."

On November 15, Barratt attended services at a small mission in New York. Lucy Leatherman and others from Azusa were in New York on their way to the foreign field. Barratt received the "full Pentecostal baptism." He said, "Immediately I was filled with light and such a power that I began to shout as loud as I could in a foreign language. Between that and four o'clock in the morning, I must have spoken seven or eight languages…I stood erect at times preaching in one foreign tongue after another, and I know for the strength of my voice that 10,000 might easily have heard all I said." Those who prayed for him saw a crown of light over his head and cloven tongues like fire in front of the crown.[721]

Barratt became one of the Pentecostal movement's most tireless leaders. He established Filadelfia Church in Oslo, Norway, and helped spread the message across Europe and around the world.

Soon after his return from the United States, Barratt was visited by Alexander A. Boddy. Boddy was the vicar of All Saints Church in Sunderland, England. He, too, was hungry for more of God. When Barratt visited All Saints in September of 1907, the fire fell in England. On October 28, the pastor of Bowland Street Mission in Bradford received his baptism in Boddy's home. This master-plumber-turned-pastor, Smith Wigglesworth, would be one of the greatest Pentecostal ambassadors. He traveled on five continents preaching and healing the sick.[722]

These stories, too, could be repeated thousands of times. Only the faces and places would change. An early participant in the revival wrote:

This great movement is like a little mustard seed planted in Los Angeles. It took root in a humble place which proved to be good soil and watered with rivers from heaven, it soon put forth its branches to nearby towns like Long Beach and out to Oakland. Soon the limbs spread north and far over the eastern states, and then clear over into Sweden and India. Now it is spreading all over the world, and how beautiful and green it is, and how the birds are coming to lodge in its branches.[723]

19

THE FIRST CHALLENGE: OPPOSITION

Despite all that God was doing at Azusa Street, there were still critics, skeptics, and scoffers. *The Apostolic Faith* reported, "The religion of Jesus Christ is no more popular now than it was when Jesus was here. Many are rejecting the truth and are not going to receive it. The word not only says that signs shall follow them that believe, but that 'They that live godly in Christ Jesus shall suffer persecution.' This is also being fulfilled."[724] Another observer wrote, "It would be unlike Satan not to stir up derision and opposition."[725]

Secular newspapers had a field day. The first reporter to visit the mission described a "wild scene last night on Azusa Street." Another called the faith "weird fanaticism." A cartoon ridiculed the worshippers as "holy rollers," "holy jumpers," and "holy kickers."[726]

From April of 1906 until the end of 1908, more than one hundred related articles appeared in the area newspapers. In July of 1906, at the height of the revival, the stories averaged almost one per day.[727]

When Della Cline, a "pretty" twenty-three-year-old Los Angelean, received the baptism of the Holy Spirit, *The Los Angeles Daily Times* carried a front page story with the headline, "Weird Fanaticism Fools Young Girl." According to the report, before attending services at Azusa Street,

Miss Cline "thought but little on religious matters." After she received the baptism evidenced by tongues, she spent so much time in her room waiting on more of God that her "friends" became worried about her.[728]

The following newspaper account of what took place in the mission is especially descriptive:

> Disgraceful intermingling of the races, they cry and make howling noises all day and into the night. They run, jump, shake all over, shout to the top of their voice, spin around in circles, fall out on the sawdust blanketed floor jerking, kicking, and rolling all over it. Some of them pass out and do not move for hours as though they were dead. These people appear to be mad, mentally deranged, or under a spell. They claim to be filled with the spirit. They have a one-eyed, illiterate, Negro as their preacher who stays on his knees much of the time with his head hidden between wooden milk crates. He doesn't talk very much but at times he can be heard shouting "Repent," and he's supposed to be running the thing...They repeatedly sing the same song, "The Comforter Has Come."[729]

Another article in *The Los Angeles Daily Times* was especially critical of the racial makeup of what the reporter called "the strangest service ever held in this city." Seymour is described as "the one-eyed Negro leader" who was surrounded by a motley company who shouted and moaned, screeched, and prayed themselves hoarse in their frenzy.

According to the article, one young white woman "engaged in whispered conversation with the black leader and appeared to press her face against his perspiring chops in her eagerness to tell her story." The reporter said, "Pandemonium reigned supreme when the meeting was practically turned over to the Negroes at 10 o'clock. Black wenches threw themselves on the floor and cackled and gabbled." The racial bias is evident throughout the article. The author even criticized how "whites and Negroes clasped hands and sang together." His greatest surprise was that "any respectable white person would attend such meetings as are being conducted on Azusa Street."[730]

Some items reported in the press went beyond the ridiculous. *The Los Angeles Express* repeated a "rumor" that Pentecostals in Monrovia, California, were contemplating "making sacrifices of children, to appease the wrath of God." According to the paper, "timid" women were keeping a close watch over their children.[731]

Reporters who came to critique the services were sometimes caught by surprise. One such reporter was sent by his editors to write a comical description of the services. After witnessing the power of God on the service, his attitudes changed dramatically. During the service, a woman stood and began to speak in tongues. She had no idea what she was saying, but she spoke in the native language of the immigrant reporter. Looking straight at him, she described his sinful life in a "holy torrent of truth."

After the meeting, he pressed his way through the crowd and asked the woman if she knew the language she had spoken. "Not a word," was her response. At first he doubted her honesty, but he was finally convinced by both her sincerity and the grammatical perfection and fluency of her speech. He told her what she had said and that he believed it was God's call for his salvation, a call that he pledged to answer.

Returning to the newspaper, he told his boss he could not deliver the type of article he had been sent to write. He would, on the other hand, be glad to submit a truthful piece on the virtues of the meeting. Not only was he not allowed to give a positive report, but he was also informed of his dismissal from the paper.

Bartleman wrote, "The newspapers began to ridicule and abuse the meetings, thus giving us much free advertising. This brought the crowds. The devil overdid himself again."[732] Another writer, commenting on the critical reports, said hungry people came because they understood "the devil would not fight a thing unless God was in it."[733]

Azusa Street worshippers were cursed, egged, jailed, and physically assaulted. Owen "Irish" Lee was a rough customer before he was saved in the mission. This former Catholic had been a bartender and street fighter both in his homeland of Ireland and later in New York City. Once, he fought four police officers because he had seen them abuse a drunkard.

After Owen's conversion, a Catholic woman and her "giant" accomplice came to the mission with a stout rope to hang Owen from a streetlamp. They were upset that he had left his old religion and accepted Christ as his Savior. The man spit in Owen's face and then punched him in the face. By the grace of God, Owen turned the other cheek.

When the man tried to hit Owen again, his fist was stopped by the power of God, which then threw him backward into the gutter. Owen prayed for his enemies and was thrilled a few nights later when he saw them both enter the mission and receive salvation from their sins.[734]

In the face of growing opposition, the mission's periodical courageously proclaimed, "We are ready, not only to go to prison, but to give our lives for Jesus." This was not just cheap talk. Many, many of the Azusa faithful were arrested for their faith. According to *The Los Angeles Times*, the entire congregation had been "subject to threats of arrest for the disturbances made."[735]

One brother was arrested for speaking in tongues before two police officers. Convinced that he was "crazy," they put him in the emergency hospital and brought insanity charges against him. At the police station, the emergency room, and later in the county hospital and courtroom, he continued to speak in tongues. Some, including the judge, recognized the language he was speaking. Although several people came to testify on his behalf, he was released without needing to call a single witness.

Not long afterwards, the same worker was arrested for disturbing the peace while conducting a street meeting. Among other things that went on in the courthouse, he rebuked the antagonistic city attorney with a message in tongues. The jury deliberated for more than eight hours but did not reach a verdict. The charges against him were eventually dropped.[736]

Henry Prentice, a Black brother, went from Azusa to Whittier, where he conducted an open-air meeting. Following Azusa's example of not receiving offerings, Prentice could demonstrate no "visible means of support," so the police arrested him for vagrancy.

This was not the first time Prentice had encountered the heavy hand of the law. In June of 1906, he was arrested after he disrupted a tent meeting at First Street and Cummings Street. Prentice "nearly caused a riot" when he pointed his finger at Emma Robinson, the daughter of a white preacher, J. S. Robinson of the Church of God, and told the young lady she was a sinner. Some in the congregation wanted to "hang" Prentice. Someone summoned the police, who arrived and arrested the preacher for disturbing the peace. Prentice was tried and sentenced to thirty days on the chain gang.[737]

Prentice had received only one year of formal education, but on the occasion of his arrest for vagrancy, he insisted on representing himself in a jury trial. He also claimed his legal right to participate in the selection of the jury. He read Matthew 10 to every prospective juror and explained that Jesus told His disciples to go out and preach without taking gold, silver, or brass in their purse. (See Matthew 10:9.) He emphasized verses 14 and 15, *"And whosoever shall not receive you, nor hear your words, when ye depart out of the house or city, shake off the dust of your feet. Verily I say unto you, it shall be more tolerable for the land of Sodom and Gomorrah in the day of judgment, than for that city"* (Matthew 10:14–15 KJV).

The judge became exasperated with Prentice and angrily threatened to throw a chair at him. After every outburst from the bench, the defendant would reply, "The Lord bless you, judge."

After Prentice had selected his twelve jurors and read Matthew 10 twelve times, he told the judge to proceed with the trial. The prosecuting attorney, however, had a different plan. He said he would not face Prentice for "all the money in the United States." The case was dismissed, and the attorney and judge both found their way to Azusa, where they were born again.[738]

Henry McClain, a husband and the father of three little children, did not fare as well as Prentice. He was arrested in Whittier for having a prayer meeting in his home. The police said they were making "unusual noise and disturbing the peace of the neighborhood." McClain was sentenced to thirty days of hard labor on a chain gang.

Not discouraged, he said, "I never had such power of God on me as when I was in that jail." A number of Mexicans were in jail with McClain, and McClain preached to them in Spanish, a language he did not know. Only after he was through did someone tell him that he had spoken the words of Isaiah 55, a chapter of Scripture he also did not know. McClain said, "There was not a one of them but was weeping bitterly."[739]

In Pasadena, Ansel Post and his Household of Faith congregation were harassed by the civil authorities after neighbors complained of the noises coming from their "big tent." It was reported that the "'Householders' hold meetings frequently until after midnight and that they make so much noise that it is impossible for anyone within two blocks to sleep. One of the features of their services is the casting out of devils. These devils invariably depart from the bodies of their victims to the accompaniment of unearthly shrieks and groans."

At first the authorities gave them three days to tone down their services or move their tent. Defiant, Post announced, "We have received a message from the Lord and He tells us not to move our tent." Their injunction ignored, police raided the tent on July 12. Post was arrested, hauled into court, ordered to take the tent down, and fined fifty dollars.[740] When Post moved the tent, the *Pasadena Daily News* reported, "Buffeted about from pillar to post, with no one caring for their presence in the vicinity, followed by crowds of the curious and, according to their complaint, 'beset by ruffians on all sides,' the members of the 'Household of God' sect are now without home and friends and minus a place to lay their heads, figuratively speaking."[741]

The most stinging attacks did not come from the secular media or law enforcement, but from the Christian community. E. P. Ryland, pastor of Trinity Methodist Episcopal South Church and president of the Los Angeles Church Federation, visited the mission and reported to the newspaper that what was going on was nothing worse than "modern religious fanaticism." Ryland expressed his concern, however, that "certain of the enthusiasts might lose their reason through over zeal and become dangerous."[742]

The Azusa meetings did, however, have a positive impact on the established churches in Los Angeles. In response to the Azusa success, the denominational churches operating as the Church Federation began a series of street meetings and campaigns in the summer of 1906. *The Los Angeles Express* reported, "This movement is an outgrowth of a sentiment on the part of Rev. Ryland and his associates, that the orthodox churches are falling behind other religious organizations in missionary effort, and that, for this reason, the people are drawn away from the beaten paths of established faiths." The paper also reported that it was the revival at Azusa Street and Smale's church that "aroused the federation to action."

Ryland commented, "This effort must not be construed into a fight against the new creeds…New creeds are springing up here and there, and the promoters are imbued with the spirit of missionary work to such an extent that they never rest. On the other hand, the orthodox churches in many cases are content with enjoying the light they have received."[743]

Holiness churches, Baptist churches, and conservatives that lost so many members to the Pentecostal movement were even harsher critics. Holiness papers called the Pentecostals "deluded," "heretical," "counterfeits," "fad worshippers," and much worse.[744] The members of these churches were asked to leave if they were caught attending the Azusa Street services.[745]

William Pendleton, pastor of Hawthorne Street Holiness Church, and some of his members received the Pentecostal experience early in the meetings. Their church then had a visit from W. M. Kelly, an overseer, who informed them they had "obtained strange fire and had thereby come under the influence of a deceiving, lying spirit and were under a strong delusion." Soon afterwards a denominational meeting was held at the church, and Pendleton was told not to teach "a third blessing."

A few weeks later, Kelly returned and found the Spirit moving, with people lying on the floor and others speaking in tongues. They asked him if he wanted to receive the baptism of the Holy Spirit, and he replied, "Another Holy Ghost? No. I would have to deny Him who is living in my heart, to receive another." Mrs. McGowan, of the congregation, shook her finger at him and rebuked him while speaking in tongues. Mrs. Lemoine said the Spirit was grieved. Kelly stayed until the meeting ended at five o'clock in the morning but was convinced that he had seen the fulfillment of 2 Thessalonians 2:11 (KJV): *And for this cause God shall send them a strong delusion, that they should believe a lie.*

On August 27, 1906, the elders of the church, led by Asa Adams, forced Pendleton and twenty-eight members to withdraw from the Holiness church for "being out of harmony with the doctrines and rules of the church, they holding that the evidence of receiving the baptism of the Holy Spirit was always the gift of languages; also teaching that the disciples were sanctified before the day of Pentecost, and did not receive the baptism of the Holy Ghost until receiving the gift of tongues, this being in direct opposition to the teaching of the Holiness Church as set forth in the book of rules." According to the Holiness leaders, Pendleton and the other Pentecostals "denied their faith."[746]

The Burning Bush lambasted A. G. Garr when he received his baptism. According to the editor, Garr was "led away by the people known in Los Angeles as the 'Tongues' people, who profess to receive unknown tongues as an evidence of a third blessing." Further, it was reported that "the light has left the eye, the fire is gone and we can see clearly that he has lost the Holy Ghost." The editorial concluded, "It is with great personal regret we record this downfall of a man of good gifts and success as a soul winner."[747]

W. M. Collins, a Baptist preacher, reflected on his Pentecostal experience in *The Upper Room*, a periodical published by Elmer Fisher in 1910. He wrote, "What has it meant to me? On the one hand it has meant loss—loss of friends, loss of money, loss of position, loss of reputation. On the other hand gain. Here I fail. I cannot tell the heights, the depths, the lengths, the breadths of the riches which this blessing has brought into my experience."[748]

It seems paradoxical that those who had the most in common with the Azusa worshippers were the most critical and violently opposed to the outpouring of the Holy Spirit. Donald Gee, a leader of the Pentecostal movement in Europe, once wrote, "there seems to be a law which students are compelled to observe, that the last wave of spiritual revival in the church nearly always seems to offer the greatest opposition to the oncoming wave of blessing and advance."[749]

Before the great revival began in Los Angeles, a resident of the city had a very descriptive vision of the coming movement. He saw individual fires springing up and then gathering to form a solid wall of flames. A preacher was trying to put the fire out with a gunny sack, but his futile labors were useless against the growing inferno. *The Apostolic Faith* reported the vision and commented, "The man with the wet gunny sack is here also, but his efforts only call attention to the fire."[750]

20

THE SECOND CHALLENGE: DIVISION

Anna Hall, one of Charles Parham's workers, came to Los Angeles from Texas in the summer of 1906. Parham had sent here there to help with the growing work on another new field. She would be the first missionary of the Apostolic Faith to enter the Lone Star State.

She was soon followed by the Walter J. Oyler family and Mr. and Mrs. Quinton.[751] The Oylers were residents of Orchard, Texas, and had visited Parham's meetings in Kansas and Missouri. Both had received the baptism of the Holy Ghost and asked that a worker accompany them to Texas to assist in spreading the Pentecostal message. Oyler was a brother-in-law to A. A. Ayler, one of Parham's strongest allies. The Oylers and Aylers had extended an invitation to Parham to preach the Apostolic Faith message at Orchard. He accepted and began his successful Texas mission.[752] These were people whom Parham trusted and, no doubt, they were sent to the West Coast as his representatives. It is noteworthy that they were all white.

This, however, did not satisfy Seymour, who was anxious for Parham, his "father in this gospel of the Kingdom," to visit Los Angeles and put his stamp of approval on the work.[753] Seymour wrote the Apostolic Faith offices in Texas on July 12, 1906, requesting ministerial credentials and

Apostolic Faith pins.[754] W. F. Carothers sent a note to Parham that the credentials had been sent and noted this was the "first colored mission."[755]

In August, Seymour wrote Parham, acknowledging Hall's arrival and inviting him to Los Angeles for a large meeting. He was expecting a spiritual "earthquake" as God would shake the city.[756] The faithful at Azusa also looked forward to Parham's visit. One remarked that he wanted to see the white "father of the black son."[757]

There was hope that Parham would arrive in Los Angeles on September 15 and conduct the city-wide revival in the early fall.[758] When he agreed to the campaign, the Azusa paper heralded his coming. He was announced as "God's leader of the Apostolic Faith Movement."[759] Parham, however, was giving his attention to ministry in Zion, Illinois, and the Midwest, and he postponed his visit to Los Angeles.

When Parham finally arrived at Azusa Street in late October, he felt especially threatened. A few months earlier, he had been accused of a moral failure in League City, Texas. These charges had followed him for years. One of his lieutenants, Warren Carothers, was demanding accountability and questioning his leadership of the movement.[760]

With all this on his mind, and already fearing he was losing control of the movement he founded, he arrived in Los Angeles to find a revival equal to or greater than any he had led. Instead of offering a right hand of friendship, he swatted the saints with a heavy dictatorial hand.

To say that he was not pleased with the Azusa Street meetings would be a gross understatement. Before entering the building, he heard "chatterings, jabberings and screams." Without introduction, Parham walked to the front of the mission, greeted Seymour, and pronounced, "God is sick at His stomach!"[761] This was not what the Californians had expected!

No doubt, Parham was turned off by the emotionalism at the mission. This, however, does not completely explain his repulsion. Early in Parham's meetings there were manifestations of emotion, including violent shaking.[762] Parham, who by today's standards would probably be considered a racist, was most offended by the interracial composition of the meetings.[763] He described the Azusa upper room by saying, "men and women, whites and blacks, knelt together or fell across one another; frequently a white woman, perhaps of wealth and culture, could be seen thrown back in the arms of a big 'buck n-----,' and held tightly thus as she shivered in freak imitation of Pentecost."

Later, Parham wrote that the worship at Azusa was a "cross between the old-fashioned Negro worship of the South, and Holy-Rollerism."[764] Throughout the remainder of his life, he never ceased to criticize the work of the Los Angeles mission.

The congregation was as unhappy with Parham as he was with them. A. G. Osterberg said, "We didn't like that he told us that he was above us."[765] It was reported by Glenn Cook that Parham almost "discouraged" Lucy Farrow by telling her that Black people could not be part of the bride of Christ.[766] After only a couple of services, two of the elders at Azusa asked Parham to leave, and Seymour "closed the door" against him.[767] According to E. S. Williams, in the only reference Seymour ever made to race, he lamented, "You know, it is my color."[768]

Parham started another mission at the Women's Temperance Christian Union building at Broadway Street and Temple Street in Los Angeles and drew away some of the Azusa devotees.[769] When Parham left California, W. F. Carothers was placed in charge of his mission. This Texas lawyer's racial views were even more extreme than Parham's. He believed that hatred and animosity between the races was a work of the Holy Spirit, a gift of God to prevent the mixing of racial groups.[770] Though the ministerial work of both Parham and his successor in California was unsuccessful, the founder of the Apostolic Faith had succeeded in causing the first major division at Azusa.

Seymour totally severed his relationship with Parham and the parent organization, incorporating as "the Apostolic Faith Mission." An interracial group of Richard Asbery, Louis Osterberg, James Alexander, John Hughes, and Reuben Clark served as the incorporating trustees. According to the articles of incorporation, the organization was formed "to do evangelistic work; conduct, maintain and control missions, revivals, camp meetings, street and prison work."[771]

Carothers wrote, "The work in Los Angeles separated from us, under circumstances which the present writer believes justified them, but about which it would be painful to write."[772] On another occasion he wrote, "We have felt that God's permissive providence was in all of this. They discovered before we did that the man we all supposed to be an apostle raised up to lead in the great work of restoration manifestly in progress was not an apostle."[773]

The Azusa Street Mission began to issue credentials and recognized the ordination of many ministers, including E. S. Williams.[774] Although these early Pentecostal ministers were highly suspect of any organization, and especially hierarchic authority, they gladly accepted ordination because it gave them a discount with the railroads.

Because Parham would not answer to the charges of immoral conduct, Carothers and Howard Goss disfellowshipped him from the organization he had founded.[775] In July of 1907, Parham was arrested in San Antonio, Texas, and charged with sodomy.[776] Although he denied the accusations until his death, his ministry never fully recovered. For decades, a number of Pentecostal historians did not even mention his name.[777]

On August 12, 1906, before Parham's visit, Frank Bartleman had left the Azusa Mission and started a work at Eighth and Maple. He rented a building that had been occupied by The Pillar of Fire Church, some of Pentecost's most vociferous critics. Always an independent, Bartleman was offended when Azusa elected elders and began to "organize." He was also offended when he saw a sign stating "Apostolic Faith Mission" outside the building. This, to Bartleman, was evidence of a "party" spirit that he said God showed him would come to Azusa.[778] Bartleman was soon joined by William Pendleton who, with several in his congregation, had been turned out of the Hawthorne Street Holiness Church for embracing the Holy Spirit baptism evidenced by tongues.[779]

Elmer Fisher, the pastor of Glendale's First Baptist Church, received the baptism on his second visit to Azusa Street. He continued to work with his friend Pastor Smale at the New Testament Church, and Bishop Seymour at Azusa. Fisher led the Azusa Mission for four months while Seymour conducted his mission in the South. Fisher's motto was "Exalt Jesus Christ; honor the Holy Ghost."

When a group of people left the First New Testament Church, Fisher joined them in starting The Upper Room Mission. After the revival first exploded at Azusa, so many of Smale's members were worshipping at the mission that he had to go there to look them up. Smale invited his congregation back and promised them greater "liberty" in the Spirit.

One of Smale's members reported, "They drove our pastor...from the First Baptist Church because he had the power and now, he has brought it to us. We are speaking with tongues, and we are enjoying the religion those numbered in the big church might have had if they had not turned that good man out."[780]

Smale became a strong advocate of the Pentecostal message and wrote a pamphlet, *A Tract for our Times*, endorsing the movement. Later, unfortunately, Smale recanted and became an even stronger critic, forcing the "baptized" members to leave the First New Testament Church.

Fisher's Upper Room Mission, which met in an upstairs hall at 327 1/2 South Spring Street, not only received the remnant from the First New Testament Church, but also drew "most" of the whites away from Seymour. George Studd joined Fisher and taught a morning Bible study at the new mission.[781]

By the end of 1906, the movement founded on unity and love was already becoming splintered. A critic wrote, "Some were saying, 'We are with Seymour;' others were saying, 'We are with Parham;' and still others, 'We are with Bartleman.'"[782]

Early in 1907, the mission faced another major challenge. The Stevens A.M.E. Church continued to make the building available for purchase. In fact, for some time, the "For Sale" sign remained on the structure. With the real estate market booming in Los Angeles, the faithful were concerned that if they did not move expeditiously to buy the old Azusa Street building, another interested party might acquire the property, forcing them to vacate quickly and leaving them without an alternative house of worship.

The landholders requested that $15,000 be paid in three years. Late in 1906, a sum of money had been given toward either purchasing the mission or relocating, but the reserves were not sufficient to meet the owners' demands. However, within days of Seymour's announcement of the need, $4,000 was raised for a down payment on the purchase. In less than two years, the building was completely debt free.[783] Cecil Polhill gave the last $1,500 on February 2, 1908.[784] Despite this great blessing from God, some attendees were offended because a tradition had been broken: money had been mentioned in the mission, and an offering had been received.[785]

The first serious internal challenge to Seymour's leadership came from one of the trustees, Professor Charles C. Carpenter.[786] Carpenter insisted that Seymour give an account for all the funds that had been given to the mission. The money had flowed so freely that Seymour had not kept any books, not even "the scratch of a pen." A full accounting was impossible. Seymour said, "I have done the best I could with the funds. I can't remember where it was all spent." He recalled giving $100 to one effort and perhaps $500 to another. He mentioned as many as fifty names that had received offerings but could not "cover all the ground." Certainly uncomfortable trying to defend himself, Seymour said, "I sent it out as the Lord told me and as the need required, and before God, I never misspent or kept one cent of it."

Seymour never owned property and lived and died in near poverty, yet Carpenter was not satisfied. He continued to insist on a full accounting, causing a "different spirit" to creep in—a spirit that was "destructive to the place."[787]

Azusa broke new ground in the summer of 1907 when they sponsored a camp meeting. One can only imagine how uncomfortable the Southern California summers would have been in the crowded mission. This testimony described the previous summer: "During the hot days when the crowds would fill Azusa Mission all day, people would often get up and say they praised God for what He was doing 'this morning;' not realizing that the sun was going down in the evening. They had not eaten all day, and yet they were so taken up with sitting at the feet of Jesus that they lost track of the time and would sit there in the heat, wiping the perspiration from their faces."[788] For the summer of 1907, the mission provided more comfortable quarters.

The idea of a camp meeting originated with Rachel Sizelove. She dreamed one night that she saw scores of white tents pitched at the foot of a hill in Hermon, where she lived. She shared the dream with a group at the mission. R. J. Scott, a Canadian who had been Holy Spirit baptized at the mission, became a principal organizer of the event.[789]

The camp meeting at the Arroyo Seco, near the neighborhood of Hermon, was attended by thousands. They erected a tabernacle to seat one thousand and had an "upper room" tent for seekers. More than two hundred living tents and a number of large tents were set up for pilgrims. Black and white attendees had separate accommodations but worshipped together as they did at Azusa. A large number of attendees were saved, healed, and baptized in the Holy Ghost. Over one hundred converts were baptized in a nearby stream.

The power of God was evident throughout the camp. An attendee actually saw fire "issuing out of the tabernacle." One morning after breakfast, ten praying workers were slain in the Spirit. They could not get away until noon.[790]

In the meantime, services continued all summer at Azusa, affectionately called, "the old manger home." An observer who attended the regular services held back at the mission wrote, "The pillar of fire still rests there."[791]

Early in 1908, the church reported, "The meetings have been going on every day since the work started and God's Word and the Holy Spirit are just as fresh and new as ever." Nevertheless, another group of dissenters had left the mission because of Seymour's hard preaching on divorce.[792] The pastor not only believed that divorced people could not remarry without committing adultery, but he also held that those couples who had been previously divorced and remarried should separate and live apart.[793]

On May 13, 1908, over the objections and protests of some of his helpers, Seymour married Jennie Evans Moore. According to their marriage license, Seymour was thirty-eight, and Jennie was also in her thirties. They were united by one of their most faithful friends, Edward S. Lee. Edward's wife Mattie and Richard Asbery witnessed the happy event.[794] Seymour had preached several sermons on marriage, perhaps getting the congregation ready for what was ahead, and The Apostolic Faith had printed an article that explicitly stated, "It is no sin to marry."[795] Despite these preparatory efforts, several workers left the mission.[796]

One of the first missionaries to leave Azusa was Florence Crawford. She first preached in Portland, Oregon, on Christmas Day, 1906. Two years later she gave up her home in Los Angeles, returned to Portland, established a mission, and spent the remainder of her life there.[797] The Portland Apostolic Faith Mission accused the Azusa Street Mission of letting "down the standard of holiness" and ceasing to teach sanctification as a second work of grace. No basis was given for these charges, and they appear to be blatantly false, at least by any established standards of holiness.[798]

After Seymour's marriage, Clara Lum, who had served as the editor of *The Apostolic Faith*, left Los Angeles to assist Crawford. In June of 1908, the fourteenth edition of the paper was printed without the familiar "Apostolic Faith" mast on the front page. The second page of the paper carried this message: "For the next issues of this paper address: The Apostolic Faith Campmeeting, Portland, Oregon."[799] Lum wrote the following in the July/August edition: "We have moved the paper which the Lord laid on us to begin at Los Angeles to Portland, Oregon, which will now be its headquarters." She also asked that money should be sent to the Apostolic Faith in Portland. An article on the front page described the outpouring of the Holy Spirit in Los Angeles, but Seymour's role was conveniently omitted.[800] By late 1908, the entire publication was moved to Portland.[801]

Without permission, Clara Lum had removed the paper and, more importantly, the national and international mailing lists to Portland.[802] This was devastating to the Los Angeles work. Seymour tried to print at least one edition, and perhaps more, of the paper, but it was impossible to continue without the mailing lists or the financial contributions that had been misdirected to Portland. In an October/November 1908 edition published in Los Angeles, Seymour said,

> I must for the salvation of souls let it be known that the editor is still in Los Angeles…and will not remove *The Apostolic Faith* from Los Angeles, without letting subscribers and field workers know. This was a sad thing to our hearts for a worker to attempt to take the paper which is the property of the Azusa Street Mission to another city without consent, after being warned by the elders not to do so.[803]

In the summer of 1910, the Portland paper carried a weak apology: "This paper would be No. 21 from the beginning in Los Angeles, but it is No. 7 of Portland. We said it was moved from Los Angeles when we should have stated we were starting a new Apostolic Faith in Portland."[804] Neither the paper nor the mailing lists were returned to Los Angeles. The revival at the mission never fully recovered from the loss.

Seymour journeyed to Portland during the period of crisis to try to bring the mission back into the fold, but he was met by resistance from Florence Crawford and Will Trotter, the former leader of a rescue mission in Los Angeles and a former participant at Azusa Street. As he was leaving the mission, without having reached a reconciliation, Seymour met E. S. Williams on the stairs and asked him, "Are you going to continue to preach here?"

When Williams answered, "Yes," Seymour said, "I'll have the railroad take away your clergy book."

"If that is necessary," Williams replied. The fact that the usually conciliatory Seymour followed through with his threat is an indication of the depth of the pain caused by the split.[805]

George Studd regularly attended the Azusa Street Mission and the other Pentecostal missions throughout 1908, and his daily diary gives some detail as to the services. He was at Azusa when Cecil Polhill gave the great offering to pay off the mortgage. He wrote, "What a Sunday at Azusa! Dispute as to taking collection. How the devil tried to get in and how the Lord defeated him!"

On February 16, he said there were "very good meetings all day." Studd was "greatly blessed," and the meeting was "packed to the doors at night." Sunday, March 15, found Studd at the mission at half past ten in the morning; he stayed at the altar until three o'clock in the afternoon.

Most often, Studd described the services as "pretty good," "good," "splendid," "excellent," or "very good." On only one occasion, March 21, did he report, "meeting not very good."

On April 9, the mission celebrated the second anniversary of Pentecost in Los Angeles. Studd said there were "many good solid testimonies." In the afternoon service, Studd himself was given "great liberty" in his testimony.

Studd joined Richard Asbery and Joseph Warren at the Security Savings Bank on April 16, where they finished legal work on the deed to the Azusa property.[806] That night, he met with the board of trustees. The following Sunday, April 19, was Easter. Seymour and Edward Lee oversaw the services at Azusa.

Studd said that Seymour "spoke well" in the morning meeting on May 3. The message was followed by a "good time 'tarrying' in upper room." A week later, Studd said the pastor "seemed to throw away his message (if he had one)." Seymour had opened the service "for everyone to talk." Studd complained, "And some did, too."

A Mrs. Kallaway spoke at the mission on Sunday, May 17. She "spoke splendidly with great power and unction." Brother Seymour also delivered a message, speaking of his "wedding and wife."

Lucy Farrow left the mission on May 20, and there was a farewell service for her. There was an enjoyable time of tarrying for the Lord in what Studd called the "after meeting." Seymour and a Brother Stewart from Phoenix, Arizona, spoke on Sunday, June 28. Stewart spoke from John 15.[807]

During the summer and fall, Studd's visits to the mission became much less frequent. He hardly mentioned Azusa Street in his diary. In August, he wrote to *Confidence* and reported that even though white people still attended the services, the mission was "entirely controlled (humanly speaking)" by Black people.[808]

Things were cooling significantly by the beginning of 1909. A frequent attendee, Ned Cashwell, kept a diary and often shared his thoughts about the revival. On March 7, he wrote, "Seymour is fatter. Crowd was smaller but still good." The next Sunday his diary said, "Today was fine and sunny. At Azusa St. there was a small crowd. Seymour and his wife leading, and not much doing."[809]

Apparently, there was still glory in the house even as the revival waned and the crowds diminished. Bartleman visited the mission on the same Sunday as Cashwell and said, "The Lord met me in great power." He attended Azusa regularly and preached or testified often. By the end of the year, however, he reported that the mission had "lost out greatly." Despite his criticism and failure to support the work, when Bartleman left for a trip to Europe, Azusa was the only mission in Los Angeles that gave him an offering.[810]

Greek scholar and translator W. B. Godbey visited Los Angeles in 1909 and found the city "all electrified" with the Pentecostal movement. The meetings at Azusa were still running night and day without intermission. Workers from the mission stayed at the depot watching the trains at all hours to receive guests visiting the revival. They would ask visitors, "Have you received the baptism of the Holy Ghost?" If the answer was "Yes," they followed with a direct question about tongues: "Have you the sign?" If the answer was "no," they invited them to the altar and prayed with them to receive.

Godbey refused an invitation from the "runner" at the station, but his ego could not resist when Seymour invited him to speak at the mission. He said there was a "large audience" at the mission. Like all guests, Godbey was asked if he had received the sign of the Holy Ghost. He responded, "I can say with Paul, 'I thank God I speak with tongues more than you all.'" From his own knowledge of biblical languages, *"Johannes Baptistes tinxit, Petros tinxit et Christus misit suos Apolstolos ut gentes tingerent."*

Godbey sarcastically reported that the people "shouted over" him and wanted to put him at the "front" of the movement.[811] It is unfortunate that he perpetrated this sham on the people, gleefully bragged about it, and then used it as fodder in a critical cannon that blasted the movement. Is it difficult to ascertain who had a Christlike spirit: the humble pastor that shared his pulpit with this skeptic, or the arrogant guest that took advantage of his host.

From the beginning there was a strong Hispanic presence at the revival. For some unknown reason, however, in 1909, the Valdez family, the Lopez family, and almost all Latinos exited the mission. Gaston Espinosa suggests some felt they were too expressive in their testimonies and worship. Espinosa says they were "ruthlessly" crushed by leaders at the mission and left en masse.[812]

Paul Bettex, a former missionary to South America, attended the mission in early 1910, where he was "basking in the presence of God." While there, he felt God calling him to China, and he soon departed as a faith missionary.[813]

In April of 1910, Bishop and Mrs. Seymour lived at the crowded mission along with J. A. Warren, Samuel Murphy, Mack Jonas, a Mrs. Jones from Oklahoma, Johanna Eibinfeldt, a Hungarian immigrant who was serving as an Apostolic Faith missionary, and Phebe Conway and her four children: Emma, Wanda, Elenore, and Albert.[814]

During the same year, George N. Eldridge said he "became interested in the old Azusa Street Pentecostal work." Although he was initially cautious, he and his wife were both baptized in the Holy Spirit. They established Bethel Temple in Los Angeles.[815]

Just four years after the opening of the mission, there were twenty-five Pentecostal churches in greater Los Angeles.[816] The movement had drifted far from the vision of nonsectarian harmony originally espoused by William J. Seymour.

Canadian A. W. Frodsham, brother of Stanley Frodsham, was in Los Angeles in late 1910 or very early in 1911. He visited Azusa, where Black and white people continued to "worship freely together." He said, "The mission has not been flourishing of late, but now there are signs of abundance of rain, and many are being blessed."[817]

On February 14, 1911, while Seymour was on a missionary trip to the East, the mission opened its pulpit to William H. Durham, the Chicago pastor who had received his Holy Spirit baptism at Azusa in 1907.[818] In the years following 1907, Durham had formed his own association, providing ministerial credentials from his Chicago church.[819]

The Upper Room Mission denied Durham the pulpit because he had developed and was preaching a new doctrine of sanctification. Durham's baptistic view emphasized the finished work of Calvary and argued that sanctification was instantaneous at conversion and continuing with spiritual maturity.[820] This position was a direct contradiction to the Holiness doctrine endorsed by Seymour and the Apostolic Faith Mission.

Despite the controversy, Durham had great success at the mission. Many of the original participants returned to the mission as huge crowds gathered. H. S. Covington endorsed Durham after seeing him in a dream before he arrived in Los Angeles. Covington went to the station, saw Durham, and said, "This is the man I saw last night in a dream."[821]

Countless souls were saved, and an average of ten people a week were receiving the Holy Spirit. In one week, more than twenty came through to the experience.[822] On Sundays the building was filled, and hundreds were turned away. Bartleman said, "The fire began to fall at old Azusa as at the beginning."[823]

Durham's doctrine disturbed the Azusa faithful because it conflicted with their firmly held position on sanctification. Previously, Sister Rubley at the mission had had a vision about the conflict. She saw the devil and his demons seated at a large table discussing the problems they were having with all the Pentecostal people and what they should do about it. Various demons suggested remedies like taking the Pentecostal people's joy or peace. But the devil responded they would still have the Holy Ghost. Finally, a demon suggested, "I have it; give them the baptism on the unsanctified life." The demons all clapped and roared.[824] Now, through the ministry of Durham, they believed the vision was being fulfilled.

The elders wrote Seymour and asked him to come home and handle the volatile situation. Receiving their reports, he wired Los Angeles for the money to return to the church. Upon his arrival, he met with Durham and asked him to stop preaching the "finished work" at Azusa. Seymour also informed Durham that "this was his work." Apparently, Durham tried to block Seymour from preaching in his own pulpit.

Instead of submitting to the pastor of the local assembly, Durham went before the congregation on Sunday morning and asked the people to vote on whether they wanted him to continue the work or turn it back to Seymour. Durham said only "ten or less" voted with Seymour. How Durham could have participated in this unethical and egotistical spiritual coup d'etat is unimaginable.

Seymour faced this challenge to his authority without flinching. He consulted with the leaders of the mission, and on May 2, 1911, Seymour locked Durham and his followers out of the mission without notice.[825] For years, the doors had never been locked. Louis Osterberg and four other members of the board tried unsuccessfully to dissuade Seymour from locking the doors against Durham. In protest, Osterberg, a long-time friend of Azusa, resigned his position as a trustee.[826]

Durham said, "While we were preaching, praying and seeking God in the mission, Seymour had been scheming and planning as to how he could get possession of the building." How unfortunate that Seymour was accused of "scheming" to regain control of his own pulpit after his pastoral authority had been usurped by a former friend.

Frank Bartleman secured a mission on Kohler Street as a temporary home for Durham's meeting, and then his followers opened their own mission in a large building on the corner of Seventh and Los Angeles, and his crowds followed him. One commentator said, "Azusa leadership had failed God."[827] Bartleman, the Osterbergs, and other Pentecostal leaders in Los Angeles gave their support to Durham. On Sundays, one thousand would attend his meetings. Unfortunately, the Apostolic Faith Mission was devastated. Bartleman said the place became "deserted."[828]

Durham was not satisfied to practically empty the mission; he personally attacked Seymour through his periodical, *The Pentecostal Testimony*. He spoke of Seymour's "failures and blunders" and said that "the power of God had entirely left him, and that he was no longer worthy of the confidence and respect of the saints." After all but destroying Seymour's work in Los Angeles and questioning his leadership, Durham lamented that all this character assassination was his "unpleasant duty."[829]

Charles Parham was also incensed by Durham's sanctification doctrine. In January of 1912, he prayed that God would show the world which teaching was correct by taking the life of the teacher who was in error. That summer, Durham died of tuberculosis. Parham believed that God had answered his prayer and the "finished work" controversy was over.[830] Durham's message, however, outlived the messenger and has become the predominant Pentecostal position.

This was not the last division to strike the fledgling Pentecostal movement. In 1913, R. J. Scott led the planning of another camp meeting at Arroyo Seco. Noted faith healer Maria Woodworth-Etter was the featured speaker. Brother Seymour attended the meeting, but "only as a spectator."

As was often the case in Etter's meetings, attendees were healed and saved. A water baptismal service was scheduled, and R. A. McAlister, a Canadian who had been Holy Ghost baptized at Azusa, was invited to teach. McAlister discussed baptismal formulas and suggested that the disciples baptized in "Jesus's name" and that the words "Father, Son, and Holy Ghost were never used by the early church in Christian baptism."

That evening, John G. Scheppe meditated on McAlister's remarks and the wonderful healings performed as Woodworth-Etter prayed in Jesus's name. The following morning, Scheppe ran through the camp shouting that God had given him a revelation that believers were to be baptized in the name of "Jesus Only."

Frank Ewart, a former associate of William Durham, attended the meeting and was taken with the idea of the "Jesus Only" issue. He, along with McAlister and Glenn A. Cook, developed the idea of rebaptizing in Jesus's name. Within two years, the Pentecostal movement that was already divided over sanctification was again splintered between Trinitarian and Oneness believers.[831] In April of 1914, at an opera house in Hot Springs, Arkansas, the Assemblies of God denomination was born. Although C. H. Mason, the Black founder of the Church of God in Christ, spoke at the first general council, it was obvious that the Assemblies of God, with very few exceptions, would be a white denomination.[832] Two other major Pentecostal denominations, the Church of God in Cleveland, Tennessee, and Pentecostal Holiness, were also predominantly white. Mason's group would remain almost exclusively Black.

Racial segregation that disappeared when the Spirit was poured out at Old Azusa was now institutionalized. Pentecostalism, which began with a utopian dream of New Testament unity, was now divided by sect, doctrine, and race.

21

THE APOSTOLIC MINISTRY: SEYMOUR'S TRAVELS

As news of the meetings at Azusa Street spread, Seymour was invited to travel and take the revival to other areas. He evangelized, established churches, and ordained ministers much like Paul and the first-century apostles did.

In November of 1906, he traveled to Oakland, California; in the next few months, he was in San Francisco and San Jose. In the spring of 1907, he was in Texas, the South, and the Midwest. In the summer of 1907, he went to Chicago, Illinois; Indianapolis, Indiana; Zion, Illinois; and points further east.[833]

We have more information about the Indianapolis meetings than all of Seymour's other evangelistic ministries. Thomas Hezmalhalch (called Brother Tom because his name was so difficult) and Glenn A. Cook started the Pentecostal work in Indianapolis. They were soon joined by J. O. Lehman, Celia Smock, Elnora Hall, and a "Brother Harry."

In April of 1907, a newspaper reporter visited the meetings held in the Murphy League Hall at Alabama Street and New York Street and listened to the Pentecostals speak in tongues. What he heard sounded like gibberish to him, and he coined the name "Gliggy Bluk" to refer to the city's

Apostolic Faith believers and their strange gift of tongues. The name stuck, and for years the newspapers used the title when referring to the group.[834]

One of the early believers in Indianapolis was Alice Reynolds, a pretty sixteen-year-old student at Shortridge High School. The *Indianapolis Morning Star* reported her involvement with the Pentecostals, including her speaking in tongues, lying prostrate on the floor, and coming "under the power."[835] One reporter said her "manipulation of the strange tongue is really a feature of the meetings." When she would rise to speak, there would be a "craning of necks," and spectators would rise from their seats.[836] Later, Reynolds married J. Roswell Flower, who became an early official in the Assemblies of God. Their son, Joseph, also served as General Secretary for the organization. The Assemblies of God Archives is named the Flower Pentecostal Heritage Center after this influential family.

The Indianapolis Pentecostals received regular attention from the secular press and the police department. A riot nearly erupted in their mission when a Black convert, Ernest Lloyd, tried to exorcise an evil spirit from Naomi Groves, a twelve-year-old white girl. Lloyd rushed to the girl, seized her by the hair with both hands, and shook her violently. Glenn Cook said Naomi had a demon, and Lloyd was trying to shake it out. However, all this attention frightened the young girl, and she began to scream hysterically.

Naomi's screams aroused a group of unbelievers who attended the meeting as skeptical observers. The angry mob shouted racial epithets and demanded that Lloyd leave. One man said, "Religion is religion, but it is another thing for a burly n----- to grab a little girl and frighten her to death." A number of policemen were called, and soon order was restored.

The paper reported that the white believers associated freely with Lloyd and even took him with them "to restaurants to get their meals."[837] Racial tolerance was not only practiced at Azusa but exported by missionaries who left Los Angeles to preach in other areas.

About a week later, the police were called again when several people fell into "trances." The lawmen threatened the believers with arrest, declaring that if they were called to the meeting again, "somebody would get a ride in the patrol wagon."[838]

Seymour was invited to Indianapolis by Sarah Cripe, one of the local worshippers. Apparently, she also financed his trip. Cripe was a "massage doctor" with considerable wealth. The Pentecostal leaders in Indianapolis lived rent free in Cripe's home at 2341 Fletcher and were supported by her generosity. In terms that would seem patronizing by today's standards, Cripe announced, "Brother Seymour is a good man. He is a Negro, but he is the discoverer of this great faith. He met with a little band in a stable in Los Angeles and discovered the wonderful power. And now just to think that this wonderful Negro is coming right here to be with us."[839]

After a long wait, the highly anticipated visit began on June 2, 1907. Seymour arrived at the mission with the E. H. Cummings family from Los Angeles. Mr. and Mrs. Cummings were traveling to Liberia, West Africa, with their eight children: Emma, Bessie, Frank, Ida May, Mattie Belle, John C., Marjorie, and Ardell.

Cook greeted Seymour with a hug and a kiss when he entered the hall. A kiss on the cheek from a member of the same sex, or the "holy kiss," as it was called, was a hallmark of the Evening Light Saints and adopted by many early Pentecostals. Not everyone in Indianapolis was accustomed to this embrace, however, and one girl in the audience gasped, "Oh, that white fellow kissed the Negro."

Cook introduced the Los Angeles leader as "my brother, Seymour." In a voice that "shook the church," Seymour said, "Let's sing 'The Comforter Has Come,'" a favorite hymn at Azusa Street. Afterward, he announced, "I have come to spread the gospel over Indianapolis."

A visiting reporter gave one of the most complete contemporary descriptions of the preacher available anywhere. He wrote, "This founder of the sect stands full six feet in height. He wears a rubber collar, decorated by no sign of a necktie. Adorning his mouth is one massive gold tooth, ranked by rows of other teeth, perfectly straight and white. The beard that he wears could be called a flowing one if it was longer. It flows—what there is of it. His voice is like the roaring of a cannon, and of all his most striking characteristics, he has but one eye."[840]

Although the believers were "wonderfully impressed by his power," Seymour's visit was marked by controversy from the beginning. Ida May Oddy of 1720 West Washington Street, wife of Tom Oddy, a prominent grain dealer, testified that her husband was going to leave her if she continued to attend the services. Oddy played the organ and sang for the meetings. She had also received the baptism in the Holy Spirit.

Seymour addressed Oddy's problem in his message on June 3 and told of one man who was "struck down" by God because he did not want his wife to attend the meetings. A tearful Oddy bowed on her knees before Seymour, who took her by the hand and prayed for her.

Oddy's comments in the service indicate that her husband's real complaint was the racial composition of the meetings. Referring to Seymour, she said, "This brother is a man of God. And after all we should not hesitate to associate spiritually with Negroes. In the great beyond the Negroes and whites will be together. We need not associate with Negroes here except spiritually. I must associate with these people, for you know what the Bible says about the man who hid his talent under a bushel."

Oddy's husband filed for divorce, claiming his wife stayed away from home from two o'clock in the afternoon until eleven o'clock at night to attend the services. He said she could have the choice of "quitting the Bluks or quitting him." Mrs. Cummings told the church that she was not surprised by the turn of events. "Way out there in California," she said, "lots of families were torn up because the women came to our meetings."[841]

Another controversy arose when Arthur Scott, a young man residing at 3313 Graceland Avenue, came under the power while working at Van Camp Packing Company. Scott shook so violently that the dispensary ambulance was called. "Don't touch me," the man told a doctor, "this is the power of God."

The skeptical doctor replied, "If that is the power of God it is giving you a devil of a shaking." Soon, the manifestation subsided, and Scott went home shouting "Hallelujah" and "Glory."[842]

Local police attended the meetings regularly after Seymour's arrival. The chief reported he had received "many complaints" even though the offended parties did not want it known that they had attended the meetings. One protest concerned the fact that "white women of good appearance attend the meeting and mingle with Negroes freely, holding hands while they call each other 'brother' and 'sister.'" Referring to the integrated meeting, one police officer said they found things "pretty mixed up there."

On one occasion, the police refused to leave when the meeting was over, and several women were still prostrate on the floor. The faithful prayed for over an hour for the "police demons."

During another meeting, Detective Billy Holtz went to the altar to feel the pulse of a young girl in a "trance." Brother Seymour explained, "It's the power of the Lord," but the detective would not accept that explanation, choosing to believe the girl was under some kind of "hypnotic" power.[843]

Seymour and the Cummings family participated in the Indianapolis meetings for weeks. The Cummings children would give messages in tongues and then interpret their meaning. Mrs. Cummings also spoke out frequently.

On June 9, the crowd was so large that two meetings were held. Seymour preached to a large assembly upstairs, and Cook spoke in the main hall. Still the throng kept coming until Cook had to request, "Will someone please go down and stop the crowd that's comin' in so that no one will get hurt?" After the preaching, the congregation merged in the upper chamber for prayer.

During the same meeting, Alice Reynolds received considerable attention when she "conversed long and earnestly" with "Frank Cummings, Negro." The newspaper also noted that during the service, Cummings sat "with a white young man on one side of him and a white girl on the other."[844]

Opposition to the meetings became so determined that Cook found himself in the reversed role of asking the police to come to the meetings and provide protection from rowdy intruders. This security was necessary as crowds grew more hostile. On one occasion, Cook was "hit several times about the head."[845]

Saturday, June 15, was an especially important day for the Pentecostals. At two o'clock in the afternoon, between two and three hundred believers and spectators gathered at Fall Creek near Indiana Avenue for a baptismal service. Seymour performed the baptism, assisted by Cook. Cook entered the waters first and waited as Seymour exhorted from the book of Luke and conducted a service consisting of hymns and prayers. Seymour said,

"People say they don't understand this strange language. No wonder, they can't understand it until they are baptized in the Holy Ghost and fire." He proclaimed there were not enough devils in Indianapolis, heaven, or hell to destroy the faith of the Pentecostal believers.

Both Seymour and Cook were dressed in long black robes. One reporter said the former resembled "authentic portraits of the King of Abyseinia."

Thirteen people were immersed in the muddy waters. They were assisted through the dangerous current by E. H. Cummings and Joseph Ingland. Mrs. Oddy was the first baptized. Seymour gave the declaration and, with Cook's help, dipped her deep into the water. She came up speaking in tongues.

Others following the Lord in baptism were Cummings, Ingland, Lloyd, Cripe, Ada Willey, Mabel Cook, Naomi Groves, Nelda Kelso, Grace Harrison, Luella McCarty, Elizabeth Shaw, and Bennett Lawrence. Lawrence would become a founding member of the Assemblies of God and wrote what was likely the first history of the Pentecostal movement.

After the baptism, the faithful returned to Murphy Hall for a foot-washing service. Visitors were not allowed in the room as about one hundred believers washed each other's feet. Men and women were discretely separated to opposite ends of the room as four large tubs of water were carried into the hall for the service. Men washed men's feet and women washed women's. Afterwards, the men hugged each other and shared the holy kiss. Women in the front of the hall did the same. Once again, the secular press made an issue of Black and white people hugging, kissing, and showing affection to one another.

When the fellowship ended, Seymour announced, "Now we will have the Lord's Supper. Praise God!"[846] Seymour, following another tradition of the Evening Light Saints, taught that baptism, foot washing, and communion were all mandatory church ordinances.[847]

News of the Saturday services brought more opposition to the meetings. Neighbors from around the hall presented a signed petition to the Board of Public Safety, asking them to close the mission. A group of two hundred "hooting, jeering" protesters surrounded the meeting threatening the safety of Cook and others inside. The police had to be called at least six times.[848]

The mayor of the city, Mr. Hookwaiter, visited the meetings and determined the group was not a nuisance and that they deserved the protection of the police. Hookwaiter said, "I want to say that I have seen just such actions as theirs indulged in hundreds of revivals and many, many prayer-meetings. True, they get worked up in their religious frenzy until they do not seem to understand what they are doing, but they do not harm anyone, and they do not interfere with any of the neighbors." The mayor also said he saw no inappropriate familiarity between Black and white people, and "I did not see a man place his finger on a woman."[849]

The Cummings family left Indianapolis for their missionary trip on June 18, and the mission hosted a farewell service.[850] The time of Seymour's departure is not known, but it must have been soon thereafter.

Later that year, Glenn Cook invited Henry Prentice to come to the city from Los Angeles and lead the work. With the help of Oddous Barber, they soon converted Garfield Thomas Haywood, who became a prominent Pentecostal pioneer and respected church leader.[851]

On the same journey to the East, while ministering with Tom Hezmalhalch in Zion, Illinois, Seymour sent this glowing report back to the mission:

> People here receive the baptism in their pews while the service is going on and sometimes scores of them receive it. It is the sweetest thing you want to see. It reminds me of old Azusa ten months ago. The people that receive the baptism seem so happy, they remind me of our people at home. There are little children from six years and on up who have the baptism with the Holy Ghost, just as we have it in Los Angeles. Praise our God. This is another Azusa. It would do you good to hear these people speak under the power of the Holy Ghost. Some of them converse in tongues. Brother Tom has never lost the spirit of the Azusa. He is still fired up the same as ever. Everywhere I have traveled among our baptized souls they seem to have such joy and freedom in the Holy Ghost.[852]

Often neglected and almost forgotten in Los Angeles, Seymour was still well-received across the country, and he continued to travel throughout his life. In the years between 1906 and 1922, he conducted preaching tours in a number of American cities, including, but not limited to, Indianapolis, Chicago, Cincinnati, New York City, Washington DC, Baltimore, and Houston.

On more than one of his numerous eastern trips, Seymour held revivals, issued ministerial credentials, and planted new churches. In 1911, he preached in Handsome, Virginia, a small community south of Franklin. There was no building, so Seymour preached in brush arbors and home prayer meetings. Several were saved and baptized in the Holy Spirit, and a congregation was formed. Elder Charles W. Lowe, a carpenter, was left in charge of the mission. Seymour appointed Lowe as Senior Bishop and Chief Apostle of the Apostolic Faith Mission. Under Lowe's leadership, the group expanded into North Carolina, Maryland, Ohio, Pennsylvania, New York, New Jersey, and Liberia, West Africa. After Lowe, the church was led by John Thomas Cox, Robert Clarence Butts, and Oree Keyes. The fruit of Lowe's and his successors' labors continue until today in the fellowship known as the Apostolic Faith Church of God, Live On.[853]

Over the decades, the eastern churches founded by Seymour and his surrogates suffered many schisms and divisions, but in 1987, several churches with ties to Seymour's ministry formed a loose knit and very fragile federation of church groups affiliated under the name The Azusa Street Mission Churches. Cooperating churches include Apostolic Faith Holiness Church of God, Apostolic Faith Churches of God, Apostolic Faith Church of God in Christ, Apostolic Faith Church of God, Live On, The Church of Christ Holiness Unto the Lord, Inc., Saints of Runney Mede Holiness Church, and Sweet Haven Church.[854]

Seymour was back in Centerville, Louisiana, in the fall of 1912. He, along with his siblings, received $5 from the Iberia, St. Mary, and Eastern Railroad Company for a right of way across the family farm. Phillis, who was staying with Jennie at the mission in Los Angeles, received $25 for her interest.[855]

In 1918, Seymour returned to Virginia again, where he preached at the Holiness church attended by Estella Cobb. The church enthusiastically received the Pentecostal message. Cobb remembered that the people "rushed" to hear Seymour.[856]

On at least one occasion, Seymour ministered with his friend John G. Lake in the Pacific Northwest. Lake said, "The glory and power of God was upon his spirit" as Seymour preached to more than ten thousand people. The impact on the audience was phenomenal as men "shook and trembled and cried to God."[857]

Seymour was a frequent visitor at the annual convocations of the Church of God in Christ. He was an honored guest of his dear friend Bishop Mason. He attended numerous meetings in Memphis and at least one in Chicago, probably in January of 1921.[858]

In 1921, on one of his last missionary journeys, Seymour preached several weeks at the Christian and Missionary Alliance Church in Columbus, Ohio. Some of the last memories of the bishop come from Mrs. Georgiana Aycock (née Pepsico) of Columbus. She said, "The glow would be on that man's face. He looked like an angel from heaven. So many wanted to hear him...He was no man to exalt himself, but a humble man. When you'd meet him at the door you could just feel...he was a real man of God...He didn't talk much. He was not a conversationalist. He'd get off about the Lord, being true to God."[859]

Possibly on the same trip, Seymour ministered in the New York City area. Bishop Frank Clemmons met Seymour at the corner of 135th Street and Lenox Avenue in Harlem. Since Clemmons was affiliated with the Church of God in Christ, Seymour asked him if he knew Mason. Clemmons answered, "Yes, as a matter of fact, Bishop Mason is in New Jersey now attending meetings." When Seymour asked to see Mason, Clemmons took him to East Orange, New Jersey. These two gospel soldiers met, for what may have been the last time, at the home of Elder James Wells, pastor of the Old Tabernacle Church of God in Christ. Clemmons saw the two giants "weeping on each other's shoulders and praising God in power and glory."[860]

At his death, Seymour's supporters reported correctly, "The world was his parish."[861] The faithful pilgrim and apostle had taken the Pentecostal message far beyond the walls of the Azusa Street Mission.

22

THE HOMEGOING: WILLIAM SEYMOUR RECEIVES HIS REWARD

One of the last detailed looks at the mission was in 1912, when English publisher A. A. Boddy visited. Seymour was on one of his evangelistic trips in the East, but Mrs. Seymour greeted Boddy at the mission. Seymour's aged mother Phillis, J. A. Warren, and his wife also lived in the upstairs apartments.[862]

Boddy noticed a sign protruding from the building with the words "Jesus Saves" and a transparency that said, *"You shall know the truth and the truth shall make you free"* (John 8:32 NKJV). There was also a chalkboard near the front door announcing service times.

Boddy was invited to preach in the mission, and he described the service in detail. Mrs. Seymour led the hymn singing, exhorting between each song. She also led the assembly in prayer and prayed "as one who knew God." The singing was "very earnest" and was without musical accompaniment. The meeting was "orderly," and both Black and white people attended the service.

The building was "brightly lit up," clean and comfortable. A board floor had been added to the sanctuary, and the building was "nicely furnished."

After Boddy's sermon, "seekers" came to the altar. One man was delivered from the "demon of drink," and some were healed and baptized in the Holy Spirit. Boddy said, "I am greatly drawn to these dear colored people."[863]

In 1914, C. H. Mason sent Eddie R. Driver to organize a Church of God in Christ church in Los Angeles. The church experienced a great revival, with souls saved, sanctified, and baptized.[864] Although Mason and Seymour remained fast friends, it could not possibly have strengthened Seymour's work to have yet another Black Pentecostal mission in the city.

On May 19, 1914, the mission held a business meeting, amended the articles of incorporation, and elected trustees. In addition to Bishop and Mrs. Seymour, the church chose Richard Asbery, Spencer James, and James Ross to serve as the official board. The new constitution required that the bishop, vice-bishop, and all trustees were to be "people of color." Seymour reluctantly excluded whites from leadership in the church, "not for discrimination, but for peace."[865]

At this time, less than twenty people attended the Apostolic Faith Mission, most of them the original seekers from Bonnie Brae.[866] There is little doubt that racial prejudice contributed to the diminished role that Seymour would play in the future of the movement. Yet, he was never bitter. An old African proverb says, "There is no medicine for hate," and Seymour lived his life with this in mind.[867] Considering the Spirit's work and not his own feelings, he wrote, "Division came through some of our brethren, and the Holy Spirit was grieved."[868]

Seymour wrote and collected a ninety-five-page book in 1915, *The Doctrines and Discipline of the Azusa Street Apostolic Faith Mission of Los Angeles*. He wrote about "all the trouble we have had with some of our white brethren," but nevertheless declared, "We love our white brethren and sisters and welcome them." He went on to say, "Our colored brethren must love our white brethren and respect them in the truth so that the Word of God can have free course, and our white brethren must love their colored brethren and respect them in the truth so that the Holy Spirit won't be grieved. I hope we won't have any more trouble and division spirit."[869]

The book served as a church administration and minister's manual for the home church in Los Angeles and the congregations Seymour had established in the East. It provides both doctrinal sections and church help dealing with family life, finances, membership, deacons, ordination, ministerial ethics, and much more. There is also help for administering the sacraments, weddings, and burials.

It is obvious that much of the discipline was borrowed from other sources, with Seymour editing the material to fit the needs of the mission. For example, the "Articles of Religion," "Rules for a Preacher's Conduct," and several other passages in the book were taken from *The Doctrines and Discipline of the African Methodist Episcopal Zion Church* or another Methodist organization that may have shared a similar discipline. Sometimes the editing seems disjointed or, to be kinder, like a patchwork as Seymour added and subtracted to mold the book into a framework suited for his leadership. He omitted a number of passages, including information about infant baptism, from the A.M.E. Zion book. He also added a note on foot washing as a church ordinance.[870]

The discipline demonstrates that Seymour had become less inclusive over the years. The role of women and white people had been curtailed. Women could function in the ministry but could not baptize or ordain, and they had limited authority.[871] White people could not serve as bishop, vice-bishop, or trustees of the Apostolic Faith.[872]

B. Scott Lewis suggests that the original portions of the book rely heavily on the theology of Daniel Warner and the Evening Light Saints. Seymour uses the metaphor "the cleansing of the sanctuary" to provide "a biblical vision of the true church." The phrase comes from a book with that title written by Warner and H. M. Riggle in 1903.[873] Lewis shows how Seymour copied a chart from Warner and Riggle and titled it "The Tabernacle, a Type of Full Salvation."[874] Lewis believes this chart informs Seymour's theology on salvation, sanctification, and the baptism in the Holy Spirit.

By the time the *Discipline* was published, the Pentecostal world had been fractured by the Oneness or "Jesus Only" movement. Seymour makes his position clear: "The next, we don't believe in being baptized in the name of Jesus only. We believe in baptizing in the name of the Father, and the Son and the Holy Ghost, as Jesus taught his disciples" (see Matthew 28:19–20).

Without calling him by name, Seymour rejected Parham's doctrine on the annihilation of the wicked. He even suggested that a person was not really Spirit-filled if they "believed contrary to the teachings of the Holy Spirit."[875]

In his section on annihilation, Seymour added passages on speaking in tongues that have led many to assume that he changed his views on tongues as a necessary evidence of the Holy Spirit baptism. He wrote:

> We don't believe in the doctrine of Annihiation [sic] of the wicked. That is the reason why we could not stand for tongues being the evidence of the Baptism in the Holy Ghost and fire. If tongues was the evidence of the gift of the Holy Spirit, then men and women that have received the gift of tongues could not believe contrary to the teaching of the Holy Spirit. Since tongues is not the evidence of the Baptism of the Holy Spirit, men and women can receive it and yet be destitute of truth. It is one of the signs, not the evidence Mark 16:16–18.[876]

In an amended bylaw, he also wrote:

> The speaking in tongues being one of the signs "signs following" the baptized believers and other evidences of the Bible casting out devils, healing the sick and with the fruits of spirit [sic] accompanying the signs. (See 1 Corinthians 13; Mark 16:16–19; Acts 2:2–3; Acts 10:44–46; Acts 19:6.)

It is easy to see why some think that Seymour had "compromised" from the Apostolic Faith distinctive tying speaking in tongues with the Holy Spirit baptism. Originally, at least, Seymour believed that every Spirit-filled believer would speak in tongues. Did he change his opinion on this? This author does not think so. Seymour never once says that every believer will not speak in tongues. The verses he used for his texts in the amended bylaw all mention speaking in tongues. If he was suggesting that not all believers would speak in tongues when baptized in the Holy Spirit, he could easily have included Acts 8, the only passage in Acts that does not clearly say that those who received the baptism in the Holy Spirit spoke in tongues (although the author would argue it is implied in the text).

If Seymour's position changed, his new view was that not everyone who spoke in tongues was baptized in the Holy Spirit. He had seen inexcusable behavior in so-called Spirit-baptized Christians, including Parham. He had concluded that tongues were not the *only* evidence of a Holy Ghost baptism. This does not preclude believing and teaching it is the initial physical evidence.

As early as September of 1907, when Seymour clearly believed that tongues were the initial physical evidence, this statement was posted in *The Apostolic Faith*:

> Tongues are one of the signs that go with every baptized person, but it is not the real evidence of the baptism in the every day life. Your life must measure with the fruits of the Spirit. If you get angry, or speak evil, or backbite, I care not how many tongues you may have, you have not the baptism with the Holy Spirit.[877]

To say that not everyone who speaks in tongues has the Holy Spirit is different from saying not everyone who has the Holy Spirit will speak in tongues. Seymour believed the former but never taught the latter.

This idea is contrary to what is taught by many neo-Pentecostals, who would rather move away from the necessity of tongues-speaking as a biblical evidence of the Holy Spirit baptism. Some will go to almost any extreme to try to "prove" that Seymour changed his view.

In a 1908 sermon printed in *The Apostolic Faith*, Seymour is as clear about speaking in tongues as a person can be:

> The Azusa standard of the baptism with the Holy Ghost is according to the Bible in Acts 1:5, 8; Acts 2:4; Luke 24:49. Bless His holy name. Hallelujah to the Lamb for the baptism of the Holy Ghost and fire and speaking in tongues as the Spirit gives utterance.

If this is not plain enough, he adds, "So, beloved, when you get your personal Pentecost, the signs will follow in speaking with tongues as the Spirit gives utterance. This is true."[878]

Even these unequivocal statements do not satisfy those who are determined to change Seymour's theology. Charles R. Fox Jr. reads the same sermon, parses Seymour's words, and notes that he did not "promote a doctrine of Biblical evidence" because he used the word "sign" instead of evidence.[879] Fox fails to acknowledge that Seymour used both "sign" and "evidence" as far back as 1906. He did not make a distinction, using both in one sermon to mean the same thing.[880] Obviously, to Seymour, the sign was the evidence, and he provides several texts to demonstrate it is biblical.

Although some disagreement will persist with this thesis, Seymour's position is once again made abundantly clear near the end of the book. In a section he titled "Apostolic Faith," he wrote:

> The baptism in the Holy Ghost and fire means to be flooded with the love of God and Power for Service, and a love for the truth as it is in God's word. So when we receive it we will have the same signs to follow as the disciples received on the day of Pentecost. For the Holy Spirit gives us a sound mind, faith, love and power. 2 Timothy 1:7. This is the standard Jesus gave to the Church.[881]

Seymour is clear that he still believes, "When we receive it, we will have the same signs to follow as the disciples received on the day of Pentecost." How did the disciples receive? With evidentiary tongues. In other words, all believers will speak in tongues as the disciples did. Speaking in tongues, however, does not stand alone as the evidence of the baptism of the Holy Spirit. True Pentecostals should also walk in integrity, love, and power.[882]

There is one other significant bit of evidence that scholars have ignored. The churches that Seymour established in Virginia in 1911 also publish a discipline, or as they call it, a "manual." In "Article 12" they make a doctrinal statement which includes "Speaking in Tongues as Evidence of Baptism of the Holy Ghost, John 15:26; Acts 2:4; 10:44–46; 19:6."[883] If Seymour had changed his theology on tongues, why would he include this doctrine in a new church he helped to establish?

Skeptics who teach that Seymour changed his position on evidentiary tongues say he did so because of men like Parham, who taught tongues were the evidence but did not live an exemplary life. In view of the above statement, this logic becomes illogical. Before Seymour established the Apostolic Faith in Virginia, he had already had his unpleasant encounter with Parham, and yet he organized this church with speaking in tongues as the evidence of the Holy Spirit baptism.

No honest person can say that, at one time, Seymour preached and taught a biblical baptism in the Holy Ghost would always be accompanied with speaking in tongues. He was unambiguous about that. Furthermore, no one can point to even one plain statement when Seymour said he no longer believed that to be true—not one. It is an injustice to his memory that some would misrepresent his words to fit an agenda and claim he compromised his position on this significant Pentecostal distinctive.

William Seymour may not have been as thoroughly trained and as articulate as some modern theologians, but his position on glossolalia is straightforward enough to be understood by the simplest seeker, even if scholars struggle to understand it.

The collecting and editing from other sources and adding of original material for the publication of this book would require considerable ability on Seymour's part. Of course, he may have employed help, but still the book seems to show a level of skill higher than many historians have accorded him.

The passage of time would continue to bring more transitions. Long-time friend F. W. Williams broke with Seymour and the Los Angeles organization in October OF 1915. He changed the name of the churches he founded to Apostolic Faith Mission Church of God.[884]

A sizable number of Seymour's family members spent time in Los Angeles. Some lived in the apartments in the mission. His brother Isaac and his mother were living on Hemlock Street when Isaac registered for the World War I draft in 1917. Curiously, he was also blind in one eye.[885]

In about 1917 or 1918, Seymour called a meeting for restoring unity to the Pentecostal movement. Although he invited all the Los Angeles leaders to attend, only two showed up for the meeting. A disappointed Seymour lamented he had "done what little he could to help the movement."[886]

The meetings at Azusa Street were cut back to only one day a week, and only a couple dozen people attended. Seymour taught with a blackboard and chalk, and sometimes visitors from the glory days would stop by and visit.[887]

Money at the mission became scarce. Sometimes Seymour would have to receive a second offering just to cover mission expenses. Mrs. Seymour had to return to secular employment to help the couple make ends meet.[888]

Aimee Semple McPherson arrived in California in late 1918. Her biographer said that, at that time, "The Azusa Street Revival was little more than a memory." When she held her first campaign in Los Angeles in 1918, Seymour attended. He told a friend that "he had not been feeling completely well; his heart had been hurting him."[889]

Fourteen years after the fire fell, Azusa held an anniversary service and Bible conference. Unlike the revival of 1906, the 1920 meeting was more liturgical, with a printed program for the services. The rapture of the church was the theme for the meeting, but teaching on repentance, conversion, sanctification, the baptism of the Holy Spirit, healing, and doctrines of baptisms were also included. The selected songs for the service were a mixture of traditional hymns, revival songs, and Black spirituals. The Azusa Street favorite, "The Comforter Has Come," was also included.[890]

Some of the most important players in the Los Angeles story were still in the city and may have participated in the anniversary service. Joseph A. Warren, sixty-nine years of age, was living with his sister and brother-in-law at 1445 W. 36th Street.

Edward S. Lee, sixty years old, and his wife Mattie, thirty-seven years old, lived at 3624 Western. An eleven-year-old niece, Mary Ann Wiley, lived with the couple. Mary Ann and the Lees reared the daughter of Azusa Street missionary Ophelia Wiley. Ophelia had a very troubled life. She was divorced by her husband, and he had her institutionalized for being a religious fanatic.[891]

Richard and Ruth Asbery still lived in the house where the fire fell, but the city had renumbered the street, changing their address to 216 Bonnie Brae. Their daughter Willie Ella and two grandchildren, Ruth E. and Marian E. Pruden, lived with them in the home. Their son Morton and his wife Julya lived on the same block, at 228 1/2 Bonnie Brae. At age sixty-one, Richard maintained his position as a janitor.[892]

Two of the Asbery's sons ran into trouble with the law and spent time in the state reform school in Whittier. Richard Jr., raised in the famous

Bonnie Brae home, was first arrested at age twelve. He spent four years at the state penitentiary at San Quentin, serving a one year to life sentence for robbery.[893] Robert, also an eyewitness to Pentecost, was sent to reform school on June 29, 1906, in the heat of the revival. After he escaped from the school, stole a horse, and robbed a house, officials called him "incorrigible."[894]

Willis and Julia Hutchins continued to live in Los Angeles until she passed on July 11, 1920.[895] Ruth, the child they adopted in Africa, is not mentioned in the census.[896] Unfortunately, their only living birth child, Jethro, also lived on the wrong side of the law. By age thirteen, he was in the Whittier State School. He too spent time at San Quentin. Saddest of all, Jethro died at San Quentin on December 4, 1926. He was only twenty-two years of age.

In the records of the reform school, an officer noted, "The boy's home was a little better than the average colored boy's home—furnished comfortably, plenty of room and excellent sanitation. The parents at the first hearing appeared to be rather lenient toward the boy." In another place, Dr. Hoag wrote, "The trouble cannot be blamed to the home, excepting the parents have not begun to discipline the boy until too late."[897]

Lucy Farrow, the other major player in the outpouring, had returned to Texas to join her son and his family. After suffering from intestinal tuberculosis, she was promoted to her heavenly reward on February 21, 1911.[898]

Frank Bartleman continued to do mission work in Los Angeles. He had traveled the world preaching Pentecost. According to Synan, Bartleman joined the "Oneness" Pentecostals and was rebaptized in "Jesus's Name." He was then ostracized by most of his Trinitarian friends. There seems to be no conclusive evidence to support this claim.[899]

Bartleman continued to be an avid author, writing *My Story: "The Latter Rain"* (1909); *From Plow to Pulpit: From Maine to California* (1924); *Two Years Mission Work in Europe Just before the World War* (1924); *Around the World by Faith, with Six Weeks in the Holy Land* (1925); *The Deity of Christ* (1926); and the widely read *How Pentecost Came to Los Angeles* (1925).

Korsets Seier, a periodical from Norway, carried a report on the mission in 1920. It said the church had been through "stirring times." Its report that Seymour had returned to the mission and that the work was "resumed" led European historian Nils Bloch-Hoell to erroneously presume that the mission had been closed for a time. More probably, Mrs. Seymour or another worker oversaw the mission while Seymour took another of his mission trips. The magazine noted, "The Mission is independent. It cannot compromise. When people have tried to impose a new doctrine they have been rejected."[900]

John Matthews, a noted critic of the tongues movement, attended a convention in Los Angeles in the summer of 1922. He noticed an aged Black man in the audience. When he inquired as to his identity, he was informed that the visitor was Seymour, the "man who had introduced 'tongues' on the Western Coast." He described Seymour, who was only in his early fifties, as looking "worn, tired, (and) decrepit."[901]

On September 28, 1922, Seymour suffered serious chest pains and shortness of breath. Dr. Walter M. Boyd's presence was requested for a single visit. At five o'clock in the evening, Bishop Seymour was called home to be with the Lord he loved. His vision never waned; his last message was "a plea for love among the brethren everywhere." He spent his last day with his beloved Jennie, praying, singing, praising God, and planning for the work.[902]

Seymour died without a struggle. Smiling radiantly, he spoke his last words, "I love my Jesus so." His followers reported his death and stated, "His life was a crowning example of the believer in word and deed, self-denial, and whole consecration to God. He was true to the end, never failing in faith or lowering the standards, but standing against every tide in firm allegiance to God and the truth. He so often said, 'Never doubt your God and never disappoint him.' He walked in closest communion and fellowship, looking unto Jesus, his never failing source of comfort and strength."[903]

Seymour's funeral on October 2 was attended by about two hundred people, mostly Black. After a long service with many testimonials, Mrs. Seymour brought the service to a close. Seymour's earthly remains were laid to rest in Evergreen Cemetery in a simple wooden casket. Weeks later, he was disinterred, and his body was placed in a concrete vault. Admirers purchased a simple headstone that reads, "Our Pastor."[904]

G. T. Haywood of Indianapolis, by then a leader in the "Jesus Only" movement, and a man who differed with Seymour on both his sanctification and Trinitarian views, wrote, "Though he did not agree with the brethren in many things, yet he was loved and respected."[905]

The ancient writer of the biblical Proverbs said, *"When a man's ways please the LORD, he maketh even his enemies to be at peace with him"* (Proverbs 16:7 KJV).

23

THE END:
WHEN THE BATTLE'S OVER

After Seymour's death, his faithful wife, who was herself "an evangelist of power and note greatly loved by all," continued as pastor of the mission. Seymour had "placed" the work into her hands before his death.[906]

Lewi Pethrus, a noted Pentecostal leader from Sweden, visited Los Angeles in 1924. He reported to Swedish readers of *Evangelii Harold* that the work of the mission was continuing. Little else is known of the work of the mission for nearly ten years after Seymour's death.[907]

In 1925, Jennie hosted ten days of special services to celebrate the anniversary of the 1906 outpouring.[908] It is reasonable to assume that these commemorative meetings were held regularly but not always advertised.

In 1930, Jennie was living in the mission with several other people. Two nieces and a nephew lived with her: Julia Seymour, Miller Seymour, and Jean Seymour. All three were teenagers. There were also two guests at the mission and four "lodgers."[909]

Little is known of Miller and Jean, but we have information on Julia's life. Julia was born in Verdunville, Louisiana, the daughter of William's brother Simon and his wife Henrietta.[910] She attended high school in California and graduated in 1929. Julia also completed cosmetology school and was licensed as a manicurist.[911] Julia married Everett Porter, another native of St. Mary Parish, in 1931. Porter went to officer training school in World War II and gained the rank of captain. His marriage to Julia failed, but he became a highly respected attorney and judge in Los Angeles.[912] Julia remarried and continued to live in the city until her death in 1986.[913]

The next year, Jennie and the mission faced their biggest, ugliest, and most highly publicized challenge: Rupert D. Griffith came like a wolf in sheep's clothing and tried to usurp her authority and steal the Azusa property.

Little has been written about Griffith, but he very well could be the greatest con artist of all time. Griffith was born in Wales and immigrated to the United States when he was seven. His father was a Congregational Church missionary who founded three churches in Pennsylvania. He attended Oberlin College in 1892 and 1893.[914] In 1896, he married Ida C. King. As a young husband, he worked as a chef at various restaurants, and his talents were appreciated.[915]

After 1900, Griffith joined John Alexander Dowie's Christian Catholic Church. He preached and caused trouble throughout the northeastern United States, ending up in jail several times. That is when his life went off the rails. Because of his abusive mannerisms, which led to multiple arrests, the Dowieites disowned him, saying, "He had forfeited the right to preach, and even the respect of his fellowmen, by violating his promises and neglecting his family, and that he was a disgrace to the church and a hindrance to the work."[916]

Griffith was arrested in 1904 after he got into an argument with his landlord over failing to heal his wife as promised and making her confess to an unspecified sin. He broke the lock to illegally enter the boarding house from which he had been barred.[917]

In July of 1905, Griffith's infant daughter died of pneumonia, creating an outrage in the community. A newspaper reported, "Griffith is so given over to religious work that his family hasn't the proper support, and kindly people have been helping them."[918]

By choosing Dowie over his Zion competitor Wilber Voliva, Griffith found favor with the healing evangelist in 1906. He was promoted to Overseer of Boston.[919] Griffith gathered a small following in Zion and hoped he would be Dowie's successor.[920] After Dowie's death, the faithful disciple spent three nights sleeping on Dowie's grave. On the third night, Dowie supposedly appeared to him in a vision.[921]

Ida and Rupert separated in 1907. Although he claimed he did not "believe in divorce," they were legally divorced in 1910. That same year, he also claimed he was a widower.[922]

The enterprising Griffith announced in early 1912 that he had purchased land north of Mobile, Alabama, to build a new Zion City for Dowie's remaining followers.[923] When those plans fell through, he announced his utopian city would be built in Florida.[924]

Not to be outdone, when Alabama and Florida did not work out, the evangelist said he would open a "negro settlement" on six thousand acres that had once belonged to Dowie. He boasted, "For a long time the colored people who have looked to me to give them advice, have been seeking to get me to arrange such a settlement and at last I am able to gratify their desire."[925] Of course, all the plans came to naught. Later that year, Griffith said he had met with Abdul Baha Abbas, the Persian leader of the Bahaist faith, and was bringing him to Zion.[926]

Griffith was arrested in 1913 for allegedly swindling a poor Black man out of his property.[927] The overseer of Zion said he "preys upon the sentiment and charity of all who will listen to him."[928] In 1916, Griffith claimed to have moved south of the border and joined Pancho Villa in his war against the Mexican president.[929]

Griffith was arrested in St. Louis, Missouri, in 1917 as World War I began. He was interfering with recruitment officers by claiming the war was a "scheme of the money barons."[930]

Griffith applied for a passport to visit Abyssinia (Ethiopia) in December of 1918. On his application, he said this was his first passport application and that he would stay less than two months. It is unclear whether he ever made the trip.[931]

Less than two years later, Griffith was arrested for stoking a deadly race riot in Chicago. He claimed to be part of the Church of the True Brotherhood; the "reverend secretary of the League of Darker People," and connected with the "Black Star" society. A perceptive Black man said the better class of Black people "regarded him as a white man who lived by his wits and who, perhaps, was trying to use the negroes."[932] Two of Griffith's associates in Chicago were convicted, sentenced, and hanged for their part in the riots.[933]

On July 24, the charlatan was arrested for passing bad checks in New York City. He then claimed to be a leader in the "Back to Abyssinia" movement.[934]

Reinventing himself in 1921, Griffith moved to Indianapolis and promoted himself as an expert on the League of Nations and toured the major cities of the south. He lectured to civic organizations on the importance of the League. He advertised himself as an "able orator" and drew significant crowds.[935]

In less than ten years, Griffith was promoting himself as the bishop of the Coptic Church in America. According to his testimony, he had gone to Ethiopia in 1905 and been a missionary in Ethiopia for more than fifteen years. He had gone to convert the Ethiopians but, instead, he himself converted to the Orthodox religion, had become a priest, and was personal friends with Haile Selassie, the emperor of the African nation. He claimed to have escorted Selassie to a Paris peace conference after World War I and to a visit with President Woodrow Wilson.[936]

Throughout his illustrious career, Griffith used a number of aliases. He was Rupert Deveraux, Rupert Jonas, and Jonah the Preacher. He claimed he had a doctorate; that he was an attorney; that he was born in Africa; that his father was an Amharic language professor; that he was a lecturer on anthropology; that he was an educator; and that he was a converted Jew.[937] It seems nothing he ever said was believable. Yet, despite the glaring contradictions in his resume, he fooled influential people, newspapers, civic organizations, churches, and even a Bible college.

This is the man who showed up in October of 1930 when the church was having a prayer meeting. His request to join in the intercession was granted, and the people were impressed by the fervency of his prayer. Griffith was invited back and began to attend daily, "ingratiating himself in the affection of the membership."

Jennie had been injured in an automobile accident and was not able to give her full attention to the church while she convalesced. Griffith took advantage of the situation and the generosity of the congregation and moved his family into quarters in the upstairs of the mission and began to hold meetings. In Jennie's absence, the church gave him half the collection for filling the pulpit. To the surprise of Mrs. Seymour, Griffith announced that he had canvassed the congregation, and a majority wanted him to replace her and assume the pastorate.[938] Griffith had attracted some followers, and about forty members were attending at the time. Only about twelve of those were Black. The long-standing Black members could see through Griffith's scheme, saying the outsider "wanted to wrest control from the colored membership and secure the rich property."[939] With the growth of Los Angeles, the asset was worth as much as $50,000. That would be almost a million dollars in today's purchasing power.[940]

The conflict started on the last Sunday of 1930 when a fight broke out in the building and the police were called. Hymn books were thrown, and competing congregations tried to out shout or out sing the other until pure pandemonium broke loose. The *California Eagle*, an African American newspaper, shouted "Church Members Riot" in bold front-page headlines.

On Sunday, January 4, 1931, things reached a boiling point, and the police were called to calm the storm. Tensions were so high that a policeman warned the "piano stool must remain a piece of furniture, not a missile." The next day the struggle made headlines in several Los Angeles newspapers with a photo of police officer R. M. Clarke standing at the door of the mission.[941]

On the same day, the parties took their case before Deputy City Prosecutor W. D. Wildman, who set a date for a hearing on January 12. Seymour complained that Griffith was disturbing her meetings, and he claimed he was now the pastor.[942]

By Friday of that week, the *California Eagle* had run a photograph of both Seymour and Griffith in the church surrounded by their supporters.[943] The only known photo of the inside of the mission is not a pleasant one. The feud began to take on a racial element as a commentator for the *Eagle* described the struggle as "the Caucasian preacher wants to take the mission away from Mrs. Seymour." In another article, titled "Tramp White

Preacher Tries to Oust Colored Woman," the editor wrote, "Griffith has suggested for her a flogging and at least one member of the church informed this reporter that he has warned some of the Negro members that if they were somewhere else, they would get the rope." If the implications were not clear enough, the reporter concludes by saying, "We are suggesting that the Black men of this community go to the rescue of Mrs. Seymour and secure for her the proper protection under the law."[944]

Before the next Sunday, the parties had reached a "gentleman's agreement" to hold separate meetings, with Griffith taking the lower floor and Seymour the upper. In addition to the regular attendees, the publicity had drawn a curious group who wanted to see "a war firsthand." They were not disappointed. Griffith reportedly took most of the chairs, and when Seymour came to claim them, another ruckus ensued. Some of the members fell through the upper floor of the dilapidated structure. The police had had enough and barred both parties from worshipping in the building until the matter could be legally resolved.[945]

When they met with the prosecutor, Mrs. Seymour would accept no arbitration and repeatedly said, "I want him out." She saw Griffith for what he was—an "interloper and usurper"—and she would not compromise. Hoping the matter could be settled out of court, and wanting to gather more information, the prosecutor postponed a hearing until January 28.[946]

An already horrible situation deteriorated rapidly when Jennie accused Griffith's wife of attempting to assault her and Ruth Asbery with a knife. Jennie and Ruth were preparing a meal in the communal kitchen shared by all the tenants when Mrs. Griffith cursed them, called them "vile names," and threatened to kill them. Griffith himself was accused of striking Jennie, criminal charges were brought against him, and a warrant issued for his arrest.[947]

The *Eagle* sent forth an appeal to "all who stand for justice and fair play" to meet at the newspaper office and jointly visit the city attorney to plead Seymour's case. Seeing through the sham, they suggested that Griffith was "sailing under false colors" and should "return to the region from which he hails."[948] Mocking Griffith, the paper awarded him the 1930 "Hooey Award for Dumb Public Service."[949] The added publicity and outcry from the Black community in Los Angeles got the attention of the ministerial alliance, who formed a committee to see that "Mrs. Seymour gets exact justice."[950]

Feeling public pressure mounting, the court ousted Griffith in early February.[951] The mission had won a battle, but the war over ownership of the property was ongoing in the courts and at the property. One group would padlock the building, and the opposing faction would break the lock.[952]

The assault charges against the intruder Griffith went to trial on March 27, but a jury was unable to reach a verdict.[953] A new trial was scheduled for April, and he was acquitted.[954] Griffith had already moved on to other shams and scams. He was meeting with his new crop of adherents in a Los Angeles hotel. One of his new enterprises was "The Commonwealth of Israel, a Clearinghouse for the Poor, Distressed and Oppressed." He later made news while part of a retirement scheme and even threw his hat in the ring for mayor of the city.[955]

Still barred from the building, on April 8, 1931, the members of the church met at Jennie's house and amended their bylaws once again. There were twenty members present. They were "a majority of the voting power of the membership of said corporation" since the total membership was no more than "twenty-seven." The president of the corporation was N. H. Barragar. Jay P. Nix served as secretary. Trustees were Richard Asbery, Josephine Terry, L. G. Robinson, and Dr. H. C. Hudson.[956] Robinson was a city employee and Methodist pastor, and Hudson was a dentist. Both men were leaders in the Black community and the NAACP. It seems reasonable to assume that they were added to the board to lend their considerable credibility to bolster the mission's standing during the legal wrangling.

The changes to the bylaws weakened the office of bishop and gave more power to the trustees.[957] The amendments, however, were of little consequence. For all practical purposes, the work of the church was done.

In April, the Los Angeles County Health Board "stepped in" and declared the building "unfit for further habitation."[958] The Apostolic Faith Mission at 312 Azusa Street went dark. There would be no more services, no more sermons, no more songs, no more prayers. There would only be tears.

The City of Los Angeles took advantage of the problems at Azusa Street and condemned the building as a fire hazard. Jennie's group tore the historic building down. According to Stanley Frodsham, the building was offered to the Assemblies of God. The world's largest Pentecostal denomination rejected the offer because they were not interested in "relics."[959] The Apostolic Faith Gospel Mission was razed in 1931. Frank Bartleman visited the demolition site and took the numbers "312" that had marked the building and placed them on the wall of his Los Angeles home.[960]

While the legal battle had continued, Griffith hired Thomas De Coe to make physical improvements to the building. After the building was removed, he sued Jennie's group for his loss of time and materials. A municipal judge ordered the property sold, and De Coe, the only bidder, purchased the property for less than $2,000. Jennie appealed the ruling in superior court.[961] Municipal Judge Crawford also ordered the mission to pay $200 to Henry Douglas for the work he had done on the property and for chauffeuring Griffith around Los Angeles.[962]

Finally, in mid-June of 1932, Superior Judge Leon R. Yankwich ruled in favor of Mrs. Seymour, and she was able to retain ownership of the property. Yankwich saw Griffith for the fraud he was and decreed the current trustees were the legal heirs. The trial lasted over a week, but the case dragged on for a year and a half. Lewis K. Beeks, an aspiring young Black attorney, was lauded for his work on the settlement.[963]

The legal battle took a heavy financial toll on the church. Late in 1930, the corporation had borrowed $2,000 from Mrs. Seymour, who took a six-year mortgage on the property. Long-time supporter Richard Asbery signed the mortgage as church trustee. Florence M. Ludden was the mission's secretary.[964]

Mrs. Seymour continued meetings with the faithful in her home on Bonnie Brae. The movement that began as a cottage meeting on Bonnie Brae had come full circle and returned to the street where it had begun twenty-five years earlier.

Jennie remained as pastor of the small group until June of 1933.[965] Her dear friend and colleague Ruth Asbery died on March 14, 1934. The *Eagle* reported "Mother Asbery" was "well known and loved by all who knew her." She was also remembered as "one of a group to send for the Rev. Seymore [sic} from Texas."[966]

Facing difficult financial times, Jennie sold the mortgage on the Azusa Street property to a Los Angeles bank and mortgaged her home. Because she could not make the payments or pay past-due taxes, the bank foreclosed on the property on January 13, 1936.[967]

Jennie became ill and was admitted to Rancho Los Amigos County Hospital on February 3, 1936.[968] Realizing her weakening physical condition, on June 12, Mrs. Seymour gave her brother Henry R. Moore power of attorney to conduct her business.[969] The next day, long-time trustee and friend Richard Asbery passed from this life to his eternal reward.[970]

Just over two weeks later, on July 2, 1936, at 11:15 a.m., Jennie Evans Moore Seymour's tired, sick earthy house perished. She joined her faithful husband and her Lord Jesus Christ in heaven.[971] She was only sixty-two years of age. Jennie was buried in the same grave as William, where both await the glorious day when their souls and bodies will be united, changed in the twinkling of an eye.

Three hundred years ago, Isaac Watts wrote the hymn "Am I a Soldier of the Cross." Two centuries later, William B. Blake added a familiar refrain:

And when the battle's over

We shall wear a crown!

Yes, we shall wear a crown!

Yes, we shall wear a crown!

And when the battle's over

We shall wear a crown

In the new Jerusalem

Wear a crown (wear a crown)

Wear a crown (wear a crown)

Wear a bright and shining crown;

And when the battle's over

We shall wear a crown

In the new Jerusalem.

Life was a real battle for William and Jennie. Their reward in heaven is real too. Enjoy your "bright and shiny crown," faithful pilgrims.

After lengthy legal wrangling, the title to the property was cleared in May of 1938. The bank received the mission property on June 10. The property of 312 Azusa Street, now in the possession of Security First National Bank, was turned into a parking lot.[972]

The services at 312 Azusa Street had long since ended. The pastors were gone, promoted to their heavenly home. The building was gone, and now the property was gone too—but "old Azusa" was not forgotten. It never will be. The stories of what happened in a dilapidated building on an unpaved street in Los Angeles will be told as long as new generations of Spirit empowered believers have the breath to retell them.

24

THE LEGACY: THE FIRE
THAT STILL BURNS

Ninety years is a long time. It has been that long since the last service was held in the Apostolic Faith Mission on 312 Azusa Street. The revival itself ended more than a hundred years ago. Yet the memory of what happened at "old Azusa" is still very much alive. Just the mention of the words "Azusa Street" warms the hearts of millions of Pentecostals and Charismatics around the world. There is no doubt that more people know about the revival today than in 1906 when it was going full strength.

Over the past twelve decades there have been numerous attempts to recreate the amazing Azusa Street Revival. Bishop A. C. Driscoll and Elder H. S. Covington attempted to revive the mission, announcing the "reopening of Azusa Apostolic Faith Mission now located at 9411 Parmelee Avenue." A brochure carried testimonies from Azusa Street and pictures of the mission and Seymour. Driscoll even proclaimed himself as the successor to Seymour. Their efforts, however well intentioned, were largely unsuccessful.[973] Through the years, others have started "Azusa Street Missions" to try to capitalize on the fame and perhaps the flame of the revival.[974]

Multiple celebrations have been held to commemorate the Azusa Street Revival. Jennie Seymour tried to keep the anniversary observances going after the death of her husband.[975] Others tried when she was gone.

April 9 through 26, 1936, a thirtieth anniversary event was held at the Saints Home Church and Angelus Temple. Emma Cotton was "manager" for the event. Osterberg, Bartleman, and a number of the other Azusa faithful joined Aimee Semple McPherson and more than twenty other pastors in sponsoring the event. Guests were invited to come praying "that the Lord will send a mighty revival." A memorial service was held for "all the saints that have gone to be with the Lord these 30 years."[976]

Meetings with lesser impact were held in 1937 and 1938. Again, is it reasonable to believe they were held each year.[977] Elder Henry and Mrs. Henry (Emma) Cotton also held a 39th anniversary meeting in 1945 at Azusa Pentecostal Tabernacle, a church they pastored at 1001 East 27th Street in Los Angeles.[978]

A much larger and more spectacular event was scheduled for the golden anniversary of the revival. Angelus Temple was once again the site for this meeting, and it brought together some of the world's leading Pentecostals and surviving Azusa Street participants. Oral Roberts, William Branham, Jack Coe, David Nunn, Gordon Lindsey, and many others hosted services attended by thousands.[979]

In 1975, the students of Howard University chose the name "William Seymour Pentecostal Fellowship" to identify an ecumenical Pentecostal campus ministry. This was probably the first organization to honor the leader.[980]

Due primarily to the vision of one man, Art Glass, the Richard and Ruth Asbery house has become something of a Pentecostal shrine. Today the house belongs to the Church of God in Christ and has been fully restored to its original condition. The piano that Jennie Seymour played on April 6, 1906, is still in the house. Los Angeles renumbered the street, and now the house is at 216 North Bonnie Brae. Pilgrims can make arrangements to visit the revered site. Plans are to build a museum next door to the historic home.[981]

The Assemblies of God dedicated the first permanent home for their denominational seminary in Springfield, Missouri, in 1998. To honor the Azusa Street leader, the chapel was named the William J. Seymour Chapel. A stained-glass window depicting Seymour and the fire that fell at Azusa Street adorns the facility. A memorial plaque reads:

> William J. Seymour, pastor of the Azusa Street Mission, played a formative role in the worldwide expansion of the Pentecostal movement. The ministry of the son of former slaves was marked by sound judgment, spiritual balance, personal integrity, and faithfulness. He encouraged every member of his congregation to minister, to testify, and to share the gospel whenever God led them, regardless of race, class, gender, or age.
>
> He demonstrated the value of racial unity and cultural harmony, exhorting his congregation to seek God about all things, to exhibit the fruit of the Spirit even as they exercised the Spirit's gifts, and to measure all doctrine and experience by the word of God. He remains an eloquent model for Pentecostal ministry.

Today, the property formerly identified as 312 Azusa is part of the district of Los Angeles known as "Little Tokyo." In February of 1998, a Walk of Remembrance led by Azusa scholar Cecil M. Robeck ended with a rally at the site. Those gathered committed themselves to erecting a memorial wall and historical marker to commemorate W. J. Seymour and the Azusa Street Revival.[982]

On February 13, 1999, a memorial plaque was placed at the site. The ceremony was attended by participants from several ethnic groups and Christian denominations. Fred and Wilma Berry led worship, Cecil M. Robeck presented the history of the mission, and a number of local pastors greeted the assembly before a ribbon was cut and the marker unveiled.[983] Visitors can find the marker in Nagouchi Plaza, the entrance to the Japanese American Cultural and Community Center.

In 1999, *Christian History* magazine marked the end of the twentieth century by recognizing who they believed to be the "Ten Most Influential Christians of the Twentieth Century." Mother Teresa, Billy Graham, Martin Luther King Jr., and a couple of popes made the list. So did William

J. Seymour. Pentecostal historian Vinson Synan wrote, "By the year 2000, the spiritual heirs of Seymour, the Pentecostals, and Charismatics, numbered over 500 million adherents, making it the second largest family of Christians in the world."[984]

Members of the Religion Newswriters Association placed the Azusa Street Revival as the fourth most important religious event of the century.[985] They ranked it with the Holocaust, the invention of the printing press, the pilgrims settling at Plymouth Rock, and the Protestant Reformation as one of the top ten religious events of the millennium.[986]

In their millennium edition, *Life* listed the Pentecostal movement among the one hundred most important events of the past one thousand years, both religious and secular.[987]

Robert E. Fisher, a grandson of Elmer Fischer, planned the greatest commemoration ever for the centennial. Fischer was able to unite the many streams of the movement for a week of services in Los Angeles. Sadly, Fischer died before he could see his dream completed, but William M. (Billy) Wilson stepped into the leadership position and finished the task. Several large venues were used to accommodate the crowds until Saturday, when everyone joined together for a powerful rally featuring the world's greatest speakers and worship leaders. It is estimated that sixty thousand participants gathered from more than one hundred nations. Wilson said, "We see the Centennial as a homecoming for the movement a wonderful memory of what God did 100 years ago."[988] This author was honored to host an afternoon session on the history of the revival.

Azusa Street in Los Angeles no longer exists as a street; now it is "a service alley." Trucks for delivering goods and removing garbage access the lane where people once stood on the dirt street to try to gain entrance into the building.[989] The city, cognizant of the historical significance, kept the "Azusa Street" sign and a small historical marker on a post at the entrance. Many have had dreams of a more appropriate memorial for the spiritual landmark. Hopefully it will come soon.

Rev. Otis Clark passed on May 21, 2012.[990] He may have been the last living person who worshipped in the Azusa Mission. But the revival did not die with Otis Clark. It didn't die when William or Jennie Seymour went to heaven. It didn't die when the old building was razed.

The fire kindled on Azusa Street still burns in the hearts of millions. Time has not put out the flame. Neither did division, opposition, and persecution. Some estimate that 26 percent of the world's Christians are Pentecostal or Charismatic.

To some, it would appear that the Azusa fires were slowly extinguished by time, trials, and troubles. This, however, could only be the view of the nearsighted or narrow-minded. The Holy Ghost fires ignited at Azusa have not gone out; the breath of God merely blew them to other locations, both near and far. Today, the Spirit of Azusa continues to blaze all over the world. Like a prairie fire swept by a West Texas sirocco, the winds of God will continue to spread the flaming inferno of Pentecostal fire until Jesus returns to welcome all His children home.

Just saying these two simple words, "Azusa Street," leaves a sweet taste on the lips of thousands of believers. Almost everyone who hears the story of the revival wants to hear it again. Most want God to do it again.

I have told this story to believers all around the world. Thousands have identified with Seymour in his trials and triumphs. I love to remind audiences that if God can use one man, He can use any man. If God can move in one place, He can move in any place. If God can do anything once, He can do it again. Even so, grant it, Lord.

Often, I will teach for a time and then open the floor for questions about the revival. It is almost as predictable as "Old Faithful" that someone will ask me when the revival ended.

My answer: "It didn't. The Azusa Street Revival still lives in my heart."

I pray that it lives in yours.

ABOUT THE AUTHOR

D r. Larry Martin has given more than fifty years to gospel ministry, serving almost twenty-five years pastoring churches in Oklahoma, Texas, Florida, and Tennessee. While still in his teens, Martin launched his ministry career as a traveling evangelist. He returned to evangelism in 1997 and has continued in that work for most of the last twenty-five years through his ministry, River of Revival Ministries.

Dr. Martin has traveled in more than seventy countries, teaching in Bible schools, preaching in churches, and leading mass evangelism crusades where as many as 40,000 have professed Christ in one event. From 2001–2004, Martin served Brownsville Revival School of Ministry in Pensacola, Florida, as academic dean. He taught a number of courses in the college and was a regular speaker at the Brownsville Assembly of God Church. Prior to moving to Florida, he served as president of Messenger College in Joplin, Missouri.

Considered by many to be an authority on the origins of the Pentecostal movement and especially the revival at Azusa Street, Martin is the editor of the twelve-volume Complete Azusa Street Library and the author of *The Life and Ministry of William J. Seymour* in that series. He is also the author of *In the Beginning, We've Come This Far by Faith*, and *Kansas City, Here We Come*, histories of early Pentecostals and the Pentecostal Church of God; and *The Topeka Outpouring of 1901*. Among his other books are

For Sale: The Soul of a Nation; Have We Lost Our Mind? (an in-your-face call to Christian commitment); *The Good, The Bad, The Ugly and the Hilarious*, featuring stories from his ministry experiences; and *The Believer, The Bible and the Bottle*, a common-sense look at alcohol consumption and Christians. In 2022, Whitaker House published *Charles Fox Parham: The Unlikely Father of Modern Pentecostalism*, Martin's biography of the founder of the Pentecostal movement. He has also edited and/or contributed to several other works. Additionally, as a freelance writer, Dr. Martin has authored more than a hundred articles that have appeared in *Charisma, Ministries Today*, and a number of other publications.

In 2013, Martin launched pentecostalgold.com, a free online audio archive committed to preserving classic Pentecostal preaching. He has added more than four thousand sermons to the site which features many of the world's greatest preachers.

Dr. Martin is a graduate of several institutes of higher education and holds a doctorate in ministry from Austin Presbyterian Theological Seminary in Austin, Texas. He and Lynda Morehead Goetz were married on July 3, 2016, both having lost their spouses in 2014. Larry has two children, Matthew Martin, and Summer Jo Wiedenhoff (Quenten); Lynda also has two children, Lindsey Sandy (Justin), and Ryan Goetz (Rachel). The couple has four wonderful grandchildren, Matthew Martin Jr., Cash Wiedenhoff, Isaac, Anna, and Louisa Goetz.

ENDNOTES

1. Jessie Kratz, "The National Archives' Larger-Than-Life Statues," May 22, 2018, National Archives Pieces of History, prologue.blogs.archives.gov/2018/05/22/.

2. Larry Martin, *Charles Fox Parham: The Unlikely Father of Modern Pentecostalism* (New Kensington, PA: Whitaker House, 2022), 31. This author's biography of Parham is the most comprehensive work ever released on Parham.

3. Charles F. Parham, "The Personal Testimony of Chas. F. Parham, Editor to Divine Healing," *The Apostolic Faith* (hereafter *The Apostolic Faith* published by Parham will be cited *TAFP*), December 1926, 15, originalapostolicfaith.org; Charles W. Shumway, "A Critical Study of 'The Gift of Tongues'" (A. B. Thesis, University of Southern California, 1914), 164; Charles Parham, "My Testimony," *TAFP*, March 30, 1899, 6, Kansas Historical Society (hereafter cited as KHS).

4. Sarah E. Parham, *The Life of Charles F. Parham: Founder of the Apostolic Faith Movement* (Birmingham, AL: Commercial Printing Company, 1930), 66.

5. Charles F. Parham, *Kol Kare Bomidbar: A Voice Crying in the Wilderness*, 3rd ed. (Baxter Springs, KS: Apostolic Faith, n.d.), 18.

6. Transcripts, Southwestern College. Parham only took pre-college courses in the academy.

7. C. Parham, *Kol Kare Bomidbar*, 16.

8. C. Parham, *Kol Kare Bomidbar*, 16–17; C. Parham, "The Personal Testimony of Chas. F. Parham."

9. Martin, *Charles Fox Parham*, 39.

10. "Kansas Methodists," *Leroy (Kansas) Reporter*, March 23, 1894, 4, newspapers.com; Martin, *Charles Fox Parham*, 40–41.

11. S. Parham, *Life of Charles F. Parham*, 16–17.

12. Charles F. Parham, "Healing," in *Selected Sermons by the Late Charles F. Parham and Sarah E. Parham*, comp. Robert Parham (Baxter Springs, KS: Apostolic Faith, 1941), 25; C. Parham, *Kol Kare Bomidbar*, 40–41, *TAFP*, September 13, 1899, Kansas Historical Society.

13. Martin, *Charles Fox Parham*, 44–46.

14. Martin, *Charles Fox Parham*, 46–48.

15. "He Got Money," *Topeka State Journal* (hereafter cited as *TSJ*), October 20, 1900, 14, newspapers.com; S. Parham, *Life of Charles F. Parham*, 48.

16. Martin, *Charles Fox Parham*, 132, 154

17. "Stone Mansion Leased," *TSJ*, September 27, 1900, 8; "Parham Leaves," *TSJ*, January 21, 1901, 7, newspapers.com; S. Parham, *Life of Charles F. Parham*, 48.

18. Martin, *Charles Fox Parham*, 52–58.

19. Charles F. Parham and Sarah E. Parham, *Selected Sermons of the Late Charles F. Parham and Sarah E. Parham* (Baxter Springs: Apostolic Faith Bible College, n.d.), 75.

20. There are conflicting stories about exactly how and when Agnes Ozman received the Holy Ghost Baptism. These are beyond the scope of this article. For the accounts of the eyewitnesses to the incident, including Ozman, see Larry Martin, ed., *The Topeka Outpouring of 1901* (Joplin, MO: Christian Life Books, 1997).

21. Martin, *Charles Fox Parham*, 57–60.

22. These experiences are well documented. For examples see Carl Brumback, *What Meaneth This? A Pentecostal Answer to A Pentecostal Question* (Springfield, MO: Gospel Publishing, 1947) and Eddie L. Hyatt, *2000 Years of Charismatic Christianity: A 21st Century Look at Church History from a Pentecostal/Charismatic Perspective* (Lake Mary, FL: Charisma House, 2015).

23. Cecil M. Robeck, Jr., *The Azusa Street Mission and Revival: The Birth of the Global Pentecostal Movement* (Nashville: Thomas Nelson, 2006), 240. To say the movement was born at Azusa Street simply because it grew from there into a global movement is ignoring the fact that Parham founded the movement and Seymour actually called him his "father." One could as easily argue that Ray Kroc, who turned McDonald's into a global fast-food enterprise, was the "father" of the hamburger chain. In fact, he bought the franchise from the actual founders, Richard and Maurice McDonald.

24. Department of Commerce and Labor Bureau of the Census: E. Dana Durand, Director: *Special Reports Religious Bodies: 1906: Part 2: Separate Denominations: History Description and Statistics* (Washington, D.C.: Government Printing Office, 1910), 279, babel.hathitrust.org.

25. Martin, *Charles Fox Parham*, 63–68.

26. S. Parham, *Life of Charles F. Parham*, 99–103.

27. Martin, *Charles Fox Parham*, 71–73; Vinson Synan, *The Holiness-Pentecostal Movement in the United States* (Grand Rapids, MI: Eerdmans Publishing, 1971), 103.

28. Quoted in John W.V. Smith, *Heralds of a Brighter Day: Biographical Sketches of Early Leaders in the Church of God Reformation Movement* (Anderson, IN: Gospel Trumpet Company, 1955), 11.

29. William Joseph Seymour, Standard Certificate of Death: California State Board of Health, October 2, 1922.

30. The author has visited Centerville and St. Mary Parish on many occasions. Louisiana is divided into parishes, not counties.

31. "The Attakapas Country," *The (New Orleans) Morning Star and Catholic Messenger* (hereafter cited as *MSCM*), April 13, 1873, 7, chroniclingamerica.loc.gov.

32. Peter S. Feibleman, *The Bayous* (New York: Time-Life Books, 1973), 30, 56.

33. Samuel H. Lockett, *Louisiana As It Is: A Geographical and Topographical Description of the State* (Baton Rouge: Louisiana State University Press, 1969), 23, 101.

34. "Notes on the Teche Country," *MSCM*, May 21, 1876, 1, chroniclingamerica. loc.gov.

35. "The Free Labor Bluster," *The (Franklin, LA) Planter's Banner* (hereafter cited as *TPB*), January 11, 1849, 2, Franklin Public Library, Franklin, Louisiana.

36. United States Census, St. Mary Parish, Louisiana, 1860.

37. "Import ant Public Sale, *TPB*, January 8, 1853, 3, Franklin Public Library, Franklin, Louisiana.

38. Miscellaneous newspaper articles and advertisements from the 1853 editions of *TPB*.

39. These two paragraphs provide just one of many examples of Craig Borlace copying almost word for word from *The Life of William Seymour*. Borlace says, "The law allowed a barbaric regime that allowed a black person to be killed if that person hit a white person hard enough to bruise the skin. Permission to fire upon a fleeing slave was granted if the slave did not stop when ordered. The Louisiana Supreme Court suggested aiming to avoid inflicting a fatal wound, but if the slave died no charges were made." There is no citation crediting this author's work. This kind of "borrowing" was done again and again in Borlace's book. Page 17, footnotes 17 and 18 of Borlace's book is an example of how Borlace copied from *The Life of William J. Seymour* and then used a citation to the original source without citing *Seymour*. See Craig Borlace, *William Seymour: A Biography* (Lake Mary, FL: Charisma House, 2006), 14.

40. "The honorable Isaac Morse...," *TPB*, May 16, 1850, 2, chroniclingamerica.loc. gov.

41. Bernard Brossard, *A History of St. Mary Parish* (n.p., 1977), 20.

42. Kenneth M. Stampp, *The Peculiar Institution: Slavery in the Ante-Bellum South* (New York: Vantage, 1956), 30, 32, 62, 210, 211, 213, 214, 232, 233, 252.

43. John A. Garraty, *The American Nation: A History of the United States Since 1865*, fifth ed. (New York: Harper and Row, 1983), 408.

44. "Sugar Crop of the State," *Semi-weekly Louisianan*, 20 July 1871, 4, chroniclingamerica.loc.gov. A hogshead was 63 gallons.

45. "About 700...," *(Bellevue, LA) Bossier Banner*, 12 March 1870, 1, chroniclingamerica.loc.gov.

46. "A Correspondent...," *The Donaldsonville (LA) Chief*, 26 May 1877, 2, chroniclingamerica.loc.gov.

47. Michelle Leach, "Salaries in the 1880s," careertrend.com.

48. "Among those...," *St. Landry Democrat*, 7 August 1880, 1, chroniclingamerica. loc.gov; "Canada Labor for Louisiana," *Bossier Banner-Progress*, 26 November 1879, 2; "The Polish Immigrants Disposed of," *The New Orleans Times Picayune* (hereafter cited as *NOPT*), 4 May 1878, 2, newspapers.com.

49. Harry J. Carman, Harold C. Syrett and Bernard W. Wishy, *A History of the American People, Volume 2: since 1865*, third ed. (New York: Alfred A. Knopf, 1967), 19.

50. Joe Gray Taylor, *Louisiana Reconstructed: 1863–1877* (Baton Rouge: Louisiana State University Press, 1974), 366, 367.

51. Edwin Adams Davis, *Louisiana: The Pelican State* (Baton Rouge: Louisiana State University Press, 1975), 242.

52. Carman, et.al., *A History of the American People, Volume 2: since 1865*, 14.

53. Harry J. Carman, Harold C. Syrett, and Bernard W. Wishy, *A History of the American People, Volume 1: to 1877*, second ed. (New York: Alfred A. Knopf, 1960), 724.

54. Rebecca Brooks Gruver, *An American History, Volume 1: to 1877*, third ed. (Reading, MA: Addison-Wesley Publishing Co., 1981), 416.

55. Taylor, *Louisiana Reconstructed*, 368.

56. T. Harry Williams, Richard N. Current, and Fred Freidel, *A History of the United States: to 1877*, second ed., revised (New York: Alfred A. Knopf, 1967), 701.

57. Willie Malvin Caskey, *Secession and Restoration of Louisiana* (Baton Rouge: Louisiana State University Press, 1938), 189, 190

58. "The Black Code of St. Landry's Parish, 1865," usu.instructure.com.

59. Civil Rights Act of 1866, "An Act to protect all Persons in the United States in their Civil Rights, and furnish the Means of their Vindication," constitutioncenter. org.

60. Peyton McCrary, *Abraham Lincoln and Reconstruction* (Princeton: Princeton University Press, 1978), 199.

61. Joseph G. Dawson III, *Army Generals and Reconstruction: Louisiana, 1862–1877* (Baton Rouge: Louisiana State University Press, 1982).

62. "Louisiana's Constitutions: 1868," https://lasc.libguides.com.

63. "Platform of the Democratic Party of Louisiana in 1874," hnoc.org.

64. "Excerpts from Governor William Pitt Kellogg's 'Address to the People of Louisiana' on May 10, 1873," 42, hnoc.org.

65. "St. Mary," *The Weekly Louisianan* (hereafter cited as *TWL*), February 19, 1881, 1, chroniclingamerica.loc.gov.

66. "Poll Tax," *TWL*, February 19, 1881, 2, chroniclingamerica.loc.gov.

67. Pattersonville was incorporated as Patterson, Louisiana. It is about 10 miles southwest of Centerville.

68. "St. Mary," 1.

69. Leon Freidman, ed., *Southern Justice* (Cleveland, OH: World Publishing Co., 1965), 62.

70. Nicholas Gilmore, "The White League's Violent Insurrection in Louisiana Was Almost a Success," saturdayeveningpost.com.

71. Taylor, *Louisiana Reconstructed*, 162; Matthew Christensen, "The 1868 St. Landry Massacre: Reconstruction's Deadliest Episode of Violence," https://dc.uwm.edu/cgi/viewcontent.cgi?referer=&httpsredir=1&article=1193&context=etd.

72. "White League Literature," *New Orleans Republican* (hereafter cited as *NOR*), August 13, 1874, 1, chroniclingamerica.loc.gov.

73. Collin E. Delatte, "The St. Landry Riot: A Forgotten Incident of Reconstruction Violence," *Louisiana History*, Winter 1976, 45; Frank J. Wetta, "'Bulldozing the Scalawags': Some Examples of the Persecution of Southern White Republicans In Louisiana During Reconstruction," *Louisiana History*, Winter 1980, 49.

74. "The Freedmen of Louisiana: Final Report of the Bureau of Free Labor, Department of the Gulf, to Major General E. R. S. Canby, Commanding by Thomas W. Conway, General Superintendent of Freedmen; New Orleans Times Book and Job Office, 1865," loc.gov.

75. Taylor, *Louisiana Reconstructed*, 98.

76. "Disturbance in Franklin," *PB*, December 28, 1867, 2.

77. Taylor, *Louisiana Reconstructed*, 281.

78. Gruve, *An American History*, 423.

79. "The Louisiana Murders," *Harper's Weekly*, May 10, 1873, 396.

80. John A. Garraty, *The American Nation to 1877: A History of the United States* (New York: Harper and Row, 1963), 447.

81. "General Race News," *Indianapolis Recorder* (hereafter cited as *IIR*), August 5, 1899, 2, newspapers.library.in.gov.

82. "On the eve…," *IIR*, December 9, 1899, 2, newspapers.library.in.gov.

83. "The Lynching Evil," *IIR*, April 1, 1899, 2, newspapers.library.in.gov.

84. "Georgia Horror," *Chattanooga Daily Times*, April 26, 1899, 5, newspapers.com; "The Georgia Outrage," *IIR*, April 29, 1899, 2, newspapers.library.in.gov.

85. "Some Facts," *IIR*, June 10, 1899, 2–3, newspapers.library.in.gov.

86. United States Census, St. Mary Parish, Louisiana, 1870, 1880, 1900; Baptismal Record, William Simon, Church of the Assumption, Franklin, LA, September 4, 1870. In the 1870 census and on most family baptismal records, the family's last name is listed as "Simon." In south Louisiana, where French was often spoken in the 1870s (the Franklin newspaper was printed bilingually), the pronunciation would have been "See-mone." When the family name was permanently changed to Seymour is not known. Morris Bowens, a family friend, testified "that Simon Simon and Simon Seymour are the one and same person, said Seymour being often called and named indifferently Simon Simon and Simon Seymour." See Morris Bowens, General Affidavit, May 21, 1897, Simon Seymour Pension File (hereafter cited as SSPF), National Archives and Records Administration (hereafter cited as NARA). Jefferson Ellis also swore that "Simon Semon and Simon Seymour are one and the same person." See Jefferson Ellis, General Affadivit, SSPF, NARA. In 1870 Phillis is listed as Felicieta; in 1880 Phillis; and in 1900, Filiss. On the family baptismal records, her name is Felicie, Felicite, Felicity, and Felicien. Her last name is spelled Salassas, Celabas, and Salabas. It is likely that Simon, who could read but not write, and Phillis, who could neither read nor write, could not spell their own names, creating much of the confusion. It is also possible that they changed their surname, which was not an uncommon practice among former slaves. See "Surnames for African Americans—Former Slaves," familytree.com.

The multiple renderings of the Seymour name were discovered quite accidentally by this author. I was searching for the Seymours' marriage license at the courthouse in St. Mary Parish. I searched the list of applications and there was no Simon Seymour. I would have given up, but someone suggested I search the bride book. I was unaware there were separate lists for the bride and groom. Looking in the bride book, I found that Phillis had married Simon Simon. The change in spelling opened a whole new area of research that led to the discovery of the family's baptismal certificates, military records, etc.

87. In his biography, Rufus Sanders completely misidentifies the Seymour family. Sanders erroneously claims that Simon Seymour was a judge in Iberia Parish who was murdered by white men. He has the wrong person in the wrong place at the wrong time. Sanders creates a false narrative around his statement "American racism disallowed the honor of the 'Father' of the Pentecostal movement to be bestowed on William J. Seymour." The multiple inaccuracies in Sanders's book lend no credence to his attempt to frame the entire biography in racial overtones. See Rufus G. W. Sanders, *William Joseph Seymour: Black Father of the 20th Century Pentecostal/Charismatic Movement* (Sandusky, OH: Alexandria Publications, 2001).

88. United States Census, St. Mary Parish, Louisiana, 1870, 1880. Various places are given for Simon's birthplace, including Kentucky and New Iberia. This author has chosen St. Mary Parish because it is the place given by Simon when he enlisted in the military and where Phillis said he told her he was born. See Simon Seymour, Compiled Military Service Record, NARA; Phillis Seymour to George S. King, February 8, 1896, SSPF, NARA.

89. Not many dates for Simon's birth are the same. He may have been separated from his parents and would not have known when he was born. He said he was twenty-one when he joined the army in 1863. This would make his time of birth late in 1841 or in the first nine months of 1842. See Simon Seymour, Compiled. The 1870 and 1880 censuses would place his birth in 1837 or 1841, respectively. He was examined by a surgeon in July 1891, and the report says he was fifty-five, placing his birth in 1836. See Surgeon's Certificate, SSPF, NARA. On another form, not dated, but probably 1891, he lists his age as fifty. See Declaration for Invalid Pension, SSPF, NARA. This would confirm the years 1841 or 1842 for at least two times when he gave his own age.

90. Phillis refers to "the lady that owned him." This could be a reference to the wife of a slave master, or his owner could have been a woman. See Seymour to King. The author contacted several university professors who are experts in slavery, and all said it could be either. Some women received slaves as an inheritance from their husband or another family member. Calvin Schermerhorn to Larry Martin, email, September 12, 2023; Edward E. Baptist to Larry Martin, email, September 11, 2023; Joe Lockard to Larry Martin, email, September 11, 2023.

91. "Robert Wickliffe vs Walter Brashear," *TBP*, April 5, 1849, 3, chroniclingamerica.loc.gov; "Marshall Sale," *TBP*, January 3, 1850, 3, chroniclingamerica.loc.gov. With the difficulty ascertaining Simon's age, this child slave may have been he.

92. Simon Seymour, Compiled. On another occasion, Seymour's complexion is listed as "light." See Declaration for Pension, SSPF, NARA.

93. For a full account, see James G Hollandsworth Jr., *The Louisiana Native Guards: The Black Military Experience During the Civil War* (Baton Rouge: Louisiana State University Press, 1995).

94. Hollandsworth Jr., *Louisiana Native Guards*, 29.

95. Budge Weidman, "Preserving the Legacy of the United States Colored Troops," *Prologue: Quarterly of the National Archives and Records Administration* (Summer 1997), 91.

96. Rossiter Johnson, *Campfires and Battlefields: A Pictorial Narrative of the Civil War* (New York: Gallant Books, Inc., 1960), 237.

97. Hollandsworth Jr., *Louisiana Native Guards*, 18.

98. Simon Seymour, Compiled; 82nd Regiment Infantry, https://www.nps.gov/civilwar/index.htm; Record and Pension Office, War Department, SSPF, NARA.

99. Surgeon's Certificate; Record and Pension.

100. Seymour, Compiled; 93rd Regiment Infantry, https://www.nps.gov/civilwar/index.htm.

101. Jefferson Ellis, General Affidavit, SSPF, NARA.

102. Seymour to King.

103. Seymour to King; United States Census, St. Mary Parish, Louisiana, 1870, 1880, 1900; Bowens, Affidavit; Phillis Seymour, Standard Certificate of Death, February 3, 1940; Declaration for Pension.

104. United States Census, St. Mary Parish, Louisiana, 1870. The last name is spelled differently in various sources. In the Seymour family Bible owned by the author, the name is spelled "Salabar"; for the sake of consistency, that spelling is used throughout this book.

105. United States Census, St. Mary Parish, Louisiana, 1860.

106. Seymour to King.

107. United States Census, St. Mary Parish, Louisiana, 1870. In 1870 Michael was sixty-two years of age; Lucy, forty-eight; Polly, twenty; Antirnette, eighteen; Adaline, seventeen; Michael, fifteen. All the family ages would fit within the ages of slaves owned by Carlin in 1860.

108. Harriet Bedford, General Affidavit, September 11, 1893, SSPF, NARA.

109. Phillis Seymour, General Affidavit, February 23, 1895, SSPF, NARA.

110. Bond Certificate, St. Mary Parish, Marriage License Book 1867, 504.

111. Ann C. Loveland, "The 'Southern Work' of the Rev. Joseph C. Hartzell, Pastor of Ames Church in New Orleans, 1870–1873," *Louisiana History* (Fall 1975), 401.

112. Marriage License, Simon and Sellaba, St. Mary Parish, Marriage License Book 1867, 586; recorded in St. Mary Parish, Marriage Record Book 1863–1879, 76.

113. "Disturbance in Franklin," *TPB*, December 28, 1867, 2.

114. Marriage License, Simon and Sellaba.

115. Bowens, Affidavit.

116. Marriage License, Salabar and Sweet, St. Mary Parish, Book 1863–1879, 142. It is also possible that Lucy was a second wife and not Phillis's mother. On this occasion, Simon is listed as "Seymour" and Michael is "Salabar." On the same day, Jane Salabar, perhaps another sibling of Phillis, was married to Nat Porter. See Marriage License, Porter and Salabar, St. Mary Parish, Book 1863–1879, 142.

117. Baptismal Record, William Simon.

118. United States Census, St. Mary Parish, Louisiana, 1880; Simon Seymour, Compiled. On most records, Seymour only made "his mark." See his signature on Simon Seymour, General Affidavit, April 23, 1891, SSPF, NARA.

119. Simon Seymour, General Affidavit, April 23, 1891, SSPF, NARA. On most records, Seymour only made "his mark."

120. United States Census, St. Mary Parish, Louisiana, 1880; 1870; 1900; Baptismal Record, William Simon; Baptismal Record, Simon Simon, Church of the Assumption, Franklin, LA, September 8, 1872; and Baptismal Record, John Emmuas Simon, Church of the Assumption, Franklin, LA, June 7, 1874; Baptismal Record, Julia Simon Seymour, July 31, 1880, SSPF, NARA; Baptismal Record, Jacob Simon Seymour, Church of the Assumption, Franklin, LA, August 19, 1893; Baptismal Record, Isaac Seymour Simon, Church of the Assumption, Franklin, LA, August 19, 1893; Phillis Seymour, Affidavit, February 23, 1895; Declaration for Widow's Pension, SSPF, NARA; Interview, Lucille Seymour, August 14, 1999. Lucille is the widow of Van Seymour, son of Jacob, William's brother. Van spent time in California with "Uncle William and Aunt Jenny." See also St. Mary Parish, Louisiana, Book "3H" of Conveyances, 93, October 24, 1912.

121. United States Census, St. Mary Parish, Louisiana, 1880; 1870; Baptismal Record, John Emmuas Simon, Church of the Assumption, Franklin, LA, June 7, 1874; Phillis Seymour, Affidavit, February 23, 1895.

122. United States Census, St. Mary Parish, Louisiana, 1900. The date given on the census, October 1885, is obviously wrong, being too close to the known birth of Jacob. It seems this child could be Julia, since no other child is mentioned in any of the pension requests, and this census can be confirmed to be flawed in many ways.

123. "L. S. Clarke," *NOR*, February 6, 1875, 1; "Quarantine Proclamation," *The Meridional* (Abbeville, LA), September 28, 1878, 2; "Murder Will Out," *NOR*, October 16, 1870, 4, chroniclingamerica.loc.gov.

124. "Storm Effects," *NOPT*, September 4, 1879, 2, newspapers.com.

125. "St Mary," 1.

126. Shumway, "A Critical History of Glossolalia," 115.

127. Douglas J. Nelson, "For Such a Time as This: The Story of Bishop William J. Seymour and the Azusa Street Revival: A Search for Pentecostal/Charismatic Roots" (Ph. D. dissertation, University of Birmingham, England, 1981), 158. Douglas says the story came from an interview with Sadie Janbar, who attended the mission. Nelson conducted many interviews with eyewitnesses, none of which was available to this author.

128. St. Mary Parish, Louisiana, Book "V" of Conveyances, 581, February 14, 1884.

129. Joanna Jenkins, General Affidavit, June 14, 1893, SSPF, NARA.

130. Invalid Pension, SSPF, NARA.

131. Surgeon's Certificate, SSPF, NARA.

132. Valsin Hernandez, General Affidavit, June 14, 1893, SSPF, NARA. Hernandez's denominational affiliation is not known. In the censuses he is listed as a farmer, and this author has not yet found any reference to him as a pastor. Since Simon was buried in a Baptist cemetery and Hernandez officiated, it is reasonable to assume he was Baptist.

133. Jenkins, Affidavit.

134. Hernandez, Affidavit.

135. Invalid Pension, SSPF, NARA.

136. These young men are not mentioned in any of the pension requests. Admittedly, the omission could have been intentional to enhance the prospects of qualifying.

137. Phillis Seymour, General Affidavit, February 10, 1896, SSPF, NARA.

138. Clark Wilkerson, General Affidavit, April 30, 1895, SSPF, NARA.

139. F. P. Perret, Abstractor of Titles, St. Mary Parish, Louisiana, February 11, 1896, SSPF, NARA.

140. Phillis Seymour, Affidavit, February 10, 1896.

141. St. Mary Parish, Louisiana, Book "DD" of Conveyances, 654, November 13, 1894. Phillis bought the property back for $30 in 1907. St. Mary Parish, Louisiana, Book "UU" of Conveyances, 296, June 25, 1907.

142. Widow's Pension, 577, 804, SSPF, NARA; Widow's Pension, 472, 276, SSPF, NARA. The pension was raised to $20 in 1916 and eventually raised to $40 before Phillis's death in 1940.

143. Phillis Seymour, Affidavit, February 10, 1896.

144. Vinson Synan, *The Holiness-Pentecostal Tradition: Charismatic Movements in the Twentieth Century* (Grand Rapids, MI: Wm. B. Eerdmans Publishing Co., 1971), 93. Although Seymour's affiliation with the Baptist has not been documented, it is asserted by Synan and in many biographies. Lucille Seymour said Phillis was a member of New Providence Baptist Church in Centerville when she died, but there are no records available from the church.

145. Most of the Seymour children were baptized at the Church of the Assumption in Franklin. See Baptismal Record, William Simon; Baptismal Record, Simon Simon; Baptismal Record; Jacob Simon; Baptismal Record, Isaac Seymour Simon; Baptismal Record, Julia Simon Seymour; and Baptismal Record, John Emmuas Simon.

146. Shumway, "A Critical Study of 'The Gift of Tongues,'" 173; Shumway, "A Critical History of Glossolalia," 115.

147. Lillian Brandt, "The Make-Up of Negro City Groups," *The Survey: The Negro in the Cities of the North* (New York: Charity Organization Society, 1905), 11, 16.

148. "Negroes Coming North," *IIR*, September 9, 1899, 1, newspapers.library.in.gov.

149. "The Exodus Spirit," *NOPT*, June 10, 1897, 2, newspapers.com.

150. Brandt, "The Make-Up of Negro City Groups," 16.

151. In the first edition of this book, the author was more definite about Seymour's travel, raising questions only in the footnotes. Robeck disagreed with the scheme I developed and suggested I should make it clearer that I am only presenting a theory. I agree. Perhaps Robeck has found proof of a different journey. I have not seen this proof and continue to offer my opinion, but only as one theory. See footnote 10 below. Cecil M. Robeck Jr. to Larry Martin, December 13, 2022.

152. It does seem likely that he is the man, since he appears and disappears in the city directories at the appropriate times. See footnotes 11 and 12.

153. Lori Erickson, *Mighty Mississippi: Traveler's Guide* (Aldsaybrook, CT: The Globe Pequot Press, 1995), 132, 133.

154. Nelson, "For Such a Time as This," 159.

155. Wayman Norbury, *Life on the River: A Pictorial History of the Mississippi, the Missouri, and the Western River System* (New York: Crown Publishers Inc., 1971), 232, 233.

156. *Polk City Directories* (hereafter cited as *PCD*), Memphis, TN, 1890, 649; *PCD*, Memphis, TN, 1891, 980; *PCD*, Memphis, TN, 1892, 883, 1192; *PCD*, Memphis, TN, 1893. It is important to note that William was a boarder and the other Seymours were listed as residents, eliminating the possibility that he was part of the immediate family. According to his death certificate, Henry was born in Tennessee and lived his life in Memphis. With forced family separations common during slavery, a relationship between William and Henry is still possible. See Henry Seymour, Pre-1902 Death Records, Memphis/Shelby Co. Archives, Memphis, Tennessee.

157. *PCD*, Memphis, TN, 1892, 232, 833.

158. *PCD*, Memphis, TN, 1892, 883.

159. Gruver, *An American History, Volume 1*, 282. To the best of this author's knowledge, it has never been reported that Seymour lived in Memphis, St. Louis, or Chicago. The information was found after studying Seymour's pattern of moving north and east (Indianapolis to Cincinnati) along former routes of the Underground Railroad and then looking at Gruver's map of the former slave's northern exodus. Seymour was found by reading census records and contacting libraries in many cities along the route. Since William Seymour appears and then disappears in these cities at the appropriate times, it seems more than reasonable that he made the journey and lived in each of the cities. The author must admit, however, that the Memphis and St. Louis connections have not and cannot be proven beyond doubt with the evidence now available.

160. Brandt, "The Make-Up of Negro City Groups," 2.

161. J. A. Dacus and James W. Buel, *A Tour of St. Louis or the Inside Life of a Great City* (St. Louis: Western Publishing Co., 1878), 413, 416, 417.

162. *Gould City Directory*, St. Louis, MO, 1893–4, 1288; 1895–6, 1895.

163. John A. Wright, *Discovering African-American St. Louis: A Guide to Historic Sites* (St. Louis: Missouri Historical Society, 1994), 27.

164. Glenn A. Cook, *The Azusa Meeting: Some Highlights of this Outpouring* (n.p., n.d.), 2; Shumway, "A Critical Study of 'The Gift of Tongues,'" 173.

165. G. F. Richings, *Evidence of Progress among Colored People* (Philadelphia: George S. Ferguson, Co., 1903), 276–277.

166. Emma Lou Thornbrough, *The Negro in Indiana before 1900: A Study of a Minority* (Indianapolis: Indiana Historical Bureau, 1957), 15.

167. *IIR*, January 7, 1899; *IIR*, January 14, 1899; *IIR*, January 28, 1899, newpapers. library.in.gov. All issues beginning January 1899 are available online.

168. Indianapolis-Marion County Public Library, letter to the author, December 15, 1998; *PCD*, Indianapolis, IN, 1896, 782; 1898, 810; 1899, 835.

169. "Smith Kill His Wife, *IIR*, December 2, 1899, 2; "Said Her Husband Struck Her," *Indianapolis News*, December 23, 1898, 9, newspapers.library.in.gov.

170. Cook, *Azusa Meeting: Some Highlights*, 2; Shumway, "A Critical Study of 'The Gift of Tongues,'" 173.

171. "Negro Bluk Kissed," *Indianapolis Morning Star* (hereafter cited as *IMS*), June 3, 1907, 3; *PCD*, Indianapolis, IN, 1896, 1001.

172. "Indianapolis' Best Cafe," *IMS*, June 30, 1907, 26.

173. "National Business League Notes," *IIR*, August 27, 1904, 1, newpapers.library.in.gov.

174. "Good Advice to Waiters," *IIR*, November 10, 1900, 1, newspapers.library.in.gov.

175. "The Pastor's Eye," *IIR*, December 30, 1899, 4, newspapers.library.in.gov.

176. Nelson, "For Such a Time as This," 159; Thornbrough, *Negro in Indiana before 1900*, 354. Borlace says Seymour joined the Association of Head and Side Waiters. See Borlace, *William Seymour*, 46.

177. A waiter in Atlanta was paid from $1 to $2.50 a week, while a hotel waiter in Cambridge, MA, was paid $5 a week. See Carol D. Wright and Oren W. Weaver, eds., *Condition of the Negro in Various Cities: Bulletin of the Department of Labor* (Washington, D.C.: Government Printing Office, 1897), 305, 307, 320.

178. Brandt, "The Make-Up of Negro City Groups," 2.

179. Shumway, "A Critical Study of 'The Gift of Tongues,'" 173. Nelson says Seymour joined Simpson Chapel Methodist Episcopal Church, 160. Simpson Chapel is often misidentified as an African Methodist Episcopal congregation. For an example, see Thornbrough, *Negro in Indiana before 1900*, 370. Robeck says Seymour could have joined either Simpson, Bethel African Methodist Episcopal, or Meridian Street Methodist Episcopal. He offers no proof that Nelson is incorrect. See Cecil M. Robeck Jr., *The Azusa Street Mission and Revival* (Nashville: Thomas Nelson, 2006), 28.

180. "Louisiana Methodist Conference—Fifth Day's Session," *NOR*, January 14, 1873, 6, newspapers.com.

181. Clara Merritt DeBoer, *Blacks and the American Missionary Association*, January 6, 2009, United Church of Christ, https://web.archive.org/web/20090106042417/; http://www.ucc.org/about-us/hidden-histories/blacks-and-the-american.html; *History of the American Missionary Association*, Library of Congress, https://tile.loc.gov/storage-services/public/gdcmassbookdig/historyofamerica00amer_1/historyofamerica00amer_1.pdf.

182. Philip Stone, "How the Methodist Church Split in the 1840s," January 30, 2013, https://blogs.wofford.edu/from_the_archives/page/14/?cat=-1.

183. "End of the Central Jurisdiction," http://gcah.org/history/central-jurisdiction.

184. "History of Blacks and Methodism," asburyumcbrandywine.com/some-history-of-blacks-and-methodism/.

185. *Polk City Directory*, Indianapolis, IN, 1897, 118; 1898, 116; History of Simpson Church (n.p., 1924), 6, 7. In 1966, Simpson, Christ, and Gorman churches merged to form University United Methodist Church. See "Our Church History," typescript, Depauw University.

186. Fannie Barrier Williams, "Social Bonds in the 'Black Belt' of Chicago," *The Survey: The Negro in the Cities of the North* (New York: Charity Organization Society, 1905), 41.

187. Delilah L. Beasley, *The Negro Trail Blazers of California* (New York: Negro Universities Press, 1919), 46.

188. Shumway, "A Critical Study of 'The Gift of Tongues,'" 173.

189. Ida Webb Bryant, *Glimpses of the Negro in Indianapolis, 1863–1963* (n.p.; n.d.).

190. *Leaves of Healing* (hereafter cited as *LOH*), January 6, 1900, 336.

191. Williams, 40; Bessie Louise Pierce, *A History of Chicago: Volume III, The Rise of a Modern City, 1871–1893* (Chicago: University of Chicago Press, 1957), 48.

192. Williams, "Social Bonds in the 'Black Belt' of Chicago," 43.

193. United States Census, Cook County, Illinois, 1900. This census gives Seymour's place of birth and the place of birth for his parents as Tennessee. This is obviously incorrect, since all were born in Louisiana. However, in 1910, the Los Angeles census said his parents were born in Virginia. In 1870 his father's birthplace was Kentucky. This William Seymour is a Black male, born in May 1870 and working as a waiter. Furthermore, Seymour disappeared from the Indianapolis City Directories after 1899. There is a possible contradiction to these theories of Seymour's travels. In 1900 he is also listed with his family in the census in Louisiana. There are several explanations for this. First, Seymour's family may not have understood the enumerator and listed all family members. It is also possible, but less likely, that Seymour was visiting in Louisiana and still would have been listed in Chicago if his rent was paid at the boardinghouse. It is notable that Seymour's birth date and age are incorrect (by almost five years), as are his brother's. Seymour was probably not present, and his mother admitted she did not know the birth dates of her children, but a sister kept the "correct" records. Phillis Seymour, *General Affidavit*, February 23, 1895, Simon Seymour Pension File, National Archives and Records Administration. Robeck Jr. dismisses the Chicago census entry and says Seymour was in Centerville. I disagree. See Robeck Jr., *Azusa Street Mission and Revival*, 31.

194. Williams, "Social Bonds in the 'Black Belt' of Chicago," 40; Pierce, *History of Chicago: Volume III*, 48.

195. United States Census, Cook County, Illinois, 1900.

196. Unless Seymour had a different job and address, his name does not appear in any city directories available to the author. See *Chicago City Directory*, Chicago, Illinois, 1897, 1534; 1898, 1994; 1900, 1720; 1901, 1786; 1902, 1842; 1903, 1927. 1899 was not available.

197. *LOH*, February10, 1900, 525.

198. *LOH*, January 20, 1900, 395, 400.

199. Grant Wacker, "Marching to Zion: The Story of John Alexander Dowie's 20th Century Utopian City—Zion, Illinois," *Assemblies of God Heritage*, Fall 1996, 8.

200. John Alexander Dowie, *LOH*, June 11, 1904, 228; John Alexander Dowie, *LOH*, September 24, 1904, 803.

201. Martin, *Charles Fox Parham*, 77–78.

202. *Cincinnati City Directory*, Cincinnati, Ohio, 1901, 1576; 1902, 1637.

203. Shumway, "A Critical Study of 'The Gift of Tongues,'" 173. The Saints did evangelistic work in both Indianapolis and Cincinnati. See B. Scott, "William J. Seymour: Follower of the 'Evening Light,'" *Wesleyan Theological Journal* (hereafter cited as *WTJ*), Fall 2004, 172, 175–178, wtsociety.com.

204. Beverly Carradine, *The Sanctified Life* (Cincinnati: M. W. Knapp, Pentecostal Publisher, 1897), 17.

205. James S. Tinney, "William J. Seymour: Father of Modern-Day Pentecostalism," in Randall K. Burkett and Richard Newman, eds., *Black Apostles: Afro-American Clergy Confront the Twentieth Century* (Boston: G. K. Hall and Co., 1978), 216.

206. Emma Cotton, "The Inside Story of the Azusa Street Outpouring," 1. This author prefers Shumway's information. Glenn Gohr and I visited Anderson, Indiana, but a search of the Church of God Archives at Anderson University provided no information on Seymour. Ministerial lists from the time are no longer available if they ever existed.

207. Andrew L. Byers, *Birth of a Reformation: Life and Labors of D. S. Warner* (Anderson, IN: Gospel Trumpet Company, 1921), 264.

208. Byers, *Birth of a Reformation*, 24.

209. Smith, *Brief History of the Church of God Reformation Movement*, 12–15, 30, 33.

210. J. Gordon Melton, *The Encyclopedia of American Religions: Religious Creeds, Volume Two* (Detroit: Gale Research, Inc., 1994), 150, 152.

211. Byers, *Birth of a Reformation*, 113.

212. Smith, *Brief History of the Church of God Reformation Movement*, 32, 33.

213. Byers, *Birth of a Reformation*, 191–193.

214. J. Harvey Gossard, "John Winebrenner: Founder, Reformer, and Businessman," in Pennsylvania Religious Leaders (Historical Study No. 16, The Pennsylvania Historical Association, 1986), 89–90, quoted in Barry L Callen, "Daniel Warner: Joining Holiness and All Truth," *WTJ*, Spring 1995, 96, wtsociety.com.

215. John W. V. Smith, *A Brief History of the Church of God Reformation Movement* (Anderson, IN: Warner Press, 1976), 107, 121–124.

216. W. J. Henry, "The Color Line," *GT*, December 20, 1906, 3, cited in Lewis, "William J. Seymour: Follower of the 'Evening Light.'"

217. Charles Carroll, *"The Negro a Beast"; Or, "In the Image of God"* (St. Louis: American Book and Bible House, 1900), babel.hathitrust.org.

218. William G. Schell, *Is the Negro a Beast? A Reply to Chas. Carroll's Book Entitled "The Negro a Beast," Proving that the Negro is Human from Biblical, Scientific, and Historical Standards* (Moundsville, WV: Gospel Trumpet Publishing Company, 1901), 231, babel.hathitrust.org.

219. In the earlier edition I said Seymour was credentialed by the Saints. As I stated at the time there is no proof of that. Robeck Jr. disagrees. He could be right. During this period, most ministers sought credentials with an organization so they could get discounted train tickets. As much as Seymour traveled, it seems likely that he would have had some type of ministerial recognition.

220. Byers, *Birth of a Reformation*, 269.

221. Smith, *Brief History of the Church of God Reformation Movement*, 96.

222. Byers, *Birth of a Reformation*, 49.

223. Smith, *Brief History of the Church of God Reformation Movement*, 41, 69.

224. Henry Louis Taylor Jr., ed., *Race and the City: Work, Community, and Protest in Cincinnati, 1820–1970* (Urbana: University of Illinois Press, 1993), 115.

225. W. Laird Clowes, *Black America: A Study of the Ex-Slave and His Late Master* (London: Cassell and Co., Ltd., 1891), 98, 99.

226. Walter Havighurst, *Ohio: A Bicentennial History* (New York: W. W. Norton and Co., 1976), 8, 9, 92.

227. Nelson, "For Such a Time as This," 163, 164.

228. "In the Churches," (Washington, D.C.) *Evening Star*, December 3, 1898, 21, newspapers.com.

229. Elmer T. Clark, *The Small Sects in America* (New York: Abingdon-Cokesbury Press, 1937), 76; J. Gordon Melton, *Religious Leaders of America: A Biographical Guide to Founders and Leaders of Religious Bodies, Churches, and Spiritual Groups in North America* (Detroit: Gale Research, Inc., 1991), 255. Through a series of mergers Knapp's group became part of the Pilgrim Holiness Church and finally the Wesleyan Church.

230. Martin Wells Knapp, *Lightning Bolts from Pentecostal Skies* (Cincinnati: Office of the Revivalist, 1898), 173, quoted in Vinson Synan and Charles R. Fox Jr., *William J. Seymour: Pioneer of the Azusa Street Revival* (Alachua, Florida: Bridge Logos, 2012), 38.

231. "Deceptions and Counterfeits," GT, August 22, 1901, cited by Lewis, "William J. Seymour: Follower of the 'Evening Light.'" Lewis also cites example of where Knapp's periodical criticized the Saints.

232. William Kostlevy, *Holy Jumpers* (Oxford: Oxford University Press, 2010), 26.

233. Kostlevy, *Holy Jumpers*, 18, 29.

234. Robeck Jr., *Azusa Street Revival*, 34.

235. "Bible Students in Police Court," *The Dayton (Ohio) Herald*, July 12, 1901, 1, newspapers.com.

236. "Expects He Will Go 'Tripping into Heaven,'" *The Cincinnati Post*, July 15, 1901, 8, newspapers.com.

237. Kostlevy, *Holy Jumpers*, 18.

238. "Death Invades the Mt. of Blessing and Removes Noted Faith Curist," *Lexington (Kentucky) Leader*, December 11, 1901, 2, newspapers.com.

239. Valerie Hayes-Ross, "Pest Houses – A Necessary But Inhumane Practice," *The News-Examiner*, January 18, 2021, https://www.hjnews.com/montpelier/pest-houses---a-necessary-but-inhumane-practice/article_a6e918db-e873-57be-8e3b-85cf5db389e5.html.

240. S. Rathinam and E. Cunningham, "Vitiligo iridis in patients with a history of smallpox infection," *Eye* 24, 1621–1622 (2010), https://doi.org/10.1038/eye.2010.102; "Pesthouses," kyhi.org/pest-houses.

241. "Vitiligo Iridis in Patients with a History of Smallpox Infection," nature.com; Richard D Semba, "The Ocular Complications of Smallpox and Smallpox Immunization," archophthalmo.com. I wrote several ophthalmologists asking about this disease and its consequences. Those who responded said that losing the eyeball was possible with the diagnosis, but a film or scar on the eye or whitening or an opaque coloring of the cornea was more common. Dean McGee Eye Institute to Larry Martin, September 12, 2023; Sandeep Shah to Larry Martin, September 9, 2023.

242. "Laser Resurfacing of Smallpox Scars," pubmed.ncbi.nlm.nih.gov; D. H. Kang, S. H. Park, and S. H. Koo, "Laser resurfacing of smallpox scars," *Plast Reconstr Surg.* 2005 Jul;116(1):259-65; discussion 266-7. doi: 10.1097/01.prs.0000170093.62733.e5. PMID: 15988276.

243. Shumway, "A Critical Study of 'The Gift of Tongues,'" 173; "Weird Babel of Tongues" *LAT*, April 18, 1906, II, 1. It is often reported that Seymour had a glass eye. This may not have been the case. He could not see out of one eye, and it was obviously afflicted. A milky film or scale over the pupil of the eye would be more consistent with blindness caused by smallpox.

244. "A Modern Babel of Tongues in Kansas," *The Cincinnati Commercial Tribune*, January 20, 1901, 29, newspaperarchive.com.

245. *Cincinnati City Directory*, cited in Lewis, "William J. Seymour: Follower of the 'Evening Light,'" 170. Lewis reports there was a William Seymour living at 337 W. Front employed as a laborer.

246. Havilghurst, *Ohio: A Bicentennial History*, 138.

247. *PCD*, Columbus, OH, 1904-5, 892; *PCD*, Columbus, OH, 1905-6, 978; the listing is for William J. Seymour. Although the directory does not identify people by race, a research librarian confirmed that both addresses would be consistent with African American communities at the time of Seymour's residency; Sam Roshon, letter to Larry Martin, April 15, 1999. The odds that another Black man named William J. Seymour would appear in Columbus, Ohio, and then disappear from the directories in the years that Seymour's residence is unknown seem staggering. This is especially true since Seymour's pattern was to travel eastward.

248. E. Myron Noble, *Like as of Fire: Newspapers from the Azusa Street World Wide Revival* (Washington, D.C.: Middle Atlantic Press, 1994), vii; Shumway, "A Critical Study of 'The Gift of Tongues,'" 173.

249. Melton, *Encyclopedia of American Religions: Religious Creeds, Volume Two*, 321.

250. J. Gordon Melton, *Religious Leaders of America* (Detroit: Gale Research, Inc., 1991), 232.

251. C. E. Jones, "Church of God in Christ," in Stanley M. Burgess and Gary B. McGee, *Dictionary of Pentecostal and Charismatic Movements* (Grand Rapids: Zondervan Publishing House, 1988), 204.

252. Elmer T. Clark, *The Small Sects in America* (New York: Abingdon Cokesbury Press, 1937), 120; Melton, *Religious Leaders of America*, 232.

253. Frank S. Mead, *Handbook of Denominations in the United States, ninth edition* (Nashville: Abingdon, 1990), 77.

254. Shumway, "A Critical Study of 'The Gift of Tongues,'" 173.

255. Melton, *Encyclopedia of American Religions: Religious Creeds, Volume Two*, 321.

256. Shumway, "A Critical History of Glossolalia," 113. Shumway says Seymour was searching for his parents. There is a definite error here. Seymour was born after slavery ended, and his mother was still in Centerville. He could have been searching for other family members, or Shumway may have misunderstood.

257. Seymour is not listed in any Houston city directory, suggesting that he never established permanent residency in the city. This author believes the amount of time he spent in Houston has been greatly exaggerated. As stated in a previous chapter, he may have been listed as a resident of Columbus, Ohio, in the 1905-6 city directory.

258. *John G. Lake: His Life, His Sermons, His Boldness of Faith* (Fort Worth: Kenneth Copeland Publications, 1994), 87.

259. Nelson, "For Such a Time as This," 166, 180; Robeck Jr., *Azusa Street Mission and Revival*, 35. Robeck Jr. says Seymour visited John G. Lake in Chicago during this period. This seems very unlikely. A more probable scenario is that the meeting took place when Seymour was in Zion, Illinois, in June 1906 or at some later date when both men would have received the baptism in the Holy Spirit and embraced the Pentecostal movement. Robeck Jr. also erroneously claims that Lake received the baptism in the Holy Spirit at Azusa Street, 247.

260. "Mrs. Lucy F...," *AFLA*, September 1906; United States Census, Harris County, Texas, 1900. Whether she was born in bondage is unknown. One unsubstantiated rumor was that she had a white father and was not sold into slavery until after his death.

261. Cecil M. Robeck Jr., "The Impact of the Azusa Street Revival: The Impact on Pentecostal Missionary Vision," AGTS Spring Lectureship Audio Cassette, March 16, 1989.

262. Charles F. Parham, "A Critical Analysis of the Tongues Question," *AFP*, undated photocopy of page 3, FPHC.

263. "Louisiana Parish Marriages, 1837–1957," 126, familysearch.org. Estrada says her husband's name was James. This author has seen no evidence for that claim. See page 40.

264. United States Census, Harris County, Texas, 1900; Houston City Directories, 1899; 1900–1901; 1902–03; 1903–04; 1905–06. In the directories, Farrow's name is misspelled Farrell and Farrar. Special thanks to Rev. Calvin Durham for providing the Houston directories.

265. Cotton, "The Inside Story of the Azusa Street Outpouring," 1; Shumway, "A Critical Study of 'The Gift of Tongues;'" B. F. Lawrence, *The Apostolic Faith Restored* (St. Louis: Gospel Publishing House, 1916), 64.

266. S. Parham, *Life of Charles F. Parham*, 118.

267. C. Parham, "A Critical Analysis of the Tongues Question," 7.

268. "Pentecostal Testimonies," *AFLA*, February 6, 1907, 8.

269. Jennie C. Rutty, "The Gift of Tongues," *The Gospel Trumpet* (hereafter cited as *GT*), September 18, 1902, 3.

270. Cotton, "The Inside Story of the Azusa Street Outpouring," 1.

271. S. Parham, *Life of Charles F. Parham*, 140; Goff, 105; Ethel E. Goss, *The Winds of God: the Story of the Early Pentecostal Movement (1901–1914) in the Life of Howard A. Goss* (Hazelwood, MO: World Aflame Press, 1958), 65, 66.

272. S. Parham, *Life of Charles F. Parham*, 161.

273. S. Parham, *Life of Charles F. Parham*, 142.

274. Goss, *Winds of God*, 73; Lawrence, *Apostolic Faith Restored*, 64.

275. Goss, *Winds of God*, 65.

276. Lawrence, *Apostolic Faith Restored*, 55.

277. Nelson, "For Such a Time as This," 167.

278. S. Parham, *Life of Charles F. Parham*, 137.

279. A. C. Valdez, *Fire on Azusa Street* (Costa Mesa, CA: Gift Publications, 1980), 18.

280. "A Letter," *The Apostolic Faith* (Goose Creek, TX), May 1921, 5.

281. Shumway, "A Critical Study of 'The Gift of Tongues,'" 173; Lawrence, *Apostolic Faith Restored*, 64.

282. S. Parham, *Life of Charles F. Parham*, 161.

283. "Pentecost with Signs Following," *AFLA*, December 1906, 1; "Annihilation of the Wicked," *AFLA*, January 1907, 2. The eighth-day creation was a strange idea that the seven days in which the Bible says God created the universe were not literal days, allowing for a much longer time span. But man was created on the eighth day, separate and apart from the other days of creation.

284. Lawrence, *Apostolic Faith Restored*, 55; S. Parham, *Life of Charles F. Parham*, 142.

285. Estrelda Alexander, *The Women of Azusa Street* (Lanham, Maryland: Seymour Press, 2023), 16.

286. United States Census, Los Angeles County, California, 1900; United States Census, Los Angeles County, California, 1910; United States Census, Los Angeles County, California, 1920.

287. M. B. Terry and Josephine Harris, Application for Marriage, Harris County Texas, April 22, 1879; Alexander, *Women of Azusa Street*, 16. There is no record of the actual marriage in Harris County. The records contain no marriage license. There are several possible explanations. The couple may not have returned the license to the courthouse, or perhaps they never had a marriage. Alexander says Julia Hutchens was a witness to the wedding. This seems unlikely, since she was in Georgia, but this author has not seen a marriage license or Alexander's evidence.

288. James L. Tyson, *The Early Pentecostal Revival: History of Twentieth-Century Pentecostals and the Pentecostal Assemblies of the World, 1901–1930* (Hazelwood: Word Aflame, 1992), 95, 96; Valdez, *Fire on Azusa Street*, 18.

289. Cotton, "The Inside Story of the Azusa Street Outpouring," 1, 2.

290. James Tinney, "The Life of William Seymour," in Randall Burkett and Richard Newman, *Black Apostles: African American Clergy Confront the 20th Century* (Boston: G.K. Hall, 1978), 218, quoted in Alexander, *Women of Azusa Street*, 18, 19.

291. Lawrence, *Apostolic Faith Restored*, 64.

292. W. F. Carothers, "History of Movement," *AFP*, October 1908, 1; "Bro. Seymour's Call," *AFLA*, September 1906, 1; Goss, *Winds of God*, 73; S. Parham, *Life of Charles F. Parham*, 142. Although Mrs. Goss is wrong on many of the facts and Mrs. Parham is very biased, their works are important.

293. Stanley Wayne, "Early Revivals," in *Perpetuating Pentecost: A Look at the Formation and Development of the Southern Missouri District Council of the Assemblies of God* (Springfield, MO: Southern Missouri District, 1989), 5–13; Kathleen Joan Foster Stafford, "Pentecostal Pioneer—Opal Stauffer Wiley, typescript," FPHC; Glenn Gohr interview of Mrs. Raye Wiley Batson, Fall 1989; Mrs. Raye Wiley Batson, personal interview, November 13, 1998, FPHC; Glenn Gohr and Kathleen Stafford, personal interview, November 13, 1998, FPHC.

294. William Scarborough, "A Step Backward," *Frank Leslie's Illustrated Newspaper*, September 19, 1891, 98.

295. Bay, "Jim Crow Journeys: An Excerpt from *Traveling Black*."

296. Chris Rockwell to Larry Martin, email, July 27, 2023; John Privera to Larry Martin, email, August 2, 2023; John Privera to Larry Martin, email, August 3, 2023; John Privera to Larry Martin, email, August 12, 2023; John Privera to Larry Martin, email, August 15, 2023. John is a librarian at the California State Railroad Museum and was very gracious to provide invaluable information, schedules, and brochures.

297. Molly Alma White, *Looking Back from Beulah* (Denver: Pentecostal Union, 1902), 36–37, babelhathitrust.org.

298. Molly Alma White, *Looking Back from Beulah* (Bound Brook, NJ: Pentecostal Union, 1910), babelhathitrust.org.

299. Susie Cunningham Stanley, *Feminist Pillar of Fire: The Life of Alma White* (Cleveland, OH: Pilgrim Press, 1993), 64.

300. Stanley, *Feminist Pillar of Fire*, 86.

301. Stanley, *Feminist Pillar of Fire*, 90.

302. White, *Looking Back from Beulah*, 59–60.

303. White, *Looking Back from Beulah*, 259.

304. White, *Looking Back from Beulah*, 190; Alma White, *The Story of My Life, Vol III* (Zarephath, NJ: Pillar of Fire, 1924), 113, babelhathitrust.org.

305. "Putnam," *Hartford (CT) Courant*, January 30, 1902, 14; "Sunday School Convention," *Sioux City Journal*, August 2, 1903, 11; "Holiness Convention Begins Its Session," *(Omaha) Evening World Herald*, April 18, 1903, 7; "Wrath of God," *Boston Globe*, July 9, 1902, 3, newspapers.com.

306. Alma White, *Demons and Tongues* (Zarephath, NJ: Pillar of Fire Publishers, 1936), 67, 68. White had several reasons to be prejudiced against Seymour and the Pentecostal movement. First, after years of a troubled relationship, her husband left her when he became a Pentecostal. For more information, see Alma White, *My Heart and My Husband* (Zarephath, NJ: Pillar of Fire Publishers, 1923). Nelson's dissertation gives an excellent defense of Seymour's appearance, which White called "untidy." If Seymour was less than proper in his dress, it should be considered in light of both the Holiness tradition of plain dress and the fact that he had traveled from Houston to Denver on a train in a "colored" coach. Train travelers were advised not to wear light-colored clothes "which are more serviceable from the standpoint of coal dust." See Hallie Erminie Rives, *The Complete Book of Etiquette* (Philadelphia: John C. Winston Company, 1926), 327.

307. *El Pueblo: Los Angeles before the Railroads* (Los Angeles: Security Trust and Savings Bank, 1928), 2, babelhathitrust.org.

308. John Caughey and Laree Caughey, *Los Angeles: Biography of a City* (Berkeley: University of California Press, 1976), 3.

309. *El Pueblo*, 8.

310. Caughey and Caughey, *Los Angeles*, 41, 42, 55.

311. Caughey and Caughey, *Los Angeles*, 71.

312. Caughey and Caughey, *Los Angeles*, 66–71.

313. Charlotta A. Bass, *Forty Years: Memoirs from the Pages of a Newspaper* (Los Angeles: n.p., 1960), 2.

314. Caughey and Caughey, *Los Angeles*, 75. A mestizo is someone of mixed white and Native American ancestry.

315. Charles Dwight Willard, *The Herald's History of Los Angeles* (Los Angeles: Kingsley Barnes and Neuner, Co., 1901), 102, babel.hathitrust.org.

316. Willard, *Herald's History of Los Angeles*, 127.

317. Robert Fogelson, *The Fragmented Metropolis* (Cambridge, MA: Harvard University Press, 1967), 7.

318. Rockwell D. Hunt, *California in the Making: Essays and Papers in California History* (Westport, CT: Greenwood Press, 1953), 53.

319. Fogelson, *Fragmented Metropolis*, 1.

320. Fogelson, *Fragmented Metropolis*, 15.

321. Luther A Ingersol, *Ingersol's Century History: Santa Monica Bay Cities* (Los Angeles: Ingersol, 1908), 82, babel.hathitrust.org.

322. Willard, *Herald's History of Los Angeles*, 279.

323. Fogelson, *Fragmented Metropolis*, 21.

324. Fogelson, *Fragmented Metropolis*, 26, 27.

325. Hunt, *California in the Making*, 119.

326. Bass, *Forty Years*, 7.

327. Hunt, *California in the Making*, 119.

328. Fogelson, *Fragmented Metropolis*, 27.

329. Beasley, *Negro Trail Blazers of California*, 158–160.

330. Lynn Bowman, *Los Angeles: Epic of a City* (Berkeley: Howell-North, 1974), 203.

331. Fogelson, *Fragmented Metropolis*, 21.

332. Fogelson, *Fragmented Metropolis*, 76, 77.

333. Fogelson, *Fragmented Metropolis*, 76, 78.

334. "228,298 Is Population of this City," *The Los Angeles Express* (hereafter cited as *LAE*), April 14, 1906, 1.

335. Caughey and Caughey, *Los Angeles*, 284.

336. Bass, *Forty Years*, 15, 16.

337. Fogelson, *Fragmented Metropolis*, 199, 201.

338. Bass, *Forty Years*, 21.

339. "Negro Is Captured after Long Chase," *LAE*, April 7, 1906, 5.

340. Lawrence, *Apostolic Faith Restored*, 72, 73.

341. Frank Bartleman, *My Story: The Latter Rain* (Columbia, SC: John M. Pike, 1909), 26. A reprint of this book is available at azusastreet.org.

342. Frank Bartleman, *From Plow to Pulpit: From Maine to California* (Los Angeles: n.p., 1924), 5–132. A reprint of this book is available at azusastreet.org.

343. Bartleman, *From Plow to Pulpit*, 23.

344. Bartleman, *From Plow to Pulpit*, 18–20.

345. Joseph Smale, Standard Certificate of Death: California State Board of Health, September 16, 1926; "Rites for Churchman Tomorrow," *Los Angeles Daily Times* (hereafter cited as *LAT*), September 18, 1926, II, 1.

346. Herbert L. Sutton, *Our Heritage and Our Hope* (Los Angeles: Continental Graphics, 1974), 24.

347. Sutton, *Our Heritage and Our Hope*, 27, 28.

348. Joseph Smale, *The Pentecostal Blessing* (Springfield, MO: Gospel Publishing House, 2017), 11–12.

349. Sutton, *Our Heritage and Our Hope*, 28.

350. Sutton, *Our Heritage and Our Hope*, 29; Smale, *Pentecostal Blessing*, 13; Bartleman, *Azusa Street*, 13.

351. Sutton, *Our Heritage and Our Hope*, 29–30.

352. Sutton, *Our Heritage and Our Hope*, 30.

353. Sutton, *Our Heritage and Our Hope*, 30.

354. Smale, *Pentecostal Blessing*, 59.

355. Smale, *Pentecostal Blessing*, 72.

356. Smale, *Pentecostal Blessing*, 64.

357. Smale, *Pentecostal Blessing*, 66.

358. Smale, *Pentecostal Blessing*, 14–15; Sutton, *Our Heritage and Our Hope*, 30.

359. Sutton, *Our Heritage and Our Hope*, 30.

360. "Curb Preacher Scores Theater," *LAE*, May 1, 1906, 7; Bartleman, Azusa Street, 26. Smale's congregation left the hall in the summer of 1906 and worshipped in a tent. A controversy with their landlord arose following an outdoor service in May. The services were held outside the theater and hall every evening before the services began inside. Theater attendees would stop and listen to the preaching on their way to watch the theatrical performances. A problem arose, however, when one of the participants gave a testimony and said, "He who goes to the theater is on the road to hell." The owner of the theater and hall was not thrilled with his tenants, and the church moved when their lease was fulfilled.

361. Sutton, *Our Heritage and Our Hope*, 30; Frank Bartleman, *Azusa Street* (South Plainfield, NJ: Bridge Publishing, Inc., 1980), 13–27. This is a reprint of Bartleman's 1925 work *How Pentecost Came to Los Angeles: How It Was in the Beginning*. Although it is one man's view of the events, it is a valuable source; Lawrence, 70, 71; Stanley M. Horton, "Pentecostal Explosion," *The Pentecostal Evangel* (hereafter cited as *TPE*), October 7, 1962, 8. According to Sutton, so many leaders left First Baptist that when elections were held that week, only three officers had previously held a position in the church.

362. Horton, "Pentecostal Explosion," 8–9; Ruth Fisher Steelberg Carter, "I Remember or What Pentecost Means to Me," typescript, *TPE* Files, FPHC.

363. Bartleman, *Azusa Street*, 7; Anderson, *Vision of the Disinherited*, 64.

364. Bartleman, *Azusa Street*, 7.

365. Bartleman, *Azusa Street*, 7, 10–11, 15.

366. "Will Preach in Elk's Hall," *LAE*, March 10, 1906.

367. Demos Shakarian, *The Happiest People on Earth* (Old Tappan, NJ: Revell, 1975), 15–24.

368. Thomas G. Atteberry, "Tongues," *Apostolic Truth*, December 1906, 1, 2.

369. A. G. Osterberg, "I Was There," *Full Gospel Business Men's Voice*, May 1966, 11–13, 18–21; A. G. Osterberg, "Tears—The Secret of the Azusa Street Revival," *The Voice of Healing*, July 1954, 5, 24; Dean Osterberg, letter to the author, August 22, 1998; Dan L. Thrapp, "Pentecostal Sects Convene Here," *LAT*, September 9, 1956, III, 11.

370. Clara Davis, *Azusa Street Till Now* (Tulsa: Harrison House, 1989), 18.

371. Davis, *Azusa Street Till Now*, 16.

372. Gospel Roots: African American Churches in Los Angeles, https://scalar.usc.edu/works/will-the-circle-be-unbroken/gospel-roots-african-american-churches-in-los-angeles.

373. Sutton, *Our Heritage and Our Hope*, 26; Beasley, *Negro Trail Blazers of California*, 161.

374. Alexander, *Women of Azusa Street*, 23; United States Census, 1900; United States Census, 1910 United States Census 1920, United States Census, 1930; "New York, U.S., Arriving Passengers and Crew Lists (Including Castle Garden and Ellis Island), 1820–1957," ancestry.com. In 1900 they were still in Georgia.

375. Thomas R. Nickel, *Azusa Street Outpouring: As Told to Me by Those Who Were There* (Hanford, CA: Great Commission International, 1956), 4; Osterberg, "I Was There," 6; Shumway, "A Critical Study of 'The Gift of Tongues,'" 173.

376. Shumway, "A Critical Study of 'The Gift of Tongues,'" 172; Bartleman, *Azusa Street*, 14.

377. Davis, *Azusa Street Till Now*, 17.

378. United States Census, Los Angeles County, California, 1900.

379. United States Census, Los Angeles County, California, 1910.

380. Shumway, "A Critical Study of 'The Gift of Tongues,'" 172; Moore's address is added by Nelson, 217. Estrelda Alexander says Jennie was in the employee of Walter Cline and lived across from Julia Hutchins's mission, and that is where she was converted by an evangelistic outreach. See Alexander, *Women of Azusa Street*, 194. Robeck Jr. says she was employed as a masseuse. See Robeck Jr., *Azusa Street Mission and Revival*, 65.

381. Shumway, "A Critical Study of 'The Gift of Tongues,'" 172; Alexander A. Boddy, "At Los Angeles, California," *Confidence* (hereafter cited as *CON*), October 1912, 233.

382. Jennie Evans Seymour, Standard Certificate of Death: California State Board of Health, July 2, 1936.

383. United States Census, Los Angeles County, California, 1900.

384. "Oily Burgle of a Gurgle," *LAT*, December 15, 1906, 17; "Building Permits," *LAT*, April 30, 1911, 100, newspapers.com.

385. "Pentecost with," 1.

386. Shumway, "A Critical Study of 'The Gift of Tongues,'" 172; Shumway, "A Critical History of Glossolalia," 115.

387. Shumway, "A Critical Study of 'The Gift of Tongues,'" 172.

388. Valdez, *Fire on Azusa Street*, 18; Nickel, *Azusa Street Outpouring*, 4; Osterberg, "I Was There," 7; Tinney, "William J. Seymour: Father of Modern-Day Pentecostalism," 218. Osterberg says Terry "had been in a Pentecostal revival down there where they spoke in tongues according to Acts 2:4." Tinney says Terry was also a student at Parham's school. Nelson doubts that Terry received or even heard about speaking in tongues while in Houston. He also ignores Shumway's claim that Lee had learned about Pentecost from Charles F. Parham. It is this author's opinion that Nelson demonstrates an obvious bias toward Seymour's role and a design to downplay Parham's more significant role in the foundation of the movement. Unfortunately, this indefensible bias permeates much of the literature.

389. Lawrence, *Apostolic Faith Restored*, 55, 73; Nickel, *Azusa Street Outpouring*, 4; Tyson, *Early Pentecostal Revival*, 95, 96; Cotton, "The Inside Story of the Azusa Street Outpouring," 1; W. J. Seymour, *The Doctrines and Discipline of the Azusa Street Apostolic Faith Mission of Los Angeles, CA* (n.p., 1915), 12. It is often reported that Seymour came to Los Angeles to assume the pastorate of the church. This does not seem to be true. Seymour himself said he only came to give Bible teaching, and he also said the saints in Texas were expecting him to return from Los Angeles in one month. See "Azusa Mission," *The Apostolic Faith* [Los Angeles] (hereafter cited as AFLA), April 1907, 2.

390. Cotton, "The Inside Story of the Azusa Street Outpouring," 2.

391. "Pentecost with Signs Following," *AFLA*, December 1906, 1.

392. Seymour, *Doctrines and Discipline*, 12.

393. Shumway, "A Critical Study of 'The Gift of Tongues,'" 173.

394. "Pentecost with," 1.

395. "Pentecost with," 1.

396. Shumway, "A Critical History of Glossolalia," 115; Shumway, "A Critical Study of 'The Gift of Tongues,'" 173. It is often stated that Seymour was locked out of the building after his first sermon. This is not true. Shumway says it was the fifth meeting, and Seymour himself says, "One night they locked the door against me." See "Bro. Seymour's Call." Hutchins later embraced Pentecost, was baptized in the Holy Spirit, and took the message to Liberia, West Africa.

397. United States Census, 1910; Texas, U.S., Select County Marriage Index, 1837–1965, ancestry.com.

398. "The Sudden death of...," *Highland Park Herald*, November 6, 1909, 4, newspapers.com.

399. "J. M. Roberts," *LAH*, February 28, 1897, 10, newspapers.com.

400. "Mr. Maynard Chatteron…," *Highland Park (California) News-Herald and Journal* (hereafter cited as *HPNH*), December 29, 1906, 8, cdnc.ucr.edu; "Garvanza," *Los Angeles Herald* (Hereafter cited as *LAH*), 14 December 1902, 5, cdnc.ucr.edu; "The Sudden death of…"; "Dr J.M. Roberts, Dentist," *HPNH*, December 26, 1908, 4, newspapers.com; "Garvanza," *LAT*, December 8, 1902, 5, newspapers.com.

401. "New Camping Grounds for Holiness Churches," *LAT*, August 20, 1903, 7, newspapers.com.

402. Charles Edwin Jones, "The 'Color Line' Washed Away in the Blood? In the Holiness Church at Azusa Street, and Afterward," *WTJ*, Fall 1999, 255, wtsociety.com.

403. "Holiness Camp-Meeting," *LAT*, April 21, 1894, 11, newspapers.com.

404. "Holiness Hosts," *LAT*, April 6, 1902, 28, newspapers.com; "New Camping Grounds for Holiness Churches."

405. "New Camping Grounds for Holiness Churches," 7.

406. "Bro. Seymour's Call," 1; Bartleman, *Azusa Street*, 71. Bartleman reports that Roberts was a seeker for the Holy Spirit at his mission.

407. As the reader will learn, Lee was very influential in the meetings. Without a doubt Lee's experience as a pastor would have been a stabilizing force for Seymour, who was much less experienced. Lee would be the first one baptized in the Holy Spirit. He officiated at the marriage ceremony between Seymour and his wife. He preached regularly at the mission.

408. United States Census, 1870, ancestry.com; United States Census, 1880, ancestry.com; United States Census, 1860. This record was sent to author by Hannah Lane, an archivist specializing in "Study of the Legacy of Slavery" at the Maryland State Archives. This census would indicate Edward was born in 1856. Hannah P. Lane to Larry Martin, email, September 13, 2023.

409. "Wealth Mobility in the United States," muse.jhu.edu.

410. *Statistics of the United States, (including mortality, property, &c.,) in 1860: Comp. from the Original Returns and Being the Final Exhibit of the Eighth Census, under the Direction of the Secretary of the Interior* (Washington, D.C.: Government Printing Office, 1866), 512, babel.hathitrust.org.

411. "Slavery and Freedom in Maryland," lib.guides.umd.edu; "A Guide to the History of Slavery in Maryland," msa.maryland.gov.

412. Henry Louis Gates Jr., "Free Blacks Lived in the North, Right?" https://www.pbs.org/wnet/african-americans-many-rivers-to-cross/history/free-blacks-lived-in-the-north-right/.

413. Hannah P. Lane to Larry Martin, email, September 13, 2023.

414. Zoe Phillips to Larry Martin, August 3, 2023; Zoe Phillips to Larry Martin, August 7, 2023. Zoe Phillips is the executive director of the Dorchester County Historical Society. Ms. Phillips and her volunteers were most helpful in providing records from Dorchester County.

415. Zoe Phillips to Larry Martin, August 7, 2023.

416. U.S., Federal Census Mortality Schedules, 1850–1865, Jones Soules Price Boswell Lovell Family Tree, ancestry.com.

417. California, U.S., Voter Registers, 1866–1898, ancestry.com. Amateur genealogists on ancestry.com have mistaken Lee for a man in Carson City, Nevada, from the 1880 Census. This is impossible, since he was in Maryland and the name of the mother is incorrect. Another genealogist says Lee married Ophelia Wiley, who was actually his niece.

418. United States Census, 1900, ancestry.com; "Queer Soul Saving Enterprise Launched," *LAT*, December 28, 1901, 9, newspapers.com; "Concluded Its Business," *The (Sacramento) Record-Union*, August 24, 1897, 4, newspapers.com.

419. "African Methodists," *LAT*, August 24, 1897, 3, newspapers.com; "A.M.E. Church Conference," *LAH*, August 18, 1898, 12, newspapers.com; "Third Day's Doings," *LAT*, August 20, 1898, 6, newspapers.com; "A.M.E. Conference," *LAE*, August 22, 1898, 8, newspapers.com.

420. "Queer Soul Saving…," 9.

421. "Queer Soul Saving…," 9.

422. "Queer Soul Saving…," 9.

423. Many historians argue that the main burden of Seymour, and the primary focus of the revival, was the love that removed the color line. If their thesis is correct, perhaps Edward Lee should be given more credit for the nature and composition of the meetings.

424. Family genealogists suggest 1904 for the marriage date, but none offers any evidence. See ancestry.com.

425. Although he was many years her senior, apparently Edward outlived Mattie by many years. She died on October 26, 1930. She was only fifty-four. Edward lived to be a hundred and nine, passing on February 6, 1969. California Death Index, 1905–1939, ancestry.com; California Death Index, 1940–1997, ancestry.com.

426. United States Census, 1900, ancestry.com.

427. "He Wouldn't Jump," *LAT*, May 21, 1905, 18, newspapers.com.

428. "Peniel Mission," https://www.nps.gov/klgo/learn/historyculture/peniel.htm.

429. California, U.S., Voter Registers, 1900–1968, ancestry.com.

430. Cotton, "The Inside Story of the Azusa Street Outpouring," 1; Shumway, "A Critical Study of 'The Gift of Tongues,'" 174; Shumway, "A Critical History of Glossolalia," 115; Frank J. Ewart, *The Phenomenon of Pentecost* (Hazelwood, Missouri: Word Aflame, 1992), 72; United States Census, Los Angeles County, California, 1910. The circumstances of the meeting between Parham and Lee are not known. Parham had not yet visited California. Those who want to mark Seymour and the Azusa Street Revival as the birth of the modern Pentecostal movement ignore the fact that Parham had an undeniable influence on Lee as well as Seymour, Farrow, and others who were leaders in the Azusa outpouring.

431. Cotton, "The Inside Story of the Azusa Street Outpouring," 2.

432. Shumway, "A Critical History of Glossolalia," 115.

433. Shumway, "A Critical Study of 'The Gift of Tongues,'" 174.

434. John G. Lake, "Origin of the Apostolic Faith Movement," *The Pentecostal Outlook*, September 1932, 3. This article was originally written in 1911; see also *John G. Lake: His Life*, 87, 88.

435. Cotton, "The Inside Story of the Azusa Street Outpouring," 2.

436. Cotton, "The Inside Story of the Azusa Street Outpouring," 2.

437. Cotton, "The Inside Story of the Azusa Street Outpouring," 2.

438. Cotton, "The Inside Story of the Azusa Street Outpouring," 2.

439. "Music from Heaven," *AFLA*, May 1907, 3.

440. Cotton, "The Inside Story of the Azusa Street Outpouring," 2.

441. Shumway, "A Critical History of Glossolalia," 115.

442. Bartleman, *Azusa Street*, 41.

443. Lawrence, *Apostolic Faith Restored*, 56, 64; "Pentecost with," 1; "Mrs. Lucy F. Farrow...," *AFLA*, September 1906, 1; Cotton, "The Inside Story of the Azusa Street Outpouring," 2.

444. Lawrence, *Apostolic Faith Restored*, 66; Goss, 98. See also Cotton, "The Inside Story of the Azusa Street Outpouring," 2.

445. "Divinely Healed," *AFLA*, September 1906, 4; United States Census, Los Angeles County, California, 1910.

446. Houston City Directories, 1899; 1900–1901; 1902–03; 1903–04; 1905–06. Special thanks to Rev. Calvin Durham for providing copies from the Houston directories.

447. "Pentecost with," 1.

448. Lawrence, *Apostolic Faith Restored*, 74; Shumway, "A Critical Study of 'The Gift of Tongues,'" 174.

449. Cotton, "The Inside Story of the Azusa Street Outpouring," 2.

450. Cotton, "The Inside Story of the Azusa Street Outpouring," 2; Shumway, "A Critical History of Glossolalia," 116. Douglas Nelson questions Cotton's account, accusing her of "gender" bias.

451. "Fair Weather the Forecast," *LAE*, April 9, 1906, 1.

452. Shumway, "A Critical Study of 'The Gift of Tongues,'" 175; Nickel, *Azusa Street Outpouring*, 5; "Music from Heaven," 3; Nelson, "For Such a Time as This," 190, 191. The piano that Moore played is still in the Asbery home, which is now maintained by the Church of God in Christ as a museum and a place of prayer.

453. Shumway, "A Critical Study of 'The Gift of Tongues,'" 174; Nickel, 5; Shumway, "A Critical History of Glossolalia," 116; Nelson, "For Such a Time as This," 190–191.

454. "Big Crowds Attend Revival Services," *LAE*, April 10, 1906, 7.

455. Cotton, "The Inside Story of the Azusa Street Outpouring," 2.

456. Nickel, *Azusa Street Outpouring*, 5, 6.

457. "The Same Old Way," *AFLA*, September 1906, 3.

458. C. L. Witherspoon, Houston Ward, Suzie Matthews, and Lola Robinson, typescript, Apostolic Faith Mission Church of God, 1.

459. Ewart, *Phenomenon of Pentecost*, 77; Shumway, "A Critical Study of 'The Gift of Tongues,'" 175.

460. Nelson, "For Such a Time as This," 57, 70.

461. "Pentecost with," 1.

462. Nelson, "For Such a Time as This," 58.

463. Russell Chandler, "Pentecostals: Old Faith, New Impact," *LAT*, January 11, 1976, I 22,

464. Lake, "Origin of the Apostolic Faith Movement," 3. Lake is attempting to describe the April 9 meeting, but the facts of his account seem to fit better with April 12.

465. A. A. Boddy, "At Los Angeles, California," *Confidence*, October 1912, 233.

466. A. G. Osterberg, interview by Jerry Jensen and Jonathan Ellsworth Perkins, March 1966, tape 1, page 5, transcript by Mae Waldron, Flower Pentecostal Heritage Center (FPHC). For many years, Osterberg served the Assemblies of God as a District Superintendent in Southern California.

467. A. G. Osterberg, "From the Personal Writings of A. G. Osterberg," typescript, FPHC; Osterberg, interview, tape 1, pages 5–6.

468. Osterberg, interview, tape 1, page 6.

469. Osterberg, interview, reel 3, page 10 (there are 2 transcripts of tape 3. This one is labeled "reel 3").

470. Osterberg, interview, reel 3, page 10.

471. Osterberg, interview, reel 3, page 15.

472. Osterberg, interview, reel 3, page 14.

473. Osterberg, interview, reel 3, page 17.

474. Osterberg, interview, reel 3, page 17.

475. Osterberg, interview, reel 3, page 10.

476. Cecil M. Robeck Jr., "The Use of Public Materials for Instruction on Pentecostal Origins," unpublished manuscript, n.d., 4, FPHC.

477. Mortgage Deed, 31 December 1930, Book 10511, 277, 278, Los Angeles County, California.

478. Takeshi Nakayama, "African American Roots of Little Tokyo," *The Rafu Shimpo*, February 13, 1998, 1; Bass, *Forty Years*, 23, 24; Beasley, *Negro Trail Blazers of California*, 90, 109.

479. Shumway, "A Critical Study of 'The Gift of Tongues,'" 175.

480. Robeck Jr., "The Use of Public Materials for Instruction on Pentecostal Origins," 4.

481. See the photos of the church.

482. "Strayed," *LAT*, March 23, 1899, 6, newspapers.com.

483. Beth McDonald, "Gospel Roots: African American Churches in Los Angeles," Will the Circle Be Unbroken: The Sacred Music of the African American Diaspora, California State University, Dominguez Hills Gerth Archives and Special Collections, https://scalar.usc.edu/works/will-the-circle-be-unbroken/gospel-roots-african-american-churches-in-los-angeles.

484. Beasley, *Negro Trail Blazers of California*, 160.

485. "Deaths," *LAH*, October 4, 1905, 8, chroniclingamerica.loc.gov; "Deaths," *LAE*, November 12, 1902, 8, newspapers.com.

486. G. F. Taylor, *The Spirit and the Bride: A Scriptural Presentation of the Operations, Manifestation, Gifts and Fruit of the Holy Spirit in His Relation to the Bride with Special Reference to the "Latter Rain" Revival* (n.p., 107), 94; "Fire Does Much Damage," *LAE*, March 7, 1904, 7; "Scoundrels Deed," *LAT*, March 11, 1904, 13; "Flames Leave a Trail of Charred Buildings in Los Angeles," *LAR*, March 10, 1904, 6, newspapers.com.

487. Bartleman, *Azusa Street*, 51; Davis, *Azusa Street Till Now*, 16; Osterberg, "I Was There," 12; Rachel A. Sizelove, "A Sparkling Fountain for the Whole Earth," *Word and Work* (hereafter cited as *WAW*), June 1934, 1.

488. Russell Chandler, "Pasadena Cleric Recalls Mission," *LAT*, January 11, 1976, II, 5; Nickel, *Azusa Street Outpouring*, 6; Florence Crawford, *The Light of Life Brought Triumph* (Portland: Apostolic Faith, 1936), 7.

489. "It Is a Counterfeit Pentecost," *The Burning Bush* (Hereafter cited as *TBB*), December 27, 1906, 4.

490. "Bible Pentecost," *AFLA*, November 1906, 1; Sizelove, "A Sparkling Fountain for the Whole Earth," 1.

491. Nelson, "For Such a Time as This," 192; "Bible Pentecost," 1; Sizelove, "A Sparkling Fountain for the Whole Earth," 1.

492. Nickel, *Azusa Street Outpouring*, 6; Shumway, "A Critical Study of 'The Gift of Tongues,'" 176.

493. Nelson, "For Such a Time as This," 193; Taylor, *Spirit and the Bride*, 94, 95; Sizelove, "A Sparkling Fountain for the Whole Earth," 1; Chandler, "Pasadena Cleric Recalls Mission," II, 5.

494. "It Is a Counterfeit," 4.

495. Clara Lum, "Miss Clara Lum Writes Wonders," *The Missionary World*, August 1906, 2.

496. Sizelove, "A Sparkling Fountain for the Whole Earth," 11.

497. Valdez, *Fire on Azusa Street*, 5; Taylor, *Spirit and the Bride*, 94; Bartleman, *Azusa Street*, 51; Ernest S. Williams, "Memories of Azusa Street," *TPE*, April 24, 1966, 7. Many have not understood the "shoebox" pulpit because they visualize contemporary individual cardboard shoeboxes. At the turn of the century, multiple pairs of shoes were shipped together in larger wooden crates.

498. This falsehood is promoted by Tommy Welchel in what seems to be a mostly fictitious book of unreliable stories supposedly from the revival. See Tommy Welchel, *They Told Me Their Stories* (Mustang, OK: Dare to Dream Books, 2008), 36.

499. Osterberg, "I Was There," 12, 13; Jensen and Perkins interview.

500. Bartleman, *Azusa Street*, 51; Taylor, *Spirit and the Bride*, 94; Jensen and Perkins interview.

501. Taylor, *Spirit and the Bride*, 94; Valdez, *Fire on Azusa Street*, 20; Jensen and Perkins interview.

502. Bartleman, *Azusa Street*, 60.

503. Bartleman, *Azusa Street*, 19.

504. Lawrence, *Apostolic Faith Restored*, 74.

505. "Pentecost Has Come," *AFLA*, September 1906, 1. With all the publicity surrounding the cottage meetings and only word of mouth to advertise the move to a new location, it seems this would be a necessity.

506. Shumway, "A Critical Study of 'The Gift of Tongues,'" 176; Boddy, "At Los Angeles," 233; Nickel, *Azusa Street Outpouring*, 4, 8; Bartleman, *Azusa Street*, 43; Carter, "Notes." Boddy says it was a Methodist church; Nickel says Peniel Hall. Bartleman, who was present, and Ruth Carter join Shumway in saying, "The New Testament Church."

507. Bartleman, *Azusa Street*, 43.

508. Leonard Lovett, "Black Origins of the Pentecostal Movement," in Vinson Synan, *Aspects of Pentecostal-Charismatic Origins* (Plainfield, NJ: Logos, 1975), 132.

509. This article was reprinted in its entirety in another volume of this series, Larry Martin, ed., *Holy Ghost Revival on Azusa Street: Skeptics and Scoffers* (Joplin, MO: Christian Life Books).

510. Wayne R. Thatcher, Peter L. Ward, David J. Wald, James W. Hendley II, and Peter H. Stauffer, "When Will the Next Great Quake Strike Northern California?" https://pubs.usgs.gov/fs/1996/fs094-96/.

511. Jack London, "The Story of an Eyewitness," reprinted from *Colliers*, May 5, 1906; available from sfmuseum.org.

512. "Earthquake and Graft Prosecution Timeline 1906," https://sfmuseum.org/hist/timeline.html, 5.

513. Lawrence, *Apostolic Faith Restored*, 74.

514. "Ye Know Not What a Moment May Bring Forth," *LAE*, April 20, 1906, 9.

515. Bartleman, *My Story*, 42.

516. A. G. Garr, "From Los Angeles," *TBB*, May 17, 1906, 3.

517. Sizelove, "A Sparkling Fountain for the Whole Earth," 11.

518. Cotton, "The Inside Story of the Azusa Street Outpouring," 4. Apparently there were some short breaks in the schedule to allow the leaders to "meet alone, daily, with the Father, Son and Holy Spirit for instruction." See Manley, "True Pentecostal Power with Signs Following," 7.

519. Society for Pentecostal Studies Interview of Lawrence F. Catley, 1974, FPHC.

520. Bartleman, *Azusa Street*, 58.

521. Jensen and Perkins interview.

522. Bartleman, *Azusa Street*, 60.

523. Nickel, *Azusa Street Outpouring*, 9; Bartleman, *Azusa Street*, 57; Manley, "True Pentecostal Power with Signs Following," 7. "The Comforter Has Come" was written by Frank Bottome, and William J. Kirkpatrick furnished the tune. It was first published in 1890 and is based on John 14:16, 26. See Donald P. Hustad, *Dictionary-Handbook to Hymns for the Living Church* (Carol Stream, IL: Hope Publishing Co., 1978), 77.

524. Sarah Haggard Payne, "The Fulfillment of a Life Dream," *The Weekly Evangel*, January 13, 1917, 4.

525. Bartleman, *Azusa Street*, 60.

526. Jensen and Perkins interview.

527. Durham, "Personal Testimony of Brother Durham," 4.

528. Carter, "I Remember," unpublished manuscript (1964), 1. Ruth Fisher, the daughter of Elmer Fisher, was four years old when the revival began at Azusa. She later married Wesley Steelberg, an Assemblies of God General Superintendent. After his death, she wed Howard Carter, General Superintendent of the Assemblies of God in Great Britain and Ireland.

529. Bartleman, *Azusa Street*, 60.

530. Dan L. Thrapp, "Pentecostal Sects to Convene Here," *LAT*, September 9, 1956, III, 11. Sizelove says it was July when large crowds were beginning to gather.

531. Osterberg, "I Was There," 18; Jensen and Perkins interview.

532. "Women with Men Embrace," *LAT*, September 3, 1906, 11.

533. J. G. Speicher, "As Dr. Speicher Sees It," *Zion City News*, June 28, 1907, 1–2.

534. William F. Manley, "True Pentecostal Power with Signs Following," *The Household of God*, September 1906, 6–7.

535. William H. Durham, "Personal Testimony of Brother Durham," *Pentecostal Testimony* (hereafter cited as *PT*), n.d., Vol. III, Nos. 2–3.

536. Lum, "Miss Clara Lum Writes Wonders," 2.

537. Etta Auringer Huff, "A Scriptural Pentecost," *The Herald of Light*, July 14, 1906, 10.

538. "The Old-Time Pentecost," *AFLA*, September 1906, 1.

539. "Russians Hear in their Own Tongue," *AFLA*, September 1906, 4.

540. Frank Bartleman, "Letter from Los Angeles," *Triumphs of Faith*, December 1906, 248–50.

541. Huff, "A Scriptural Pentecost," 10; Lawrence, *The Apostolic Faith Restored*, 79.

542. Osterberg, "I Was There," 13; Osterberg, "From the Personal Writings of A. G. Osterberg," 2.

543. Leonard Lovett, "Black Origins of the Pentecostal Movement," in Vinson Synan, ed., *Aspects of Pentecostal-Charismatic Origins* (Plainfield, NJ: Logos, 1975), 132, 135.

544. "Sister Bridget Welch" and "A young man saved," *AFLA*, November 1906, 1; "A man who," *AFLA*, October 1906, 1; "A brother testified," *AFLA*, December 1906, 3; "A burglar," *AFLA*, May 1908, 1.

545. "A baptismal service," *AFLA*, September 1906, 4.

546. Chandler, "Pasadena Cleric Recalls Mission," II, 1; Valdez, *Fire on Azusa Street*, 5; Bartleman, *Azusa Street*, 58.

547. Lovett, "Black Origins of the Pentecostal Movement," 132.

548. "It is a blessed place," *AHLA*, December 1906, 3.

549. Rachel Sizelove, "The Temple," *WAW*, May 1936, 2, 12; Bartleman, *Azusa Street*, 59.

550. Bartleman, *Azusa Street*, 59; "Bible Pentecost," 1.

551. Sizelove, "The Temple," 12; Stanley Horton, "Twentieth-Century Acts of the Holy Ghost," *TPE*, October 21, 1962, 18.

552. Bartleman, "Letter from Los Angeles," 251; Ewart, *The Phenomenon of Pentecost*, 78.

553. Lawrence, *The Apostolic Faith Restored*, 79–80.

554. Bartleman, "Letter from Los Angeles," 251–52.

555. Tinney interview of Williams.

556. Nickel, *Azusa Street Outpouring*, 14; Valdez, *Fire on Azusa Street*, 11; Bartleman, *Azusa Street*, 63.

557. "This gospel cost," *AFLA*, Feb–March 1907, 1.

558. Del Tarr, "Hold It Gently," *TPE*, November 8, 1998, 20.

559. William J. Seymour, "Gifts of the Spirit," *AFLA*, January 1907, 2.

560. Lawrence, *The Apostolic Faith Restored*, 86.

561. Sizelove, "The Temple," 2; Lawrence, *The Apostolic Faith Restored*, 86; Chandler, "Pasadena Cleric Recalls Mission," II, 5; Nelson, "For Such a Time As This," 235.

562. Bartleman, *Azusa Street*, 55.

563. *John G. Lake: His Life*, 252.

564. Lum, "Miss Clara Lum Writes Wonders," 2. This is a very significant quote, especially since some have tried to discount the importance of Seymour's role and define Azusa Street as a lay revival without ministerial leadership.

565. Stanley M. Horton, "A Night at Azusa Street," *TPE*, October 14, 1962, 6.

566. Central Bible College Student interview of E. S. Williams, n.d., FPHC.

567. "Says Elders Threw Him from Church," *LAH*, March 24, 1908, 5, chronicalingamerica.loc.gov.

568. Valdez, *Fire on Azusa Street*, 9.

569. Taylor, *The Spirit and the Bride*, 94; Ewart, *The Phenomenon of Pentecost*, 80.

570. Chandler, "Pasadena Cleric Recalls Mission," II, 1; Valdez, *Fire on Azusa Street*, 9.

571. "In Azusa Mission," *AFLA*, May 1907, 2.

572. Cotton, "The Inside Story of the Azusa Street Outpouring," 4.

573. Osterberg, "From the Personal Writings of A. G. Osterberg," 3.

574. Florence Crawford, *A Witness of the Power of God* (Portland: Apostolic Faith Church, n.d.), 5–6.

575. "A baby that," *AFLA*, January 1907, 1.

576. Deborah Sims LeBlanc, *Like a Rose: Life, Times and Messages of the Late Bishop Frank R. Bowdan, D.D., 1910–1976* (Los Angeles: DLB Associates), 2–3.

577. Fred T. Corum and Hazel E. Bakewell, *The Sparkling Fountain* (Windsor, OH: Corum and Associates, Inc., 1983), 39.

578. Society for Pentecostal Studies interview of Lawrence Catley, 1974.

579. "Tongues of Fire—Gift of Languages and Holiness Union," *DOS*, October 4, 1906, 6.

580. Sizelove, "The Temple," 12; Valdez, *Fire on Azusa Street*, 5; Cook, *The Azusa Meeting: Some Highlights of this Outpouring*, 3; Nelson, "For Such a Time As This," 262.

581. Ewart, *The Phenomenon of Pentecost*, 78.

582. Sizelove, "The Temple," 12.

583. Lawrence, *The Apostolic Faith Restored*, 78.

584. Josephine M. Washburn, *History and Reminiscences of the Holiness Church Work in Southern California and Arizona* (South Pasadena: Record Press, 1912), 383–90, https://archive.org/details/historyreminisce00wash/page/388/mode/2up?view=theater&q=brightest.

585. Gee, *The Pentecostal Movement*, 48.

586. L. F. Wilson, "George B. Studd," in Burgess, *Dictionary of Pentecostal and Charismatic Movements*, 834.

587. Gee, *The Pentecostal Movement*, 50; *Heroes of the Faith* (Springfield, MO: Assemblies of God Division of Foreign Missions, 1990), 78; "From a Missionary to Africa," *AFLA*, September 1906, 3.

588. John Worrell, letter to Larry Martin, November 24, 1998.

589. A. S. Worrell, "The Movements in Los Angeles, California," *Triumphs of Faith*, December 1906, 256.

590. "Young Girl Given Gift of Tongues," *LAE*, July 20, 1906, 1. See also "Queer Gift Given Many," *LAT*, July 23, 1906, 5.

591. Horton, "Pentecostal Explosion," 9.

592. Bartleman, *Azusa Street*, 54, 58.

593. Bartleman, *Azusa Street*, 54.

594. Nelson, "For Such a Time As This," 234; Lovett, "Black Origins of the Pentecostal Movement," 133.

595. Jensen and Perkins interview.

596. "One token," *AFLA*, Feb–March 1907, 7.

597. Nelson, "For Such a Time As This," 13. I disagree with Nelson's contention that "Seymour championed one doctrine above all others: there must be no color line or other division in the church of Jesus Christ because God is no respecter of persons." A reading of all of Seymour's statements and writings does not support this position. I would be more inclined to agree with Bishop J. Ramsey of Gloster, Mississippi, who argues that Seymour's message was primarily a call to biblical holiness—the Holy Spirit would only fall on a sanctified life.

598. Nelson, "For Such a Time As This," 13, obtained from FPHC.

599. Cecil M. Robeck, *The Colorline Was Washed Away in the Blood: A Pentecostal Dream for Racial Harmony* (Costa Mesa, CA: Christian Education Press, 1995), 12.

600. Max Wood Moorhead, "A Short History of the Pentecostal Movement," *Cloud of Witnesses to Pentecost in India*, November 1908, 15.

601. Ewart, *Phenomenon of Pentecost*, 70.

602. Seymour, *Doctrines and Discipline*, 12.

603. G. B. Cashwell, "Came 3,000 Miles For His Pentecost," *AFLA*, December 1906, 3; R.J. Scott, "What The Pentecost Did for One Family," *AFLA*, Feb–March 1907, 7.

604. "Some People," *AFLA*, December 1906, 3.

605. Richard Crayne, *Pentecostal Handbook: A Reference Guide to the Origins, Personalities and Doctrines of the Pentecostal People in the United States of America* (n.p., 1989), 195; Valdez, *Fire on Azusa Street*, 5, 10; Ewart, *Phenomenon of Pentecost*, 79. Crayne quotes Fred Anderson, an eyewitness. Ewart was an associate of William H. Durham and succeeded him as pastor in Los Angeles.

606. "Tongues of Fire—Gift of Languages and Holiness Union," *DOS*, October 4, 1906, 6.

607. Bartleman, *Azusa Street*, 58.

608. Shakarian, *The Happiest People on Earth*, 24.

609. Cook, *The Azusa Meeting: Some Highlights of this Outpouring*, 3.

610. Fred T. Corum, "Azusa's First Camp-Meeting," *WAW*, January 1936, 1.

611. Cook, *The Azusa Meeting: Some Highlights of this Outpouring*, 1–2; Corum, "Azusa's First Camp-Meeting," 1; "Sister Mary," *AFLA*, December 1906, 3; Nils Bloch-Hoell, *The Pentecostal Movement: Its Origin, Development, and Distinctive Character* (Oslo: Scandinavian University Books, 1964), 48.

612. "Oregon, U.S., State Deaths, 1864–1971," United States Census 1870, ancestry.com; "Lumm Services Are at Evansville," *The (Madison, Wisconsin) Capital Times* (hereafter cited as *MCT*), April 15, 1947, 8, newspapers.com.

613. Edith L. Blumhofer, "Clara E. Lum," *Assemblies of God Heritage*, Summer 2001, 17, ifphc.org.

614. "Lumm Services Are at Evansville," *MCT*, April 15, 1947, 8, newspapers.com; Ruth Ann Montgomery, "Evansville Seminary," evansvillehistory.net.

615. "Commencements," *LAT*, June 23, 1892, 9, newspapers.com.

616. "Orange County," *LAT*, August 20, 1893, 6, newspapers.com.

617. "Orange County," *LAT*, June 28, 1894, 9, newspapers.com.

618. "Untitled," *The (Palo Alto, CA) Peninsula Times Tribune*, April 26, 1895, 3, newpapers.com.

619. Blumhofer, "Clara E. Lum," Orange County, August 20, 1893.

620. Blumhofer, "Clara E. Lum."

621. Blumhofer, "Clara E. Lum"; "Pentecostal Testimonies," *AFLA*, February–March 1907, 8.

622. "Portland Is Stirred," *AFLA*, January 1907, 1; "The Lord has," *AFLA*, May 1908, 2; Nelson, "For Such a Time As This," 234.

623. "The Lord has," 2.

624. "The Gift of Tongues," *The Nazarene Messenger*, December 13, 1906, 6.

625. Donald Gee, *The Pentecostal Movement* (London: Elim Publishing Co., Ltd., 1949), 12.

626. James Tinney interview of E. S. Williams, November 8, 1978, FPHC.

627. Jensen and Perkins interview.

628. Thrapp, "Pentecostal Sects Convene Here," III, 11.

629. John G. Lake, *The Collected Works of John G. Lake*, 20, https://christiandiet.com.ng.

630. Lake, *The Collected Works of John G. Lake*, 670.

631. Lake, *The Collected Works of John G. Lake*, 337.

632. Manley, "True Pentecostal Power with Signs Following," 6.

633. E. W. Mason, *The Man…Charles Harrison Mason: Sermons of His Early Ministry (1915–1929) and a Biographical Sketch of His Life* (n. p., n.d.), 6–7.

634. "Bible Pentecost," 1.

635. Crawford, *The Light of Life Brought Triumph*, 9–10.

636. A. B. Simpson, *The Holy Spirit or Power from on High* (New York, NY: Christian Alliance Publishing, 1896), 4, FPHC.

637. Simpson, *The Holy Spirit or Power from on High*, 367.

638. Simpson, *The Holy Spirit or Power from on High*, 372.

639. See Noble, *Like as of Fire: Newspapers from the Azusa Street World Wide Revival*. All of the sermons credited to Seymour are published in William J. Seymour, *Azusa Street Sermons: The Words that Changed the World* (Duncan, OK: Christian Life Books, 2017).

640. See the sermon "The Marriage Tie," in Noble, *Like as of Fire: Newspapers from the Azusa Street World Wide Revival*, 43.

641. Seymour, *Azusa Street Sermons*, 24–25. See Isaiah 53:5; Exodus 15:26; Psalm 103: 1, 3; and Isaiah 53:4.

642. Seymour, *Azusa Street Sermons*, 36. See 1 Corinthians 16:1–2.

643. Seymour, *Azusa Street Sermons*, 65. See Acts 2:3–4; and Romans 10:10.

644. Seymour, *Azusa Street Sermons*, 46. See Matthew 25:6.

645. Saint Anonymous, "My Experience in the Baptism with the Holy Ghost," *TPE*, January 3, 1931, 2.

646. Saint Anonymous, "My Experience in the Baptism with the Holy Ghost," 2.

647. C. M. Robeck Jr., "Ernest Swing Williams," in Burgess, *Dictionary of Pentecostal and Charismatic Movements*, (Grand Rapids: Zondervan, 1988), 886.

648. Ernest S. Williams, "Forty-Five Years of Pentecostal Revival," *TPE*, August 19, 1951, 3.

649. Saint Anonymous, "My Experience in the Baptism with the Holy Ghost," 2.

650. Saint Anonymous, "My Experience in the Baptism with the Holy Ghost," 2.

651. Ernest S. Williams, "Memories of Azusa Street Mission," *TPE*, April 24, 1966, 7.

652. Ernest S. Williams, "My Personal Experience at the Azusa Mission," in Wayne Warner, ed., *Touched by the Fire: Patriarchs of Pentecost, Their Lives, Their Visions, Their Ministries* (Plainfield, NJ: Logos, 1978), 45.

653. Williams, "Memories of Azusa Street Mission," 7.

654. Williams, "Memories of Azusa Street Mission," 7; Saint Anonymous, "My Experience in the Baptism with the Holy Ghost," 2.

655. Williams, "Memories of Azusa Street Mission," 7; Saint Anonymous, "My Experience in the Baptism with the Holy Ghost," 2; Williams, "My Personal Experience at the Azusa Mission," 46.

656. Saint Anonymous, "My Experience in the Baptism with the Holy Ghost," 2.

657. Williams, "Forty-Five Years of Pentecostal Revival," 3.

658. Robeck, "Ernest Swing Williams," 887.

659. Wayne Warner, "The Men Who Have Led the A/G," *Assemblies of God Heritage*, Winter 1981–1982, 3, https://ifphc.org; C. M. Robeck Jr., "Ernest Swing Williams," in Stanley M. Burgess, *The New International Dictionary of Pentecostal Charismatic Movements* (Grand Rapids: Zondervan, 2002), 1197–98.

660. E. W. Mason, *The Man…Charles Harrison Mason*, 6–7.

661. I. C. Clemmons, "Charles Harrison Mason," in Stanley M. Burgess and Gary B. McGee, eds, *Dictionary of Pentecostal and Charismatic Movements* (Grand Rapids: Zondervan, 1988), 585.

662. Clemmons, "Charles Harrison Mason," 586.

663. Clemmons, "Charles Harrison Mason," 586.

664. E. W. Mason, *The Man…Charles Harrison Mason*, 8–9.

665. Clemmons, "Charles Harrison Mason," 586.

666. E. W. Mason, *The Man…Charles Harrison Mason*, 11–13.

667. E. W. Mason, *The Man…Charles Harrison Mason*, 14, 16; Witherspoon et al., 1; C. H. Mason, "Tennessee Evangelist Witnesses," *AFLA*, March 1907, 7.

668. E. W. Mason, *The Man…Charles Harrison Mason*, 14.

669. E. W. Mason, *The Man…Charles Harrison Mason*, 15–19.

670. C. H. Mason, "Tennessee Evangelist Witnesses," 7.

671. Hans A. Baer and Merrill Singer, *African-American Religion in the Twentieth Century: Varieties of Protest and Accommodation* (Knoxville: University of Tennessee Press, 1992), 153.

672. E. W. Mason, *The Man…Charles Harrison Mason*, 14, 19; I. C. Clemmons, "Charles Harrison Mason," in Stanley M. Burgess, *The New International Dictionary of Pentecostal Charismatic Movements* (Grand Rapids: Zondervan, 2002), 865–67.

673. G. B. Cashwell, "Came 3,000 Miles for His Pentecost," *AFLA*, December 1906, 3.

674. H. V. Synan, "Gaston Barnabas Cashwell," in Stanley M. Burgess and Gary B. McGee, eds, *Dictionary of Pentecostal and Charismatic Movements* (Grand Rapids: Zondervan, 1988), 109–10.

675. Joseph T. McCullen Jr., "Gaston B. Cashwell Once a Prodigal Son," in *The Heritage of Sampson County, North Carolina: 1784–1984* (Winston-Salem: Hunter Publishing, Co., 1984), 87–88.

676. Synan, "Cashwell," 110.

677. Oscar M. Bizzell, "The North Carolina Holiness Association Started Here, 1897," in *The Heritage of Sampson County, North Carolina: 1784–1984* (Winston-Salem: Hunter Publishing, Co., 1984), 85–86.

678. Synan, "Gaston Barnabas Cashwell," 110; Cashwell, "Came 3,000 Miles for His Pentecost," 3.

679. Vinson Synan, *The Old Time Power: A History of the Pentecostal Holiness Church* (Franklin Springs, GA: Advocate Press, 1973), 97.

680. Synan, *The Old Time Power*, 97–98; Cashwell, "Came 3,000 Miles for His Pentecost," 3.

681. Joseph E. Campbell, *The Pentecostal Holiness Church: 1898–1948; Its Background and History* (Franklin Springs, GA: The Publishing House of the Pentecostal Holiness Church, 1951), 239–43; Vinson Synan, *The Holiness-Pentecostal Tradition: Charismatic Movements in the Twentieth Century* (Grand Rapids: Eerdmans, 1997), 112–22; Synan, *The Old Time Power*, 99–104; Synan, "Gaston Barnabas Cashwell," 110.

682. Charles W. Conn, *Like a Mighty Army Moves the Church of God* (Cleveland: Church of God Publishing House, 1955), 84–85.

683. S. Clyde Bailey, *Pioneer Marvels of Faith* (Morristown, TN: n.p., n.d.), 49.

684. H. V. Synan, "Gaston Barnabas Cashwell," in Stanley M. Burgess, *The New International Dictionary of Pentecostal Charismatic Movements* (Grand Rapids: Zondervan, 2002), 457–58; Bailey, *Pioneer Marvels*, 49.

685. "The Comforter Has Come," in *Azusa Street Mission: Fourteenth Anniversary of the Outpouring of the Holy Spirit In Los Angeles, California* (Los Angeles: W. H. Giles, 1920), 6.

686. Lawrence, *Apostolic Faith Restored*, 80.

687. James L. Dodd III, letter to Larry Martin, December 17, 1998, with photocopies of a history of First Christian Assembly of God.

688. "Pentecost in Portsmouth," *AFLA*, December 1906, 1.

689. Conrad Dottin, "How Pentecost Came to Cambridge, Mass.," *Apostolic Messenger*, December 1920, 12.

690. "Converts Claim Strange Powers," *The (East Liverpool, OH) Evening Review*, January 7, 1907, 1, 3; "'Gift of Tongues' is Satan's Work," *Los Angeles Record*, January 10, 1907, 2.

691. "Spreading the Full Gospel," *AFLA*, November 1906, 1; "Slow to Arrive," *Daily (Salem) Oregon Statesman* (hereafter cited as *DOS*), October 10, 1906, 2; "Sister Crawford Departs," *(Salem) Daily Capital Journal* (hereafter cited as *DCJ*), December 29, 1906, 5; "Healed Blind Woman," *DCJ*, December 24, 1906, 6.

692. Wiley is described as "a mulatto or quadroon" and "yellow." "New Tongues," *DOS*, November 20, 1906, 6; "Healed Blind…," 6

693. "New Tongues," 6; "Claims Gift of Tongues," *(Dallas, Oregon) Polk County Observer*, December 28, 1906, 1; "Sister Crawford…," 5; "Healed Blind Woman," 6.

694. "Spreading the Full Gospel," 1.

695. "Fear Witchcraft; Mob Missionaries," *The Des Moines Capital*, August 7, 1907, 3.

696. Catley interview.

697. John Hall, email to Larry Martin, February 9, 1999. There are conflicting family stories about Hall's experience at Azusa Street.

698. Witherspoon et al., 1–2; "Spreading the Full Gospel," 1; "In Mobile," *AFLA*, February–March 1907, 3; "In Mobile," *AFLA*, April 1907, 1; Sherry Sherrod DuPree, *African American Holiness Pentecostal Movement: An Annotated Bibliography* (New York: Garland Publishing, Co., 1996), 246–47.

699. "Under Wings of Police," *DCJ*, November 14, 1906; "Ask Police Aid," *DOS*, November 15, 1906, 3.

700. "Young Mob Assails Bluks' Temple," *IMS*, June 17, 1907, 3; "Bluks Appeal to Police," *Indianapolis Sun* (hereafter cited as *ISU*), June 17, 1907, 7; "Mayor Will Protect 'Gliggy Bluks,'" *IIN*, June 19, 1907, 1.

701. "Color Line Obliterated," *The Morning (Portland) Oregonian*, December 31, 1906, 4; "Padded Cell Religion in Two Forms Is Rampant in Portland," *The (Portland) Evening Telegram* (hereafter cited as *PET*), December 31, 1906, 1; "Frazer after Holy Howlers," *PET*, January 1, 1907, 1; *PET*, January 2, 1907, 7; "Judge Frazer Issues Ukase," *PET*, January 3, 1907, 8; "'Bride of the Lord' Has Severe Cold," *PET*, January 4, 1907, 12.

702. "Bits for Breakfast," *DOS*, October 5, 1906, 2.

703. "Pigs Squeak," *DOS*, December 21, 1906, 1.

704. "Padded Cell Religion in Two Forms Is Rampant in Portland," 1.

705. Nickel, *Azusa Street Outpouring*," 18; C. M. Robeck Jr., "Robert James Semple," in Stanley M. Burgess and Gary B. McGee, eds., *Dictionary of Pentecostal and Charismatic Movement* (Grand Rapids: Zondervan, 1988), 776–77.

706. Osterberg, "I Was There," 19; "Missionaries to Jerusalem," *AFLA*, September 1906, 4; Andrew Johnson, "Letter from Brother Johnson," *AFLA*, October 1906, 3; A. G. Johnson, "From our Brother in Sweden," *AFLA*, January 1907, 3. Others may have arrived on the foreign field before Johnson since he stayed for some time in Colorado, Chicago, and New York.

707. "We cannot give…," *AFLA*, February–March 1907, 1.

708. "Good News from Danville," *AFLA*, September 1906, 4; William A. Ward, *The Trailblazer* (n.p., n.d.), 9.

709. "Fire Still Falling," *AFLA*, October 1906, 1.

710. "Sister Florence Crawford…," *AFLA*, November 1906, 2.

711. "Testimonies of Outgoing Missionaries," *AFLA*, October 1906, 1; "From Los Angeles to Home and Foreign Fields," *AFLA*, December 1906, 4; "Latest Report from our Missionaries to Africa," *AFLA*, January 1907, 3.

712. David Bays, "Missionary Establishment and Pentecostalism," in Edith L. Blumhofer, Russell P. Splittler, and Grant A. Wacker, *Pentecostal Currents in American Protestantism* (Champaign, IL: University of Illinois Press, 1999), 53–56.

713. William Taylor, *The Flaming Torch in Darkest Africa*, (New York: Eaton and Mains, 1898), 485; "From a Missionary to Africa," *AFLA*, September 1906, 3; "New Tongued Missionaries for Africa," *AFLA*, November 1906, 3. Taylor, the bishop of Africa, said, "If there were a thousand such trainers as Samuel Mead and Ardel, his wife, there would in a few years be twenty thousand native evangelists and pastors in Africa under the leadership of our all conquering King."

714. Robeck, "The Impact of the Azusa Street Revival Series: The Impact on Pentecostal Missionary Vision."

715. *Heroes of the Faith* (Springfield, MO: Assemblies of God Division of Foreign Missions, 1990), 78–84.

716. Nelson, "For Such a Time As This," 1.

717. "An editor…," *AFLA*, September 1906, 2.

718. "As soon as…," *AFLA*, January 1908, 4.

719. Lawrence, *The Apostolic Faith Restored*, 77.

720. E. S. Hanson, "Called and Baptized," *Apostolic Light* (hereafter cited as *AL*), November 19, 1906, 2.

721. "Baptized in New York," *AFLA*, December 1906, 3; "Missionaries to Jerusalem," *AFLA*, September 1906, 4; Thomas Ball Barratt, *When the Fire Fell and an Outline of My Life* (Oslo: Alfons, Hansen and Soner, 1927), 98–130.

722. Gee, *The Pentecostal Movement*, 20–25.

723. "This great…," *AFLA*, September 1907, 1.

724. "The religion," *AFLA*, November 1906, 1.

725. Lawrence, *The Apostolic Faith Restored*, 79.

726. "Weird Babel of Tongues," *LAT*, April 18, 1906, 1; "Weird Fanaticism Fools Young Girl," *LAT*, July 12, 1906, 1; "Summer Solstice Sees Strenuous Sects Sashaying," *Los Angeles Examiner* (hereafter cited as *LAX*), July 23, 1906, 1.

727. The author has collected dozens of these articles in a volume. See Larry Martin, *Wild and Weird: William J. Seymour, Azusa Street and Early Pentecostalism as Reported by the Los Angeles Secular Newspapers* (Pensacola, FL: Christian Life Books, 2012). Available at azusastreet.org.

728. "Weird Fanaticism Fools Young Girl," *LAT*, July 12, 1906, 1.

729. Art Glass, "The Comforter Has Come," bonniebrae.org.

730. "Women with Men," 11.

731. "Weird Fanaticism Fools Young Girl," 1. The author published a collection of newspaper articles in Los Angeles during the revival.

732. Bartleman, *Azusa Street*, 48.

733. "The secular papers," *AFLA*, September 1906, 1.

734. Valdez, *Fire on Azusa Street*, 12.

735. "Weird Fanaticism Fools Young Girl," 1.

736. "Arrested for Jesus' Sake," *AFLA*, December 1906, 3.

737. "Negro Preacher on Trial in Police Court," *LAE*, June 12, 1906, 2; "Abusive Preacher Convicted," *LAE*, June 13, 1906, 6; "Negro Preacher to Work in Chain Gang," *LAE*, June 14, 1906, 1.

738. Nickel, *Azusa Street Outpouring*, 15–18. In 1908, Prentice was working in Indianapolis, Indiana, when he was arrested for interrupting the services at a Methodist church. This was the twenty-third time he was arrested for preaching the gospel. Again, Prentice represented himself. About one hundred believers were in the courtroom and sang "I'm on the Hallelujah Side" as the trial began. Prentice interviewed every prospective juror, asking if they were Christians. The jury, however, fined Prentice $25. The judge fined him $10 for calling the Methodist pastor a lawyer and another $25 for contempt for saying, "The Lord bless you." For more details, see "'Tongues' at Allen Chapel," *IIN*, April 24, 1908, 7; "Bluks Invade Allen Chapel and Stop Sermon," *IMS*, April 24, 1907, 1; "Invade the Bluk's Temple," *IIS*, April 25, 1907, 1; "'Gliggy Bluks' Are Fined," *IIS*, April 26, 1907, 3; "For Disturbing Service," *IIN*, March 4, 1908, 7; "Gliggy Bluk Pleads Own Case and Pays 3 Fines," *IMS*, March 5, 1908, 1; "Gliggy Bluk Preacher Fined for Contempt," *IIN*, March 5, 1908, 16.

739. "Arrested," 3; "In Jail for Jesus' Sake," *AFLA*, November 1906, 4.

740. "Says House of God Is Noisy," *Pasadena Daily News* (hereafter cited as *PDN*), July 3, 1906, 1; "Tongues Gift Given Many," *PDN*, July 5, 1906, 1; "Lord's Advice Hold the Fort," *PDN*, July 9, 1906, 1; "Council Orders Tent of Household Moved," *PDN*, July 10, 1906, 1; "Heed Divine Injunction," *PDN*, July 12, 1906, 10; "Head of Sect Is Disturber," *PDN*, July 13, 1906, 12; "Sect Leader Is Fined $50," *LAE*, July 13, 1906, 15.

741. "Household Is On Move Again," *PDN*, July 18, 1906, 12.

742. "Weird Fanaticism Fools Young Girl," 1.

743. "Churches Aroused to Action," *LAE*, July 18, 1906, 12. See also "Church Census for City," *LAE*, July 13, 1906, 6; "Church Workers to Meet Tonight," *LAE*, July 24, 1906, 12; "Praying Bands for Churches," *LAE*, July 25, 1906, 6; "Open-air Service at Trinity Successful," *LAE*, July 31, 1906, 4; "Praying Bands Are Forming," *LAE*, August 1, 1906, 7; "Open-air Meeting at Trinity Tonight," *LAE*, August 2, 1906, 3; "Plan for Religious Crusade," *LAE*, August 3, 1906, 7; "Outdoor Religious Services in Westlake," *LAE*, August 4, 1906, 15.

744. "The Gift of Tongues," 6; "About Tongues," *The Church Herald and Holiness Banner* (hereafter cited as *CHB*), July 27, 1907; R. L. Averill, "The Apostolic Faith Movement," *The Holiness Evangel*, January 1, 1907, 1. There are literally more cases than can be cited. For a few examples, see Larry Martin, ed., *Skeptics and Scoffers: The Religious World Looks at Azusa Street: 1906–1907* (Pensacola, FL: Christian Life Books, 2004). Available at azusastreet.org.

745. Valdez, *Fire on Azusa Street*, 10.

746. Washburn, *History and Reminiscences of the Holiness Church Work in Southern California and Arizona*, 383–90.

747. "A. G. Garr," *TBB*, July 19, 1906, 4.

748. Reprinted in "Impressions of Pentecost 35 Years Ago," *TPE*, February 24, 1945, 2.

749. Gee, *The Pentecostal Movement*, 19.

750. "Before the fire," *AFLA*, November 1906, 1.

751. S. Parham, *Life of Charles F. Parham*, 148; "Bible Pentecost," 1.

752. Goff, *Fields Ripe Unto Harvest*, 94.

753. J. G. Campbell, "History of the Apostolic Faith Movement: Origin, Projector, etc.," *The Apostolic Faith* (Goose Creek, TX), May 1921, 7. Campbell is quoting K. Brower from a 1909 letter from Los Angeles.

754. This pin is a mystery. For decades this author has searched for one in antique and thrift stores. Seymour seems to be wearing the pin in one of his photos. In a photo taken at Brunner Tabernacle in Houston, most of the Apostolic Faith workers were wearing the pin. The search continues.

755. William J. Seymour to Warren F. Carothers, July 12, 1906.

756. S. Parham, *Life of Charles F. Parham*, 154–55.

757. Campbell, "History of the Apostolic Faith Movement: Origin, Projector, etc.," 6.

758. S. Parham, *Life of Charles F. Parham*, 154.

759. "Letter from Brother Parham," *AFLA*, September 1906, 1.

760. Martin, *Charles Fox Parham*, 175–76.

761. Shumway, "A Critical Study of 'The Gift of Tongues,'" 178.

762. For one such example, see Lawrence, *The Apostolic Faith Restored*, 60.

763. Although it offends some, it is hard for this author to refer to Parham as anything less than racist. He held to a British-Israelism theory that amounted to little less than white supremacy. His doctrinal positions condemned interracial marriages, and he apparently denied that Black people could be part of the bride of Christ. In later years he associated with the Ku Klux Klan. In fairness, it should also be noted that Goff, a Parham biographer, argues that Parham's view of Black people was not racist, but patronizing. He admits, however, that his prejudices increased as he grew older. For a complete study of Parham and his views, see Martin, *Charles Fox Parham*.

764. Charles F. Parham, "Free Love," *AFP*, December 1912, 4; Charles F. Parham, *The Everlasting Gospel* (Baxter Springs: n.p., n.d.), 118.

765. Jensen and Perkins interview.

766. Campbell, "History of the Apostolic Faith Movement: Origin, Projector, etc.," 6.

767. Campbell, "History of the Apostolic Faith Movement: Origin, Projector, etc.," 6; S. Parham, *Life of Charles F. Parham*, 163.

768. Tinney interview of Williams.

769. S. Parham, *Life of Charles F. Parham*, 163.

770. Goff, *Fields White Unto Harvest*, 109, quoting *AFP*, March 1906, 12.

771. Articles of Incorporation, Apostolic Faith Mission, Los Angeles County, California, March 9, 1907.

772. Carothers, "History of the Movement," 1.

773. W.F. Carothers, *Church Government* (Houston: n. p., 1909), 62.

774. Tinney interview of Williams.

775. Lawrence, *The Apostolic Faith Restored*, 67.

776. Goff, *Fields White Unto Harvest*, 136.

777. Stanley H. Frodsham, *With Signs Following* (Springfield, MO: Gospel Publishing House, 1946). Frodsham edited the Parham name out of quotations.

778. Bartleman, *Azusa Street*, 67–69.

779. "Spreads the Fire," *AFLA*, October 1906, 4; Bartleman, *Azusa Street*, 82.

780. "Rolling on Floor in Smale's Church," *LAT*, July 14, 1906, II, 1.

781. Shumway, "A Critical Study of 'The Gift of Tongues,'" 176; Bartleman, *Azusa Street*, 54, 84; Horton, "Twentieth-Century Acts of the Holy Ghost," 18; Stanley Horton, "Elmer Kirk Fisher," in Burgess, *Dictionary of Pentecostal and Charismatic Movements*, 310; Carter, "I Remember," 1; Carter, "Notes"; Ruth Carter, "An Unusual Experience in the Upper Room Mission," *TPE*, August 7, 1966, 9. Smale's First New Testament Church became Temple Baptist Church, and he later founded Grace Baptist Church.

782. "Speaking with Tongues," *CHB*, December 15, 1906, 1.

783. Clara E. Lum, "Wonderful News from Los Angeles," *AL*, November 19, 1906, 3; "The Purchase of the Azusa Mission," *AFLA*, February–March 1907, 2; "What God Hath Wrought," *AFLA*, May 1908, 1.

784. George B. Studd, personal diary, FPHC.

785. Sizelove, "The Temple," 10.

786. Although a first name is not given, it seems likely that this is Charles C. Carpenter. He later served as superintendent of schools in Azusa, California. See "Institute Sessions Finished," *LAT*, December 19, 1928, 8, newspapers.com.

787. Osterberg, "From the Personal Writings of A. G. Osterberg," 3; Jensen and Perkins interview.

788. "Los Angeles Campmeeting of the Apostolic Faith," *AFLA*, May 1907, 1.

789. Fred Corum, "Azusa's First Camp-Meeting," *WAW*, January 1936, 1.

790. Carter, "Notes"; "Everywhere Preaching the Word," *AFLA*, September 1907, 1.

791. "Everywhere Preaching the Word," 1.

792. "From Azusa Mission," *AFLA*, January 1908, 1.

793. "The Marriage Tie," *AFLA*, September 1907, 3.

794. William Joseph Seymour and Jennie Evans Moore, Certificate of Marriage: California State Board of Health, May 13, 1908; Marriage License, May 27, 1908, Los Angeles County. The marriage license says Jennie was thirty. According to her death certificate, she would have been thirty-four. According to the 1900 census, she would have been thirty-two.

795. "Bible Teaching on Marriage and Divorce," *AFLA*, January 1907, 3.

796. There is a theory that Clara Lum and Florence Crawford, both white women, left the mission because they had romantic feelings toward Seymour and felt rejected when he married Moore. I have seen no evidence of this. Clemmons does say that in 1908, Seymour met with C. H. Mason, who advised him not to marry a white woman. See Ithiel Clemmons, "True Koinonia: Pentecostal Hopes and Historical Realities," *Pneuma: The Journal of the Society for Pentecostal Studies* (Spring 1982): 54. Two other possibilities for the fissure seem more reasonable. First, many early Pentecostals felt that it was not advisable to marry because of the nearness of Christ's coming (1 Corinthians 7). There could also have been a conflict between the departing women and Mrs. Seymour. E. S. Williams described Florence Crawford as "a strong minded woman." He said of Mrs. Seymour, "She was the backbone of his trying to push himself," and she "wanted to put Brother Seymour in his place." See Tinney interview of Williams.

797. Crawford, *Light of Life Brought Triumph*, 11–12; "Azusa to Portland, A Moment in History Revisited," *Higher Way*, November–December 1996, 7.

798. *A Historical Account of the Apostolic Faith: A Trinitarian Fundamental Evangelistic Organization* (Portland: Apostolic Faith, 1965), 70. Until his death, Seymour was a strong proponent of sanctification. See the end of this chapter for the division with William Durham. Further, how could anyone accuse this pious man of compromising on holiness? No moral stain was ever found on his spotless record. Some feel this compromise could have been his decision to marry. Since Bartleman was offended by a church sign, and others were offended when an offering was taken to pay for the building, these charges could amount to nothing. Allowing the readers to draw their own conclusions, it is also interesting to note that the Upper Room Mission, which from the natural point of view would be a serious competitor to Azusa, was very supportive of the Portland work. See "We are glad to see…," *The Upper Room* (hereafter cited as *TUR*), August 1910, 2; "Portland, Oregon," *TUR*, May 1910.

799. "For the next…," *The Apostolic Faith* (Portland, OR) (hereafter cited as *AFPO*), June 1908, 2.

800. "We have moved…," *AFPO*, July/August 1908, 2; "The Promised Latter Rain," *AFPO*, July/August 1908, 1.

801. Number 18, the January 1909 edition, says, "The last paper…was the first to be published in Portland." The author has not seen Number 17.

802. J. C. Vanzandt, *Speaking in Tongues* (Portland, OR: Vanzandt, 1926), 34–37. Richard Crayne and others argue that Lum had permission to move the paper. This cannot be the case. They cite the incorporation papers of the Portland Apostolic Faith, which say, "Vested by said mission with authority to publish at various times issues of the official organ, 'Apostolic Faith,' a paper devoted to principles and doctrines of said cause and distributed without charge." There are two major problems with this argument. First, these articles were dated October 11, 1909, nearly a year and a half after Lum moved the paper. Furthermore, these articles were signed by Jennie Seymour and Edward Doak, Azusa workers—not Lum or Crawford. It seems to me this was an attempt by the Azusa workers to reclaim the work in Portland. The articles say the Portland work is "auxiliary spiritually" to the mission in Los Angeles. This harmonizes with Allan V. McPherson, who remembered, "Mr. Seymour came to Portland, Oregon, about 1911, with some of his helpers and tried to take over Sister Crawford's work at Front and Burnside Street but met with complete failure." See Crayne, *Pentecostal Handbook: A Reference Guide to the Origins, Personalities and Doctrines of the Pentecostal People in the United States of America*, 203; and Richard Crayne, *The Mailing List Controversy* (Morristown, TN: Self Published, 2004).

803. Vanzandt, *Speaking in Tongues*, 37. To the author's knowledge, no copy of this Los Angeles paper exists. Some have said that because Vanzandt is a critic of Pentecostalism, he created this story. This is not plausible. Vanzandt first wrote in 1911, when his work could have been validated or invalidated by the participants. Further, he is accurate when quoting the Portland paper.

804. Vanzandt, *Speaking in Tongues*, 36.

805. Tinney interview of Williams.

806. According to the Los Angeles County Records, the sale of the property was originally recorded in December 1906 and finalized April 15, 1908. See pages 266–67 of Los Angeles County Records, photocopies in Azusa Street File, FPHC.

807. Studd, diary, FPHC.

808. George B. Studd, "Los Angeles," CON, August 15, 1908, 10.

809. Robeck, *The Azusa Street Mission and Revival*, 311. This author has not seen the Cashwell diaries and relies solely on Robeck.

810. Bartleman, *Azusa Street*, 143–46.

811. White, *Demons and Tongues*, 119–21.

812. Gastona Espinosa, "The Silent Pentecostals," *Christian History*, churchhistoryinstitute.org. Loaded to the web without magazine format and page numbers.

813. *Heroes of the Faith*, 78.

814. United States Census, Los Angeles County, CA, 1910.

815. George N. Eldridge, *Personal Reminiscences* (Los Angeles: West Coast Publishing, Co., 1930), 40–41.

816. Thrapp, III, 11.

817. A. W. Frodsham, "A Pentecostal Journey in Canada, British Columbia, and the Western States," *CON*, June 1911, 139.

818. William H. Durham, "The Great Revival at Azusa Street—How it Began and How it Ended," *PT*, n. d., Volume I, Number 8, 3.

819. Arthur G. Osterberg, *Certificate of Ordination*, Full Gospel Assembly, September 25, 1909.

820. For a fuller treatment on Durham, see Larry Martin, *In the Beginning* (Duncan, OK: Christian Life Books, 1995), 31–36. This author hopes to write a complete biography of Durham in the future.

821. Untitled brochure published by A. C. Driscoll, 1, Historical Center, United Pentecostal Church.

822. Durham, "The Great Revival at Azusa Street—How it Began and How it Ended," 3.

823. Bartleman, *Azusa Street*, 150.

824. Crayne, *Pentecostal Handbook: A Reference Guide to the Origins, Personalities and Doctrines of the Pentecostal People in the United States of America*, 207–08.

825. Durham, "The Great Revival at Azusa Street—How it Began and How it Ended," 4; Shumway, "A Critical Study of 'The Gift of Tongues,'" 179; Max A. X. Clark, *Latter Rain and Holy Fire: The Beginnings of the Pentecostal Movement* (n. p., n. d.), 28.

826. Osterberg, "From the Personal," 4; "Notes from A. G. Osterberg May 24, 1956," typescript, Flower Pentecostal Heritage Center. A. G. Osterberg remembered the dispute as a racial issue. He said, "The colored folks began to fight the whites because they said the whites were going to try to come in and take over Azusa." He added that, "Seymour himself was very humble about it." Laying the blame at Mrs. Seymour's feet, he said she "antagonized all the colored people. The colored folks believed in an inter-racial church as long as they had a Negro pastor."

827. Clark, *Latter Rain and Holy Fire: The Beginnings of the Pentecostal Movement*, 29; Shumway, "A Critical Study of 'The Gift of Tongues,'" 179.

828. Bartleman, *Azusa Street*, 151.

829. Durham, "The Great Revival at Azusa Street—How it Began and How it Ended," 4.

830. Goff, *Fields White Unto Harvest*, 152.

831. Shumway, "A Critical Study of 'The Gift of Tongues,'" 191; Edith L. Blumhofer, *The Assemblies of God: A Chapter in the Story of American Pentecostalism, vol. 1* (Springfield: Gospel Publishing, 1989), 222–23; D. A. Reed, "Oneness Pentecostalism," in Burgess, *Dictionary*, 644; J. L. Hall, "Frank J. Ewart," in Burgess, *Dictionary of Pentecostal and Charismatic Movements*, 290; Anderson, *Vision of the Disinherited*, 177.

832. Former General Superintendent E. S. Williams says a decision was made to discourage the ordination of Black people to appease Southern pastors who questioned having to share their pulpits with African Americans. They feared this would cause an uproar in the strictly segregated Southern states. See Tinney interview.

833. "Spreading the Full Gospel," *AFLA*, October 1906, 4; "Pentecost Both Sides the Ocean," *AFLA*, February–March 1907, 1; "Missions in Los Angeles," *AFLA*, April 1907, 1; Corum, "Azusa's First Camp-Meeting," 1.

834. "Seek New Religious Speech," *IMS*, February 1, 1907, 5; "Gliggy Bluks Meet," *IMS*, April 17, 1907, 1; "Stutterer Speaks at 'Glug' Service," *IMS*, April 18, 1907, 15; "'Bluks' Pay No Rent," *IMS*, April 19, 1907, 1, 3; "Trance Followed Sermon by Cook," *IMS*, April 24, 1907, 3. See also "'Bluk' Followers Grow," *IMS*, April 22, 1907, 7; "Bluk's Faith Fades," *IMS*, April 23, 1907, 11; and other articles that appeared almost daily in Indianapolis newspapers.

835. "Stutterer Speaks," 15; "Young Girls, Mere Children, Speak 'Tongue' of the Bluks," *IMS*, May 19, 1907, 40; "Bluk Crowd Runs Over," *IIS*, June 10, 1907, 12.

836. "Tongues Crush Idols," *IMS*, April 27, 1907, 5.

837. "Negro Bluk Beats Demon from Girl," *IMS*, May 5, 1907, 1.

838. "Police Visit 'Bluks,'" *IMS*, May 13, 1907, 12.

839. "'Bluks' Pay," *IMS*, 1; "Gives Bluks $8,000," *IMS*, April 21, 1907, 1, 7; "Negro Bluk Coming," *IMS*, May 5, 1907, 3.

840. "Negro Bluk Kissed," 3.

841. "Bluks Divide Home," *IMS*, June 4, 1907, 1; "Negro Bluk 'Blows,'" *IIS*, June 5, 1907, 20; "Woman Sticks to Bluks; Husband Asks Divorce," *IIN*, June 5, 1907, 4; "Oddy Asks Divorce Because of Bluks," *IMS*, June 6, 1907, 3.

842. "Oddy Asks Divorce Because of Bluks," 3.

843. "Bluks Fail in Efforts to Rout 'Police Demon,'" *IIS*, June 9, 1907, 16; "Police Are Spectators at 'Bluks' Meeting," *IIN*, June 11, 1907, 4; "Police after Bluks," *IIS*, June 11, 1907, 15.

844. "Bluk Crowd Runs Over," 12.

845. "Brother Cook Was a Real Bad Man," *IIS*, June 15, 1907, 3; "Hit Brother Cook," *IIS*, June 17, 1907, 3.

846. "Bluks to Wash Feet," *IIS*, June 12, 1907, 3; "Bluk Feet, Little and Big, Scrubbed," *IIS*, June 16, 1907, 10; "Gliggy Bluks Bathed in Fall Creek Waters," *IIN*, June 17, 1907, 7.

847. Seymour, *Doctrines and Discipline*.

848. "Desire the 'Bluks' to Go," *IIN*, June 17, 1907, 1; "Young Mob Assails Bluks' Temple," *IIS*, June 17, 1907, 3; "Bluks Appeal to Police," *ISU*, June 17, 1907, 7.

849. "Mayor Will Protect 'Gliggy Bluks,'" *INN*, June 19, 1907, 1; "Police Have No Power to Stop Bluks' Meetings," *INN*, June 20, 1907, 18.

850. "Hit Brother Cook," 2.

851. Victoria M. Peagler, "Garfield Thomas Haywood—1880–1931: From a Migrant's Son to an Internationally Renowned Churchman" (dissertation, Wright State University, 1993), 10–14.

852. "In the Last Days" *AFLA*, June to September 1907, 1.

853. DuPree, *African American Holiness Pentecostal Movement: An Annotated Bibliography*, 138–40; Otis J. Smith and Oree Keyes, *Manual of the Apostolic Faith Church of God* (Franklin, VA: General Assembly AFCOG, n. d.), 8, 9; "Our Birth," liveonministries.org; Matthew E. Guillen to Larry Martin, email, September 7, 2023. Guillen is a researcher at the Virginia Museum of History and Culture.

854. DuPree, *African American Holiness Pentecostal Movement: An Annotated Bibliography*, 138–40. The author made dozens of telephone calls, wrote many letters, and even visited Franklin, VA, to learn more about this federation and the history of Seymour's eastern ministry. Unfortunately, the sparse history, if any exists, is guarded more securely than Fort Knox. The one pleasant exception was Bishop Oree Keyes, who sent a copy of the group's manual with important photographs of Seymour and Lowe and copies of the most recent convention programs. He has promised to share more information in the future.

855. St. Mary Parish, Louisiana, *Book "3H" of Conveyances*, 93, October 24, 1912; St. Mary Parish, Louisiana, *Book "3H" of Conveyances*, 93, November 12, 1912.

856. DuPree, *African American Holiness Pentecostal Movement: An Annotated Bibliography*, 473.

857. *John G. Lake: His Life, His Sermons, His Boldness of Faith*, 88. Lake does not say if this was at his church in Portland or later when he moved to Spokane.

858. Sherry DuPree, personal interview, February 25, 1999. The dates and circumstances of these meetings cannot be confirmed. Unfortunately, the minutes from many of the Church of God in Christ convocations were destroyed in a flood.

859. Nelson, "For Such a Time As This," 269.

860. Clemmons, "True Koinonia: Pentecostal Hopes and Historical Realities," 55.

861. "Brother Seymour Called Home," *The Pentecostal Herald*, October 1, 1922, 1.

862. Boddy, "At Los Angeles," 232–34. Phillis lived in Los Angeles for some time. In 1915, she listed 312 Azusa as her address when asking for an increase in her widow's pension. See Widow's Pension, 472, 276, Simon Semour Pension File, National Archives and Records Administration. She returned to Verdunville when she became ill. Her daughter Julia apparently traveled to California to bring her home. Phillis died on January 30, 1940, from chronic myocarditis, a heart ailment. Also see Interview, Lucille Seymour; St. Mary Parish, Louisiana, Book "3H" of Conveyances, 93, November 12, 1912; and Phillis Seymour, Standard Certificate of Death, February 3, 1940.

863. Boddy, "At Los Angeles," 232–34; A. A. Boddy, "A Meeting at the Azusa Street Mission, Los Angeles," *CON*, November 1912, 244–45.

864. Aaron Howard, "Southern California Is the Cradle of our Rich Pentecostal Heritage," May 28, 1998, 3, bonniebrae.org.

865. Seymour, *Doctrines and Discipline*, 12, 48–49; Articles of Incorporation, Apostolic Faith Mission, Los Angeles County, California, June 3, 1914.

866. Shumway, "A Critical Study of 'The Gift of Tongues,'" 179.

867. A. O. Stafford, "The Mind of the African Negro as reflected in his Proverbs," *The Journal of Negro History*, January 1916, 46.

868. Seymour, *Doctrines and Discipline*, 12. This book is published by this author. See William J. Seymour, *The Doctrines and Discipline of the Azusa Street Apostolic Faith Mission of Los Angeles* (Joplin, MO: Christian Life Books, 2000).

869. Seymour, *Doctrines and Discipline*, 10, 12–13.

870. G. L. Blackwell, ed., *The Doctrines and Discipline of the African Methodist Episcopal Zion Church* (Charlotte: A. M. E. Zion Publication House, 1916), 25–34; Seymour, *Doctrine and Discipline*, 85.

871. Seymour, *Doctrine and Discipline*, 91.

872. Seymour, *Doctrine and Discipline*, 49.

873. Lewis, "William J. Seymour: Follower of the 'Evening Light,'" 179.

874. Seymour, *Doctrine and Discipline*, 11; Lewis, "William J. Seymour: Follower of the 'Evening Light,'" 180.

875. Seymour, *Doctrine and Discipline*, 52–56.

876. Seymour, *Doctrine and Discipline*, 52.

877. "To the Baptized Saints," *AFLA*, September 1907, 2.

878. "The Baptism of the Holy Ghost," *AFLA*, May 1908, 3.

879. Vinson Synan and Charles R. Fox Jr., *William J. Seymour: Pioneer of the Azusa Street Revival* (Newberry, FL: Bridge Logos, 2012), 81–82.

880. "Tongues as a Sign," *AFLA*, September 1907, 2.

881. Seymour, *Doctrine and Discipline*, 94.

882. This author admits a bias to the classical Pentecostal position but believes his analysis of Seymour's writing is objective and unbiased. Believing strongly in the "initial physical evidence" of tongues speaking, I have no argument with what Seymour wrote, although I might have phrased it differently. I have often said the fruit of the Spirit is a better evidence of Spirit baptism than speaking in tongues.

883. *Manual of the Apostolic Faith Church of God* (Franklin, VA: General Assembly AFCOG, n.d.), 15.

884. Witherspoon et al., 2.

885. Isaac Seymour, Registration Card, ancestry.com.

886. Nelson, "For Such a Time As This," 41.

887. Nelson, "For Such a Time As This," 261–62.

888. Nelson, "For Such a Time As This," 62.

889. Daniel Mark Epstein, *Sister Aimee: The Life of Aimee Semple McPherson* (New York: Harcourt Brace Jovanovich Publishers, 1993), 152; Nelson, 267.

890. *Azusa Street Mission: Fourteenth Anniversary of the Outpouring of the Holy Spirit in Los Angeles, California* (Los Angeles: W. H. Giles, 1920), 6.

891. Interview, Larry Martin to Anjetta Adkins, August 11, 1923. Mary Ann Wiley was Anjetta's grandmother.

892. United States Census, Los Angeles County, California, 1920.

893. Richard Asbery 32735, California, U.S. Prison and Correctional Records, 1851–1950; U. S. Census 1920, ancestry.com.

894. California Secretary of State to Larry Martin, September 28, 2023. Correspondence included records of Robert Asbery's incarceration and an undated and unsourced newspaper clipping: "Dwyer and Asbury Are Bad: Threaten to Decamp Again."

895. California Death Index, ancestry.com.

896. U.S. Census 1910; U.S. Census 1920, ancestry.com.

897. Jethro Hutchins, 40145, California, U.S. Prison and Correctional Records, 1851–1950; U. S. Census 1920, ancestry.com.

898. Anne Douglass to Larry Martin, June 9, 1999; Lucy Farrow, *Standard Certificate of Death*, February 22, 1911. Farrow's son died on April 14, 1929. See James M. Pointer, *Standard Certificate of Death*, April 16, 1929.

899. Vinson Synan, introduction to *Azusa Street* by Frank Bartleman (South Plainfield, NJ: Bridge Publishing, Inc., 1980), xxiii. In the original version of this book, the author followed Synan's view. I no longer believe Bartleman was Oneness. Richard Crayne presents a very valid counterview. See Richard Crayne, *Did Frank Bartleman Go Oneness?* (n. p., 2006).

900. Bloch-Hoell, *The Pentecostal Movement*, 54.

901. John Matthews, *Speaking in Tongues* (n. p., 1925), 14.

902. "Brother Seymour Called Home," 1; "Home-going of Rev. W. J. Seymore," *The Bridegroom's Messenger*, November and December 1922, 3; Nelson, "For Such a Time As This," 270; W.J. Seymour, Standard Certificate of Death.

903. "Brother Seymour Called Home," 1.

904. Nelson, "For Such a Time As This," 270.

905. "Death of W. J. Seymour," *The Voice in the Wilderness* 2, no. 13 (n.d.), 7.

906. "Brother Seymour Called Home," 1.

907. Bloch Hoell, *The Pentecostal Movement: Its Origin, Development, and Distinctive Character*, 54.

908. "Anniversary Meeting," CE, April 3, 1925, 6, newspapers.com.

909. US Census, 1930, ancestry.com.

910. US Census, 1920, ancestry.com

911. "Application for an Examination as Manicurist," State Board of Cosmetology, ancestry.com.

912. "California, U.S., County Birth, Marriage and Death Records, 1849–1980," ancestry.com; "Porter, Everett M.," *LAT*, May 12, 1984, 66; "Los Angeles Boy Commissioned 'Second Lieutenant,'" *(Los Angeles) California Eagle* (hereafter cited as *CE*), May 24, 1943, 5, newspapers.com.

913. "California, U.S. Death Index," 1940–1997, ancestry.com. It is unfortunate, but to my knowledge Julia was never interviewed by any researchers.

914. "U.S. Schools Catalogs, 1765–1935," ancestry.com.

915. "'Bishop of Ethiopia,' Former Resident of this City, Dies in Los Angeles," *The (Allentown, PA) Morning Call* (hereafter cited as *AMC*), April 30, 1942, 2; "Rupert D. Griffith Married, *Pottsville (PA) Republican*, May 19, 1896, 1; "Chat about Your Friends," *AMC*, December 1, 1900, 4; "Will Engage in Business in Redding," *AMC*, March 23, 1900, 1, newspapers.com.

916. "Griffith Not a Dowiete," *AMC*, October 31, 1904, 7, newspapers.com.

917. Dowie Missionary in Jail," *Pottsville (PA) Republican*, July 9, 1904, 1; "Rupert Griffith," *Reading (PA) Times*, July 14, 1904, 3, newspapers.com.

918. "Taken to the Hospital," *The Allentown (PA) Leader* (hereafter cited as *APL*), July 18, 1905, 1; "Child's Sad Death," *AMC*, July 22, 1905, 1, newspapers.com.

919. "Honors May Be for R.D. Griffith," *AMC*, June 1, 1906, 1, newspapers.com.

920. "Jonas Arrested on Phony Check Charge in East," *Libertyville (IL) Independent*, July 29, 1920, 5, newspapers.com.

921. "Planning New Zion," *Kenosha (WI) News* (hereafter cited as *KWN*), January 13, 1912, 1.

922. "Agreed to Separate," *APL*, April 19, 1907, 1; "Other Circuit Matters," *Waukegan (IL) News-Sun* (hereafter cited as *WNS*), November 18, 1910, 1, newspapers.com; U.S. Census, 1910.

923. "Planning New Zion," *Kenosha (WI) News*, January 13, 1912, 1, newspapers.com.

924. "Robert Deveraux Abandons Scheme of Alabama City," *WNS*, January 22, 1912, 1, newspapers.com.

925. "Site of Dowie's Once Palatial Home during the Summer to Be Converted into Negro Settlement," *WNS*, July 23, 1912, 1, newspapers.com.

926. "Expect Abdul Baha Will Visit Zion City Soon," *WNS*, September 14, 1912, 4, newspapers.com.

927. "'Jonah the Preacher' Arrested," *Chicago Tribune*, December 12, 1913, 5; "Rupert Griffith Arrested in Zion City by Walker," *WNS*, December 11, 1913, 1, newspapers.com.

928. "Zionists on an Apostate's Trail," *The Dayton (OH) Herald*, September 8, 1914, 13, newspapers.com.

929. "Resident of Waukegan Is Believed to Be with Villa," *WNS*, March 13, 1916, 1, newspapers.com.

930. "Chicago Race Riot Prisoner Spoke on St. Louis Street," *The St. Louis Star and Times*, June 22, 1920, 1, newspapers.com.

931. "U.S. Passport Applications, 1795–1925," ancestry.com.

932. "Chicago Race Riot Prisoner Spoke on St. Louis Street."

933. "Pay Penalty for Chicago Murder," *Leavenworth (KS) Post*, June 24, 1921, 1, newspapers.com.

934. "Ten Years Ago," *WNS*, July 24, 1930, 4; "Jonas Arrested on Phony Check Charge in East."

935. "Rev. Rupert Griffith Will Discuss League of Nations," *(Greensboro, NC) News and Record*, July 30, 1921, 6; "League Speaker Here for Work," *The Charlotte (NC) News*, July 18, 1921, 2; "Indianapolis Man Defends League," *The Montgomery (AL) Advertiser*, 3, newspapers.com.

936. "'Bishop of Ethiopia,' Former Resident of this City, Dies in Los Angeles."

937. "Second Baptist Church," *Monrovia (CA) News-Post*, September 7, 1935, 2; "Chicago Race Riot Prisoner Spoke on St. Louis Street"; "Site of Dowie's Once Palatial Home During the Summer to Be Converted into Negro Settlement"; "Again in the Limelight," *The Zion City (IL) Independent*, October 25, 1912, 1; "As the Tide Ebbs,"*(San Pedro, CA) News-Pilot*, March 14, 1941, 13; "Haile Selassie Representative Sees Bright Future for Blacks; Says War with Russia False," *The (Oklahoma City) Black Dispatch*, August 9, 1941, 12; "To Help the Negro," *The Champaign (IL) Daily Gazette*, June 20, 1917, 9; "The Co-operative Educational Congress," *The (Springfield, IL) Forum*, June 30, 1917, 4, newspapers.com.

938. "Tramp White Preacher Wants to Oust Colored Woman," *CE*, January 16, 1931, 2; "Pastor's Widow Wins Battle Over Church," *LAD*, June 13, 1932, newspapers.com.

939. "Shout, Sing, Pray to Oust Pastor," *CE*, January 2, 1931, 1, newspapers.com.

940. dollarstimes.com.

941. "Competition," *Los Angeles Daily News* (hereafter cited as *LDN*), January 5, 1931, 3; "Church Service Develops Riot," *LAT*, January 5, 1931, 17; "Church Faction Renews Efforts to Oust Pastor," *CE*, January 9, 1931, 1, 3; "Riot Squads Again Visit Singing Church Militants," January 5, 1931, 3, newspapers.com.

942. "Church Row Is Taken to Court," *Los Angeles Evening Post-Record* (hereafter cited as *LAR*), January 6, 1931, 7, newspapers.com.

943. "Open Warfare," *CE*, January 9, 1931, 3, newspapers.com.

944. "Upton Says," *CE*, January 16, 1931, 11; "Tramp White Preacher Wants to Oust Colored Woman," newspapers.com.

945. "Close Church as Result of Court Fight," *LAR*, January 12, 1931, 1; "Police Halt Riot at Church," *LDN*, January 12, 1931, 2; "Ban Church Meetings," *CE*, January 16, 1931, 1, newspapers.com.

946. "Prosecutor Delays Church-strife Action," *LAT*, January 13, 1931, 34; "Peace Hope Seen in Church Split," *LDN*, January 13, 1931, 6, newspapers.com.

947. "Minister Hailed into Court, Faces Battery Charges, CE, January 30, 1931, 1; "Warrant Issued for Church Head," *LAT*, January 29, 1931, 36; "Assault Charges To be Asked for 'Bishop,'" *CE*, January 23, 1931, 1; "Woman Bishop Accuses Pastor," *LAR*, January 29, 1931, 2; "Bishop Accused of Swatting Widow," *LAD*, January 29, 1931, 8, newspapers.com.

948. "We Are Sending," *CE*, January 23, 1931, 1, newspapers.com.

949. "Thought Signals," *CE*, January 30, 1931, 8, newspapers.com.

950. "Minister Hailed into Court, Faces Battery Charges."

951. "Preacher Ousted from Mission Church," *CE*, February 6, 1931, 1, newspapers. com.

952. Robeck, "The Use of Public Materials for Instruction on Pentecostal Origins," 9.

953. "Jurors Fail to Agree on Suit Against Preacher," *LAD*, March 28, 193, 4; "Jury Unable to Decide in Church Row," *LAT*, March 28, 1931, 22; "Pastor Case Waits," *LAD*, February 27, 1931, 6; "Jury Disagrees," *LAR*, March 28, 1931, 1; "Parson Gives Up, Fight Trial Set," *LAD*, January 30, 1931, 8, newpapers.com.

954. "Bishop Freed in Battery Retrial," *LAD*, April 29, 1931, 7; "'Bishop' Griffith Acquitted," *CE*, May 1, 1931, 1, newspapers.com.

955. "Method Change Asked," *The Pasadena Post*, February 27, 1931, 2; "Ex-Townsend Aide Starts New Plan," *LAD*, May 14, 1936, 3; "Ford Silent on Mayor's Race," *Los Angeles Evening Citizen News*, August 3, 1938, 3, newspapers.com.

956. "Founder Fights to Save Church from Usurpers," *CE*, June 3, 1932, 1, newspapers.com.

957. Articles of Incorporation, Apostolic Faith Mission, Los Angeles County, California, May 14, 1931; "Meetings of Various Kinds," *LAT*, April 4, 1931, 24, newpapers.com.

958. "Founder Fights to Save Church from Usurpers."

959. Bloch-Hoell, *The Pentecostal Movement: Its Origin, Development and Distinctive Character*, 39.

960. Nelson, "For Such a Time As This," 273.

961. Robeck, "The Use of Public Materials for Instruction on Pentecostal Origins," 9–10.

962. "Judge Rules Mission Must Pay Chauffeur," *LAT*, May 25, 1932, 28, newspapers.com.

963. "Founder Fights to Save Church from Usurpers," "Pastor's Widow Wins Battle Over Church," *LAD*, June 13, 1932, 18; "Mrs. Seymour's Rights Upheld," *LAT*, June 13, 1932, 12; "Successful," *CE*, June 17, 1932; "Famous Church Fight Ends, Mrs. Seymour Victor," *CE*, June 17, 1932, 1; "Church Fight Ends in Victory for Mrs. Seymour," *CE*, July 3, 1932, 1, newspapers.com.

964. Mortgage, December 31, 1930, Los Angeles County.

965. Jennie Evans Seymour, *Standard Certificate of Death.*

966. "Church Worker Succumbs to Long Illness," *CE*, March 30, 1934, 5, newspapers.com.

967. Nelson, "For Such a Time As This," 43, 45, 273–74.

968. Nelson, "For Such a Time As This," 45, 274.

969. *Power of Attorney*, June 12, 1936, Book 14128, p. 288, Los Angeles County, California.

970. "California, US, Death Index, 1905–1939," ancestry.com.

971. J. E. Seymour, *Standard Certificate of Death*; "Wife of Brother Seymour Taken by Death," *CE*, July 3, 1936, 2, newspapers.com.

972. Nelson, "For Such a Time As This," 45, 274; "Early Church Life Recalled in Court Here," *CE*, May 5, 1938, 7, newspapers.com.

973. Driscoll, Untitled Brochure, 4, FPHC.

974. "Azusa St. Mission in Anniversary Services," *CE*, April 6, 1939, 18, newspapers.com; "Our Leadership," azusastreetmission.org.

975. "Anniversary Meeting."

976. Great Anniversary, flyer, FPHC.

977. "Rev. Fullerton to Speak at Mission," *Wilmington (CA) Daily Press Journal*, May 18, 1938, 3; "Visiting Ministers to Fill Many Pulpits Sunday; Burroughs Here," *CE*, July 21, 1938, 6; "Azusa St. Mission in Anniversary Services," newspapers.com.

978. The Golden Anniversary, flyer, FPHC; Thrapp, "Pentecostal Sects Convene Here," III, 11.; Nickel, *Azusa Street Outpouring*, 20–27.

979. Great 39th Anniversary of "Old Azusa," flyer, FPHC.

980. Tinney, "William J. Seymour: Father of Modern-Day Pentecostalism," 223–24; "Seymour House: Intercollegiate Pentecostal Conference-International, Inc.," *Jet*, May 18, 1987, 14.

981. Mark Kendall, "The House of the Spirit," *LAT*, January 8, 2006, latimes.com. Loaded to the web without magazine format and page numbers. Jeff Struff, "115 Years after Fire First Fell on Bonnie Brae House, Glory Beckons from Azusa Street Revival," charismanews.com.

982. Takeshi Nakayama, "African American Roots of Little Tokyo," *The Rafu Shimpo*, February 13, 1998, 1, 4.

983. joshuam.org.

984. Vinson Synan, "Pentecostalism: William Seymour," *Christian History Magazine*, Issue 65, christianhistoryinstitute.org. Loaded to the web without magazine format and page numbers.

985. "Century's Important Religious Events Marked by Horror, Cataclysms," *The (Memphis, TN) Commercial Appeal*, December 18, 1999, 9, newspapers.com.

986. "Top Religious Stories of the Millennium and Century," *The (Benton Harbor, MI) Herald-Palladium*, December 25, 1999, 6, newspapers.com.

987. "Facts You Should Know about Azusa Street," 312azusa.com.

988. "Pentecostal Enthusiasm Is Spreading," *LAT*, April 28, 2006, 8; "Pentecostal Centennial," *The Bangor (ME) Daily News*, April 29, 2006, 32, newspapers.com.

989. "The Tom Bradley Legacy Foundation," Discover Nikkei, devmedia. discovermikkei.org.

990. "Otis Clark," uncrownedcommunitybuilders.com; "106-Year-Old Pastor Recalls History of Pentecostalism," jacksonville.com.

ALSO AVAILABLE

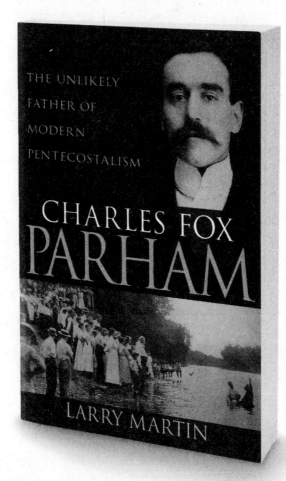

Read the absorbing, controversial biography of the man who initiated one of the most significant spiritual movements of modern times.

978-1-64123-801-4

WHITAKER
HOUSE